Gilded

Gilded

How Newport Became
America's Richest Resort

DEBORAH DAVIS

WILEY

John Wiley & Sons, Inc.

Published by John Wiley & Sons, Inc., Hoboken, New Jersey
Published simultaneously in Canada

Design by Forty-Five Degree Design LLC

For general information about our other products and services, please contact our Customer Care Department within the United States at (800) 762-2974, outside the United States at (317) 572-3993 or fax (317) 572-4002.

Wiley also publishes its books in a variety of electronic formats. Some content that appears in print may not be available in electronic books. For more information about Wiley products, visit our web site at www.wiley.com.

Library of Congress Cataloging-in-Publication Data

Davis, Deborah, date.
    Gilded : how Newport became America's richest resort / Deborah Davis.
      p.   cm.
    Includes bibliographical references and index.
    ISBN 978-0-470-12413-0 (cloth);
    ISBN 978-1-118-01401-1 (paper); ISBN 978-0-470-73022-5 (ebk);
    ISBN 978-0-470-73023-2 (ebk); ISBN 978-0-470-73024-9 (ebk)
      1. Newport (R.I.)—History.   2. Newport (R.I.)—Social life and customs.
    3. Newport (R.I.)—Biography.   4. Socialites—Rhode Island—Newport—
    Biography.   I. Title.
    F89.N5D38 2009
    974.5'7—dc22
                                                    2009033992

10 9 8 7 6 5 4 3 2

For my mother,
Jean Cianci Davis Gatto

CONTENTS

ACKNOWLEDGMENTS

At the beginning of my Newport adventure, I was fortunate to meet the delightful Ralph Carpenter, who was called Mr. Newport by his many admirers. With great charm, wit, intelligence, and insight, he told me absolutely everything I needed to know about the city. In addition to being an invaluable and indefatigable guide, he represented the very best of Newport, and it was my privilege and my great pleasure to work with him.

Three guardian angels watched over me during my frequent trips to Newport. Thank you, Kitty Cushing, Stacie Mills, and Carol Swift, for your enthusiasm, your generosity, and your ability to make every moment festive and fun. Special thanks to Cheryl and Rick Bready, Judy Chace, Pamela Fielder and David Ford, Ronald Lee Fleming, Bettie Beardon Pardee, and Rockwell Stensrud.

My thanks to Sid Abbruzzi, Yusha Auchincloss, Win Baker, Letitia Baldrige, Virginia Baldwin, Nicholas Benson, Pamela

Bradford, Minnie Cushing Coleman, Howard Cushing, Peter De Savary, Roger Englander, "Auntie Helen" Fenton, Angela Fischer, John Gacher, Richard Grosvenor, John and Mary Ellen Grosvenor, Kristine Hendrickson, George Herrick, Dyer Jones, Agnes Keating, Jerry Kirby, Didi Lorillard, Jonas Mekas, Jorey Miner, Carol O'Malley, Brian O'Neill, Leonard Panaggio, John Peixinho, Nuala Pell, Nancy Powell, Federico Santi, Marlen Scalzi, Nancy Sirkis, Carl Sprague, and John Winslow. I am very appreciative of the help I received from John Tschirch and Paul Miller at the Newport Preservation Society, and Bert Lippincott III at the Newport Historical Society. The Redwood Library and Athenaeum was an important resource, and my sincere thanks to Lisa Long, the Ezra Stiles Special Collections Librarian, for her extraordinary guidance.

I am grateful to my editor, Tom Miller, for his vision, dedication, and unfailing charm. My thanks to Dan Crissman at Wiley; Harvey Klinger at the Harvey Klinger Agency; my publicist, Robyn Liverant; and Wendy Silbert.

At home, I am indebted to my husband, Mark Urman, for his boundless creativity, optimism, and faith; my mother, Jean Gatto, for her patience and support; and my children, Oliver and Cleo, for the joy they give me every day.

Introduction

Whensplit I was a child, I thought that Newport, Rhode Island, was an enchanted place. I loved it when my family drove there on pleasant summer days to see the city's famous turn-of-the-century castles. We called them mansions, a dead giveaway that we were outsiders. Real Newporters knew the proper term was "cottage," a whimsical understatement considering they cost millions of dollars to build and had dozens of rooms and fancy exteriors. However, I discovered on these visits that most of Newport's palaces were surrounded by gates, walls, and thick shrubs that prevented all but the most fleeting glimpses of the tantalizing world inside.

The Preservation Society had taken over some of Newport's largest properties, including The Breakers and The Elms, in the 1950s and 1960s, and opened them to the public. These houses, once luxurious summer retreats for the country's wealthiest families, were fascinating monuments to a lost way of life. For the price of admission, their secrets were laid bare. Anyone could enter but, as far as I was concerned, their accessibility made them infinitely less interesting than the houses that remained impenetrable. Paying to get in, I decided, was not the same as being invited. Private Newport still beckoned me. Who lived behind those gates, I wondered, and how did they get there?

When I was a teenager and could drive myself to Newport, I finally got inside a private estate on windswept Brenton Point, a dramatic location with a stunning, unobstructed view of the sea. The main house, called The Reef, had been destroyed by a fire in 1960, and only the blackened shell of the carriage house, known as The Bells, remained. My friends and I climbed the broken staircase, holding on to crumbling walls and old beams that threatened to give way at any moment. It didn't seem particularly safe (which is why the building's charred shell is protected by a fence today) but we were young and fearless, and wanted to feel connected to the ruin's romantic past.

Just a few years later, when I left home and went out into the world, I forgot about Newport. At various times, I heard the city was in decline—that cottages were being turned into condos and shopping centers and families were leaving and not coming back. I visited the beach a few times in the 1980s. And, in the early 1990s, my husband and I spent Valentine's Day at an inn where a tuxedo-clad waiter belted show tunes while serving us a candlelit breakfast in bed. The experience was supposed to give us a taste of how the rich in Newport lived, but I was certain that real butlers did not sing, nor light candles for that matter, at morning meals.

During those years, when I thought about Newport—if I thought about it at all—I compressed it as in that famous *New Yorker* magazine cover, with just a handful of signature buildings representing the entire landscape. Then, in 2003, I was invited to give a lecture at Rosecliff, one of the city's most beautiful and historic houses. As I drove on Bellevue Avenue, the spacious, tree-lined street that the Vanderbilts, Belmonts, Astors, and Oelrichs (and even Von Bulows) called home, I was surprised to see homes in fine repair, with lush lawns, shapely shrubs, and freshly painted gates standing at attention. Since it was July, there were flowers everywhere. I actually stopped in front of an estate to admire some exotic blooms, only to realize I was looking at a bed of impatiens, the same flowers I had in my own garden in New Jersey. Somehow they looked more extravagantly colorful here in Newport. I smelled a wonderful perfume in the air, a blend of fresh grass, roses, privet hedges, and sea salt. But two other ingredients were mixed into this beguiling scent that were specific to the location: history and money. Blessed with an abundance of both, the city now looked better than ever. Newport was again an enchanted place, and the questions I'd contemplated as a child came back to me in a rush. Who lived behind those gates? And how did they get there?

These are big questions, and I went hunting for answers in the city that one nineteenth-century travel writer called "the oldest and most picturesque watering-place in this country." The public tour I took as a teenager had taught me that Newport was once a playground for self-made moguls with the Midas touch. They turned everything in the city into gold—sometimes quite literally—and ushered in America's notorious Gilded Age. But as I began to do proper research, I learned that Newport had a long history that was marked by rise and fall and rise. More than once, the city was threatened with extinction, yet somehow it always bounced back. In fact, it seemed to be in the process of bouncing back right before my eyes.

I began to spend time in the local libraries, and the details I culled from old books, magazines, and newspapers were fascinating, even revelatory. I discovered that Newport was—and is—a city defined by its women, so I wrote to Eileen Slocum,

Bellevue Avenue's leading doyenne, requesting an interview, and was thrilled when she wrote back, inviting me to tea.

This special appointment demanded special preparations. First stop, Google. An old *New York Times* interview with Mrs. Slocum revealed that she preferred a certain kind of black tea called *hu-kwa*, or at least that's what she drank fifty years earlier. I tracked down a pricey tin at an out-of-the-way emporium. I brushed up on my social pleasantries, reminding myself to say "How do you do," instead of the more common "Pleased to meet you." I packed a hardcover copy of my newest book, *Party of the Century: The Fabulous Story of Truman Capote and His Black and White Ball*, for my hostess because she had admired my previous book, *Strapless: John Singer Sargent and the Fall of Madame X*.

I was nervous when I entered one of those legendary private homes I had regarded so longingly as a child. A uniformed maid told me Mrs. Slocum was still at breakfast and would join me momentarily. I waited in a sunny living room, or sitting room, or drawing room, unsure of which word I should use to describe it. Formal portraits covered the walls, and the room was filled with furniture that was more elegantly shabby than chic.

Mrs. Slocum walked in and greeted me. She was small, definite, and surprisingly enthusiastic. It took about three breathy sentences for her to make me feel as if we were old friends, even confidantes. I mentioned I had lunched at Bailey's Beach the day before. (What a shame she didn't see me there!) I told her we had a friend in common. (Did I know he was seeing two women at the same time?) And finally, I announced that I had brought her my new book. (How lovely of me to think of her!) I proudly handed it over.

Mrs. Slocum accepted my gift and stared at the cover. "That's Truman Capote," she said. I nodded, waiting for further words of appreciation, but all she said was, "He was a nasty homosexual."

I thought I had misheard her, or that she was joking. I was wrong on both counts. She handed *Party* back to me, saying, "Oh, I wouldn't be interested in this book at all. And, dear, I don't think anyone else will be interested, either."

Having said the very worst words an author can ever hear, Mrs. Slocum continued chatting about her parents and Newport in earlier days. (They loved mah-jongg in the 1920s!) My dilemma was that I didn't want to leave the book, a full-price hardcover, with a hostile recipient. While we were talking, I pushed it behind me and slipped it into my bag, hoping she wouldn't notice.

I thought about Mrs. Slocum's behavior long after our encounter was over. Etiquette was practically a religion in Newport. There were strict rules governing introductions, invitations, thank-you notes, and every other form of interaction. Was my hostess's outspokenness a momentary lapse in manners, or an indication of something larger? Seeking an answer, I consulted Letitia Baldrige, one of America's most respected authorities on etiquette and the author of a dozen books on the subject. "Rudeness," she diagnosed, after I told her the story. "Or, maybe hardening of the arteries. No Grande Dame I know would ever speak that way."

Actually, in my research I had come across several such instances of seeming rudeness on the part of Newport's social elite, and I was convinced that this was not an isolated, or accidental, occurrence. A story still circulates about Mrs. Louis Bruguiere, Newport's reigning matron in the 1950s and 1960s. When asked if she had received an art book a friend sent her as a gift, she answered curtly, "I did, and I threw it in the wastebasket. I don't like that kind of painting." What Mrs. Bruguiere, Mrs. Slocum, and their fellow Newport colonists had in common was their unshakable sense of security. These were people who followed the rules, but who also made those rules and lived comfortably and confidently in their very own world.

The more I looked into this enchanted location, and the more time I spent there, the more I realized that there is rich and there is Newport rich, and there really is a difference. That difference seemed to me a fascinating subject for investigation, one that would result in a lively social study. The classic Newporter is an intriguing rara avis, and I began to think of myself as an enthusiastic bird watcher, one who wanted to find out everything about the species' origins, mating rituals, customs, prey, and, prospects for survival. I spent two years in the field. What follows is what I learned.

1

The Season

1913

"Newport's Season Promises to Break All Records for Gayety," predicted the *New York Times* on July 20, 1913. If the weather cooperated—and it usually did during the eight-week social season that began the first week in July and ended with the Horse Show in early September—the privileged summer residents who flocked to Newport, Rhode Island, looked forward to an uninterrupted whirlwind of activities. Every day in the "queen of summer resorts" brought a new schedule of racing, tennis, sailing, luncheons, teas, dinners, clambakes, cotillions, fantasy balls, even daybreak swims after a long night of dancing. Veteran socialites rushed from one event to another, thinking longingly of early autumn, when they could enjoy a brief respite before facing the annual round of festivities at their winter homes. But at the moment, rest was not on the schedule. Their calendars were packed with an exciting succession of engagements, and, somehow, they found the energy to do it all.

There was a long overture before the curtain could rise on this annual social extravaganza. The return of the summer colony launched Newport's service industries on a course of herculean preparations. Local merchants in the waterfront district put aside their mundane wares and stockpiled exotic provisions they knew would appeal to the rich—caviar, little hens, rare wines, candies, and other delicacies. They also raised their prices; if they played their cards right, the butcher, baker, and candlestick maker could pull in enough money during the season to support their families for the rest of the year. The tradesmen were upset whenever they heard that a wealthy regular was vacationing elsewhere: the absence of a handful of these big spenders could mean a $500,000 loss in just one summer.

On Bellevue Avenue, Newport's most fashionable street, New York department stores such as Bonwit Teller, Bergdorf Goodman, and Brooks Brothers set up summer boutiques. Their clientele did not want to miss a day of shopping, despite the fact that they were at the beach. The fancy emporium Henri Bendel was stocked with "hats, gowns, wraps, furs, sports clothes, lingerie, blouses," and anything else a woman might need on a whim, or for an unanticipated fashion emergency. Beauty salons cautioned ladies to protect their skin before they ventured into the sunlight and offered treatments to keep them looking their best. Caswell-Massey, a local apothecary founded by a Scottish doctor in 1752, sold Sarah Bernhardt's cucumber night cream and George Washington's preferred cologne. There were also stores that sold serious jewelry. The guilty husband who needed to buy—or the desperate wife who needed to sell—could depend on an agent from Van Cleef & Arpels or Tiffany to handle all transactions with the utmost discretion.

The most elaborate preseason preparations took place in the giant houses on and around Bellevue Avenue. These palatial residences were referred to as cottages, a quaint euphemism that was a throwback to the days when Newport had simple beach homes instead of French, English, and Italianate palaces. There were annual rituals that marked the June opening of a cottage. A small army of domestics—a combination of advance staff members transported from winter households in New York and other cities, and temporary help from local cleaning firms—descended on the sleeping giants with brooms, mops, buckets, and pounds of Sapolio, the preferred soap of the day. Every piece of furniture had its own custom-made linen shroud to protect it from dust and the passage of time. These covers— and little bags of camphor to ward off moths—were removed and stored neatly until the house's annual closing in September. Carpets and drapes were liberated from storage. Floors were cleaned and polished. Chandeliers were dismantled and washed with ammonia. Mattresses were turned. Hundreds of pieces of precious china and crystal were rinsed and laid out in the butler's pantry, while the family's valuable silver—and sometimes their even more valuable gold—service was shined and locked in the safe to await the first dinner party. Pots and pans, monogrammed with the family's initials or crest, were scrubbed and lined up for the chef to inspect.

Outside, the cottage's grounds and gardens were coaxed back to life. The head gardener and his staff tended the flower beds, hedges, and trees that were the hallmark of the best Newport estates. The challenge for every gardener was to orchestrate a constant array of blooms throughout the summer: this meant precise plantings that yielded different flowers at different times.

The social secretary of the lady of the house oversaw all of these activities. "Miss" (usually a single woman with a refined background but a reduced bank account) was expected to effect a seamless transition from one household to another on behalf of her mistress. It was her job to review the existing staff and to retain the summer help. She ordered the right kinds of stationery in bountiful quantities because, in polite society, communications were written and delivered by hand and the telephone was considered vulgar. She also studied the Social Index, the city's annual "who's who" and "who's where" registry of cottagers and their cottages. This would be the starting point for every Newport guest list.

The family matriarch and her daughters selected their wardrobes—approximately 280 changes for the season—months before they set out for Newport. The bare necessities for the well-dressed socialite included fourteen new evening gowns, ten afternoon outfits, and a half dozen suits, along with matching shoes, hats, parasols, and assorted accessories. Gloves, though expensive and made from the finest materials, were practically disposable. Ladies wore them everywhere, including to clambakes, and changed them several times a day. There were some traditional Newport ladies who kept their European wardrobes in storage for a year so their clothes would not look ostentatiously new.

Husbands had a much easier time packing. Their clothes were simple enough: a few good suits, formal wear, and appropriate athletic garb. Their duties never varied. They were supposed to make money—as much as possible—and show up on weekends, prepared to be the perfect escort.

The preseason frenzy ended in early July. Before the first bed had been slept in, the first invitation sent, the first champagne cork popped, or the first dinner served, the social secretary, the gardener, the butler, the housekeeper, the chauffer or the coachman, the chef, the laundress, and the assorted maids and footmen, were worn out. Their employers, on the other hand, were feeling fresh and eager to get going.

The summer of 1913, the season that promised to be Newport's most brilliant to date, was off to a fabulous start.

2

The Isle of Peace

Newport wasn't always as social as it was in 1913. Its earliest settlers—a pastor, a clerk, a farmer, four merchants, and a peace officer—were circumspect New England colonists searching for an oasis of religious and political tolerance in a world that frowned on diversity. This band of dissidents settled on the southern tip of Aquidneck Island, also known as the Isle of Peace in 1639. They paid the resident Native Americans forty-five fathoms of assorted wampum, ten coats, and twenty hoes. Their modest, little community, which they named Newport, would be a lively experiment, a place where radicals and conservatives, Christians, Quakers, and even Jews, could live side by side.

Newport was blessed with a temperate climate and one of the finest harbors in the country. Thanks to these attributes, the city grew and grew and grew until it was a thriving seaport. A major source of prosperity at the time were the many merchants who participated in the popular practice of exchanging slaves for molasses, molasses for rum, and rum for slaves, otherwise known as the triangle trade. In fact, so many slaves passed through Newport that the city laid an import tax on them, and the money was used for paving streets and building bridges.

Despite this blemish on Newport's early history, the city was considered a cosmopolitan metropolis distinguished by its vigorous intellectual life. In 1746, Abraham Redwood, a wealthy merchant who moved to Newport from Antigua, donated money for a library that would reflect the diverse interests of the community. There were volumes on navigation, geometry, philosophy, and grammar, along with how-to books about brewing beer and building a privy. There was also a popular eighteenth-century etiquette manual titled *A Young Lady and Gentleman Instructed*. The fact that this book made the list was a sure sign that Newport held good manners in high esteem even then.

Chapters such as "The Importance of Punctuality" and "Small Talk" promised to "inspire youth with noble sentiments." Young men who wanted to advance in society were advised that they had to be well versed in unimportant matters: fashionable chitchat was a must. The best way to learn the art of superficial conversation, the manual suggested, was by "frequenting the company of ladies." This was easy advice to follow because there was no shortage of ladies in Newport, especially during the summer.

Word of the city's many charms spread from Rhode Island to Pennsylvania, South Carolina, the West Indies, and other places with punishing summer climates. In fact, the very first tourists to vacation on the island were nearby Native Americans. Every summer, when the weather on the mainland became hot and oppressive, Rhode Island's Narragansett tribe relocated to the balmy shores of Aquidneck for their own version of the season.

Southerners happily followed in their footsteps. Wealthy planters and their families traveled long distances to enjoy

Newport's cool breezes, salubrious salt water, and genteel atmosphere. They found Newport to be a city of happy paradoxes. There were paved streets and magnificent, unspoiled beaches. The townspeople were fine, upstanding New Englanders, but they also had a healthy appetite for pleasure. Year-round residents and summer visitors had something in common: they both liked to have fun. Their social activities were reported in the *Newport Mercury*, the first newspaper in America to feature a regular society column. By 1774, only 135 years after its founding, Newport was the country's fifth-largest city and its most popular resort, bigger and better than Boston or New York.

Newport's star was on the rise until 1775, when King George III of England decided to reclaim the American colonies. British troops, some ten thousand soldiers, sailed into Newport's harbor and occupied the city. When the redcoats arrived, the locals left. Almost half the population—fifty-three hundred townspeople— fled from the invaders. The unfortunate souls who stayed behind were subject to one of the harshest winters in Newport's history and to the bad behavior of the British. And if the British were bad, the German mercenaries who accompanied them were even worse. Like locusts, the visiting army consumed produce and livestock, and cut down Newport's beautiful trees for firewood. They added insult to injury by stripping charming colonial homes of their signature front stoops because drunken British and German soldiers had a tendency to trip over them.

The invaders remained in Newport until 1779, when they moved on to New York. The city they abandoned barely resembled the bustling seaport that once put Boston and New York to shame. The ships were gone. The merchants were gone. Even the books in the Redwood Library were gone, some hidden by concerned citizens who wanted to protect them, others burned by enemy soldiers seeking warmth during the terrible winter.

Newport rallied with the arrival of America's French allies in 1780. General Rochambeau and his troops received a hero's welcome when they sailed into Newport. They brought arms, manpower, and most importantly, plenty of cash, a rare commodity during the Revolution. The French army stayed for almost a year, working with General George Washington on a plan to defeat the British.

Some Newporters worried that their elegant allies were pretty boys, not soldiers. One army chaplain sniffed that the French were "entirely taken up with the dressing of their hair and painting of their faces." Their elaborate toilette, combined with their dandified wardrobe of gold-braided uniforms and cockaded hats, did little to inspire confidence in their battle skills. But their skills in the parlor—and in the bedroom—were another story. Dashing soldiers, such as the Duc de Lauzen, France's handsome and silver-tongued Casanova, were romantic figures with titles, fortunes, and noble features. Rochambeau's men had exquisite manners, and they delighted in using them. "Before long . . . our politesse conquered them," boasted a proud Gaul.

The French loved Newport's charming wooden houses and wonderfully clean interiors, "so clean you can see your face in it," marveled Frenchman Jean Francois Louis Clermont-Crèvecoeur. But they saved their highest praise for Newport's women. One diarist went so far as to say that the belles of Newport had "the handsomest, finest features one could imagine." The ladies were admired for their gaiety, their independence, their fine complexions, and their dainty hands and feet. Fewer compliments were paid to their teeth because, in fact, many young American women didn't have any—the price paid for their passion for highly sweetened tea. Fortunately, it was a defect that many a Newport belle could artfully conceal behind a raised hand or a demure smile.

The French were a little puzzled by some of the local customs. For all their refinement, Americans did not use napkins at meals— instead, they wiped their hands and mouths on the tablecloth.

They also drank spirits from a common bowl, a practice the French found unhygienic. But there was one tradition that appealed to every visiting military man, from foot soldier to general. It was the quaint practice of bondle, or bundling. In Colonial times, a young man who professed his love for a young woman was permitted to go into a room alone with the object of his affection. They could get into bed together—fully clothed, of course—and caress, following the established rules of bundling. Eager to experience this novel form of seduction, the Duc de Lauzen tried his luck with two attractive sisters. When the maidens protested that he was married (bundling was an activity reserved for singles), the duc argued persuasively, "Married, oh yes, but such a very, very little bit that it is not worth mentioning."

Count Axel von Fersen, a Swedish soldier of fortune who was part of Rochambeau's entourage, was another visiting heartthrob. He was blessed with blue eyes, blond hair, a perfect nose, and a well-built body. In his native Sweden, a country famous for its statuesque blonds, Fersen was nicknamed Big Axel by his admiring king. In France, his head-turning good looks caught the eye of Marie Antoinette, the country's lovely, eighteen-year-old queen. Rumors about intimate rendezvous at her palace hideaway prompted Fersen to sail off to America with Rochambeau to squelch the gossip.

His experiences as an international courtier might have made him too big a fish for a small pond such as Newport. But Fersen felt at home in the city and found its people pleasant and well cultivated. He told his father that he admired the fact that unlike his decadent European friends, Newporters lived simply, "without luxury or display." War-torn Newport was the last place Fersen expected to fall in love, until, improbably, he met an attractive American ingenue who made him forget the notorious queen of France.

She was eighteen-year-old Eliza Hunter, colonial Newport's "It girl." In a city that was famous for its lovely young women, she was the one whom men singled out for praise. "She is without exception the most beautiful, accomplished, and elegant person . . . that I ever beheld," wrote a passionate admirer. She was also smart and spirited and came from spunky stock.

Eliza was the granddaughter of Godfrey Malbone, a wealthy settler who made a fortune in the slave trade. One widely circulated story about Malbone, who was famous for living by his own rules, concerned an unusual party he hosted at his estate. A fire broke out during the festivities, and his mansion burned to the ground. Ignoring the flames, Malbone ordered his servants to set up a table outside, and urged his guests to sit down and enjoy their meal. "If I have lost my house," he said, "that is no reason why I should lose my dinner."

Malbone's daughter, Deborah Hunter, opened up her home to the Duc de Lauzen. The womanizing Frenchman adopted a hands-off policy when it came to his hostess's lovely daughters, but Fersen, who was staying elsewhere, felt no such restrictions and instantly succumbed to Eliza's many charms. He liked to spend his evenings in the Hunters' drawing room, where he enjoyed Eliza's wit, good nature, and musical talents. She played the piano while he accompanied her on the flute. He taught her Swedish, she taught him English, and if they had trouble communicating in their native tongues, there was always French. Fersen's letters to his family included news of Eliza, whom he described as "pretty," "sweet," and "gay." Sometimes he contrived to stay after de Lauzen went to bed, just so he could spend a little time alone with her. Their flirtation was a wonderful distraction for a lonely soldier passing a long, cold winter in a place so far from home.

According to Hunter family lore, their romance became serious and Fersen proposed marriage. But Eliza regretfully declined. She had been diagnosed with a degenerative eye disease and she feared that blindness would make her a bad wife. The sweethearts parted in June 1781, when the French army set off for Yorktown to fight the British. With the help of their friends, the feisty colonies won the war in 1783.

Fersen returned to France, where he resumed his relationship with Marie Antoinette. In fact, he was the brave admirer who tried to save her from the guillotine by orchestrating her dramatic escape from the Tuileries. But he never forgot about lovely Eliza, who, as her doctors predicted, eventually lost her vision. She never married, and there was no happy ending for Fersen, either. After losing Eliza and Marie Antoinette, he dedicated himself to public service in his native Sweden. In 1810, a time of great political unrest in his country, Fersen was savagely murdered by an angry mob.

Years later, in a funny twist of fate, one of Fersen's descendants married a member of the Hunter family, and the star-crossed lovers enjoyed the reunion they were denied in life. Their miniatures—small portraits painted when Eliza and Fersen were young and beautiful—were dusted off and displayed together on a mantelpiece in Newport.

3

Reversal of Fortune

After the war, Newport fell into an economic depression that paralyzed the city for several decades. The situation was so desperate that the population barely increased and, during one dramatic slump, ten whole years passed without the construction of a single new house. "Not a pound of paint has been sold in the town since the Revolution," a townsperson griped. Eighteen sixteen was called the year without a summer because the weather was so cold. Travelers who passed through the sad little city sent reports of dilapidated houses, town squares overrun with weeds, and shops selling pauper's lots of matches and apples. Its state of "quaint and pensive decay" seemed irreversible. There was no hope in sight until, nearly a decade later, some adventurous tourists came to the rescue.

In 1825, Southerners whose families had spent happy summers in Newport in more prosperous times started trickling back. Soon they were joined by vacationers from Providence, Boston,

Philadelphia, and even faraway Cuba. They stayed in rooming houses run by enterprising housewives and in some rudimentary mom-and-pop hotels, such as Whitfield's and the Bellevue.

Many of the guests at these minimalist accommodations were accustomed to luxurious lifestyles in their year-round homes. Southern planter Thomas Middleton and his family lived on a beautiful plantation in South Carolina. But when they summered in Newport, they embraced the simple life. Mimicking country folk, they hiked along the shore, bowled on the lawn, dined on sponge cake and fresh milk, danced with their friends, and enjoyed the city's beaches, pastoral scenery, and relaxed pace. Social life was informal, even bucolic. A popular form of exercise was the joggle board, an early version of the seesaw. Chairs were attached to both ends of a plank that was balanced on a pedestal. Well-bred ladies took turns gently pushing up and down with their feet, "joggling" the board as they engaged in conversation. These women wore simple cotton frocks for both daytime and evening without anyone raising an eyebrow. At least for the moment, it was fashionable to be unfashionable in Newport.

With each successive summer, the Middletons and other regulars noticed that they were rubbing elbows with more and more tourists. They feared that the peaceful atmosphere of their little island was threatened, so they retreated to neighborhoods that were quiet and undeveloped. Some families rented houses for the summer. Others set down roots in the community by building places of their own. In 1828, local children were given the day off from school to watch a house go up on Thames Street, a sight some Newporters had never witnessed in their lifetime.

There was an interesting third option for realty. A common practice for Newport's would-be homeowners was to buy an existing house and move it to a new location. Residents grew accustomed to the comic sight of horses pulling a large house through the city streets. And, there was plenty to laugh about when one unsuspecting New Yorker bought a house that had been a popular brothel and moved it to his plot of land. The house (and its ladies) had been vilified by a local clergyman. En route to its new address, it fell off its platform and landed up against that very clergyman's church, where it sat for a few days before resuming its journey across town.

While veteran summer colonists were moving away from the city's center, a new wave of visitors called excursionists descended upon Newport. They were a demanding group who wanted activities and amenities they couldn't get at home; that was the whole point of going away on vacation. Enormous hotels were built to accommodate them. The first was the Ocean House, which opened in 1844. It was a four-story, Greek revival building with tall columns; a large dining room; a long veranda; and, most importantly, enough bedrooms to accommodate hundreds of guests.

Tourists marveled at the Ocean House's beauty, although, despite its name, it was not near the water. In the 1840s, people liked to look at the ocean, but they had mixed feelings about bathing in it. Swimming costumes of the time were heavy and uncomfortable, especially after they were soaked with seawater and covered with sand. Artist Winslow Homer created an illustration for the magazine *Harper's Weekly* depicting busy swimmers working hard to stay afloat in their stiff woolen outfits, which looked very much like the clothes they wore on dry land. Diehard bathers preferred to swim nude, and men were authorized to do so at exactly noon every day at Easton's Beach, Newport's most popular place for swimming. When their clothes came off, a red flag went up, indicating that ladies should leave the area, or be prepared to see something shocking.

The Ocean House was extremely successful, until it burned to the ground only a year after it opened. Investors immediately raised $62,000—almost three times the cost of the original building—to construct a larger and more modern hotel. The new Ocean House was completed quickly, but no matter how many hotels opened, there never seemed to be enough rooms to satisfy the ever-growing tourist trade.

The hotels built to accommodate Newport's influx of visitors were pleasure palaces designed to celebrate the newly democratized art of recreation. Guests professed to come to the resort for their health—the salt air was supposed to be a tonic—but what they really wanted was a social life. Hotels gave people the opportunity to consort with the opposite sex in a pleasant and carefree environment. Virtual strangers could spend time together under one roof, promenading, dancing, drinking tea, and even flirting in a socially acceptable way.

Nineteenth-century homes were protected environments, but hotels, with strangers sleeping in adjacent rooms, could be unsafe. Eliza Potter, an African American hairdresser who often worked the hotel circuit, liked to tell the story of a young woman who almost ruined her reputation when she mistakenly entered the right room on the wrong floor. She undressed without lighting a candle and climbed into bed, only to discover that she was under the covers with a strange man—a situation that could not have happened anywhere but in a hotel. The shocked maiden and her parents fled from the scene and ran off to Niagara Falls, hoping to stay a few steps ahead of the scandal. They were followed, not by gossip, but by the young gentleman whose sleep had been interrupted. He was so enchanted by his charming nocturnal visitor that he proposed marriage on the spot . . . and she accepted. The next year, the newlyweds legitimately shared the same room at the same establishment.

Newport's year-round residents considered these hotels, with their intensely social atmosphere, a mixed blessing. They liked having visitors who spent money, and acknowledged that this infusion of cash was responsible for pulling the city out of its slump. But there was something a little distasteful—and even threatening—about the large transient population. Tourists came to Newport to relax, and sometimes they relaxed their morals along with everything else. There was always the danger that outsiders might lower the moral tone of the community. "They bring money and gaiety to our town," said a disapproving Newporter, "but they have introduced among us . . . a very serious evil; I mean an expensive life style and a too great fondness for convivial entertainments."

The best firsthand description of resort life in Newport in the middle of the nineteenth century was reported in *Belle Brittan Here and There*, a collection of letters chronicling the adventures of a lively young woman on a road trip across America. Belle spent the summer of 1856 at the Ocean House. Caught up in the "season," she offered rapturous descriptions of the beach, musical afternoons on the hotel's veranda, and the "subscription" balls of the time. Guests paid as much as ten dollars to attend the fetes, which took place in a hotel ballroom. As for the preparations for these activities, Belle said that she changed her clothes nine times a day, complaining that "first, we put on a dress to dress in."

Belle also wrote about the reckless behavior she spied on her outings. Older women pursued younger men. Younger women chased older men. Fortune hunters of all ages ran after anyone with money. And some highly unconventional women took up with each other and were spied kissing on the lips.

Belle's whimsical (and often barbed) observations about social life at the popular watering hole are even more interesting if the reader knows that "she" was actually a he. Belle Brittan was the nom de plume of Hiram Fuller, a caustic newspaper editor at the *New York Mirror*, a counterculture publication of the time. Belle's seemingly superficial chatter about fortune hunters, desperate spinsters, gossips, and snobs was designed to lampoon tourists and their foolish, often feverish behavior. Fuller had a great sense of humor, but he found the vacationers ridiculous. Whatever he thought, Newport's tourists were having the time of their lives. They loved the city, and many of them wished that they never had to leave. Luckily, a wily land speculator named Alfred Smith was standing by, ready to make their dreams come true.

Smith was a tailor with a dream. He was born and raised in Newport, and learned how to sew there, but he was so good at his job that he landed a position with a first-rate clothier in New York. Smith was a no-nonsense type who watched his money, sometimes sleeping under his sewing table just to save a few cents. He paid close attention to his wealthy clients during their fittings, always on the lookout for a business opportunity. While Smith expertly adjusted their jackets and pinned their pants, he listened to the men chatter about their vacations in Newport. Their enthusiastic comments convinced him that there was money to be made in his old hometown.

In 1839, at age thirty, Smith moved back to Newport to explore the exciting new world of real estate. He had amassed a $20,000 nest egg and he was ready to invest it in his future. Most entrepreneurs were busy focusing on the city's hotel boom, but Smith looked ahead to a time when visitors, especially rich ones, would want to build their own summer homes. Where others saw shapeless, disconnected parcels of land that were uncultivated and inaccessible, Smith, with his tailor's eye, recognized valuable raw material that he could fashion into a bigger and better Newport.

It helped that Smith knew every inch of the city. He bought large properties in undesirable parts of town and divided them into lots. Then he added landscaping to make them more attractive, replacing the trees that were destroyed by the British during the Revolutionary War. George Noble Jones, a Savannah planter who usually installed his family in a hotel for the summer, bought property from Smith in 1841 and built a fanciful Gothic Revival house. Other vacationers followed his example, purchasing land from Smith for their dream homes. His $20,000 investment yielded great returns, but getting rich was not his only ambition. Smith considered himself a curator, handpicking each new member of the community. He championed high prices and high standards to make sure the "right" people ended up being landowners in Newport.

In 1851, Smith partnered with Joseph Bailey, another Newporter, in a potentially risky venture. They acquired a sizable property on the southern side of town—a beach area that was beautiful but undeveloped, and surrounded by sand and fields—knowing full well that it had one major drawback: it was in the middle of nowhere. Everyone thought they were crazy and Bailey regretted the purchase immediately, confiding to friends that he doubted he would get anything but "driftwood enough to keep me warm for the winter."

Smith, on the other hand, was confident that he and his partner were sitting on a gold mine. All they needed was a road. He convinced local officials to turn Bellevue Street into Bellevue Avenue, a thoroughfare that would connect the busier part of town to his remote beach property. The new Bellevue Avenue may have been little more than a wide dirt lane, but Newporters loved it. Thanks to Smith's landscaping talents, it was lined with trees that evoked the scenic boulevards of Paris. More importantly, it provided an easy route to a very beautiful part of the island.

Smith needed buyers with vision, and experience had taught him that the best way to convince rich people to part with their money was to offer them a little something extra for free. To lure buyers to his remote plots of land, he gave them access to an out-of-the-way strip of beach that became known as Bailey's. It wasn't the best beach in Newport; the water was often murky and filled with seaweed. But it was quiet and far from the annoying crowds at Easton's Beach, where tourists congregated. When landowners and their children came to Bailey's Beach, they encountered a clubby atmosphere and familiar faces.

As Smith imagined when he started buying and selling land, property values in Newport soared, especially on and around Bellevue Avenue. In 1852, Daniel Parrish, a rich southern planter, built Beechwood, a Florentine palazzo. Two years later, William Wetmore, a New Englander who made a fortune in the China trade, built an Italian-style villa he called Chateau-sur-Mer.

A few years after Chateau-sur-Mer was completed, Wetmore hosted a party that set a new record for extravagance in Newport—and everywhere else in the country. He invited more than twenty-four hundred guests to join him for a fête champêtre, a garden party held on the spectacular grounds of his estate. The splendid setting must have inspired cottage envy among Wetmore's wealthy friends. After the party, other tycoons followed his lead and bought property in the appealing resort. The 1850s brought the first wave of new money to Newport and, one by one, oversized houses sprouted, looking large and somewhat forlorn. When Newport's physical landscape changed, the city's social climate changed along with it. The old, friendly Newport, known for its relaxed pace and country pleasures, was invaded by new people with a new agenda.

4

The New Newport

S uddenly it was important to be chic in Newport. Strolls on tree-lined paths, brisk dips in the ocean, and a dress code of simple cotton gave way to citified social rituals that once would have been woefully out of place at the beach. During the day, the new breed of homeowners and tourists wore bespoke finery and paid formal visits to friends. At night they attended dances and other entertainments. The new Newport was in a constant state of celebration, a Mardi Gras without end. One unhappy old-timer wondered why no one stayed home anymore, pointing out that, in her day, it was "sometimes more agreeable to refuse than to accept an invitation."

With the tourists came the need for tourist attractions, and the two most popular ones in Newport were the Cliff Walk and the Old Stone Mill. The Cliff Walk was an elevated footpath that ran for about three and a half miles along the coast. It snaked between the rocky bluffs overlooking the Atlantic and the spacious lawns of Newport's rapidly growing estate section. The scenery, consisting

Nineteenth-century beachgoers in Newport dressed in their finest, even when frolicking in the water.

of spectacular views of the ocean on one side and cottages and their gardens on the other, delighted tourists. Some of the cottage owners weren't quite as thrilled with the Cliff Walk because it robbed them of their privacy. Thanks to an old charter that guaranteed fishermen unblocked access to the sea, the public had the right to use the coastal footpath, even when it crossed private property.

Governor William Beach Lawrence, who owned sixty acres on Ochre Point, had no intention of letting strangers roam his property. He built a stone wall to deter trespassers, a hostile act that ignited a lengthy battle with the townspeople. They pulled down his wall, so he built a new one, adding shards of cut glass. Lawrence also stationed an angry bull near his property line. But insistent Newporters continued to fight for their right to use the Cliff Walk and they won, despite Lawrence's unfriendly efforts to keep them out.

Visitors to the new Newport were also intrigued by the Old Stone Mill, a mysterious tower that stood in Touro Park, a grassy area bordering Bellevue Avenue. For centuries, most people believed that it had been built by Benedict Arnold, a Rhode Island governor and farmer whose descendant was the famous American traitor of the same name. As tourists poured into Newport, however, romantic legends supplanted the prosaic stories about the tower's origins. In 1837, Car Christian Rafn, a Danish archaeologist, suggested that the tower had been built by Vikings who came to Newport, which they called Vinland, in the eleventh century, long before Columbus discovered America. The poet Henry Wadsworth Longfellow was so inspired by the notion of a Viking visitation that he wrote a poem titled "The Skeleton in Armor" as a tribute to the tower's intrepid Norsemen.

Rafn's claims may have had some basis in science and history. The Old Stone Mill resembled some unusually shaped churches that could be found in Scandinavia and the Vikings had been in North America in A.D. 1000 because evidence of a settlement was found in Newfoundland. Furthermore, some scientists argued that the tower's measurements conformed to the Rhenish, or Hanseatic scale, using 12.35 inches to the foot, rather than the traditional English scale of 12 inches to the foot.

But scholarly discourses on the subject were not half as interesting as the fact that the Viking theory surfaced—and won acceptance—just a few years after a "sea serpent" was spotted frolicking in the waters of Nahant, a nearby Massachusetts resort that competed with Newport for summer visitors. The serpent-sighting did wonders for Nahant's tourist trade—an enterprising Austrian composer named Martin Strakosch even wrote the "Sea Serpent Polka" to commemorate the discovery. Did Newporters really believe that wandering Vikings stopped briefly in Newport, built a stone tower, and set sail without leaving a trace? Or, as the *New York Times* suggested at the time, were they promoting their own local legend to boost business? Newport's leading hotels imported "antiquarians" every year to "investigate" the Old Stone Mill question. Inevitably, the *Times* pointed out, these experts supported the tourist-friendly Viking theory (then, the cynical writer suggested, they asked to have a fresh box of cigars sent up to the room the sponsoring hotel had graciously provided free of charge).

Tourists brought in money, but Newport's literati, the city's distinctive artistic and intellectual community, made it smart. The artist John La Farge painted pastoral scenes in nearby Portsmouth, and Julia Ward Howe, an abolitionist (and later the author of "The Battle Hymn of the Republic"), maintained a salon where she debated the issues of the day with popular writers such as Bret Harte and Longfellow.

Henry James came to town as a teenager in 1858 and immediately felt at home. He took long walks on the beach and spent hours reading books at the Redwood Library. He even studied painting with artist William Morris Hunt, who had a studio in town, only to discover that he had absolutely no talent for the medium. But young James did have a talent for writing. Shy about his literary ambitions, he kept his work to himself, even though one of his brothers spied "poetically looking manuscripts" in the aspiring writer's room.

Tourists, socialites, artists, and locals managed to live side by side in Newport every summer, until 1861, when the colorful and multifaceted little community was rocked by a battle in faraway South Carolina. Confederate soldiers attacked a federal military installation at Fort Sumter, the Civil War began, and Southerners, many of whom had built homes in Newport, were prevented from coming north for their summer vacations. Fortunately, a new population stepped in to fill the void. Military strategists moved the U.S. Naval Academy from Annapolis, Maryland, to Newport because they feared it was in danger of attack by the Confederate Army, and it remained there for the next three years. The setting was so hospitable that the navy established other installations in Newport, including the country's first torpedo factory, the U.S. Naval Training Station, and the Naval War College.

The navy was good for Newport's economy because it compensated for all those absent Southerners. But Newport's women might have argued that the navy's greatest contribution to the city was the extra men—an ongoing supply of young, presentable officers who could be called upon at a moment's notice to round out a guest list at a dinner or a dance (even though smart mothers never seated a dashing military man next to their unmarried daughters).

The Civil War sparked a social and economic revolution in Newport and everywhere else in America. In antebellum days, there was a direct relationship between money and lineage, especially in New York society. The oldest families, called Knickerbockers, were wealthy, established, and notoriously exclusive. They had moved in the same small, privileged circles since birth, so they knew exactly who they were and socialized only with one another.

In the postwar 1870s, however, New York's aristocracy was assaulted by a fast-developing plutocracy. The North experienced a financial boom that spawned a population of fledgling millionaires who wanted to crash New York's innermost social circles. These upstarts had money and all that it could buy: expensive clothes and jewels, the right address, the best furnishings. But they lacked the social graces forged by generations of breeding. The nouveaux riches didn't know which fork to use at a formal dinner, the correct way to hold a teacup, or the proper form for a thank-you note. The finer points of etiquette that were second nature to Knickerbockers were a mystery to the uninitiated.

Opportunistic publishers capitalized on the paranoia of society's newcomers by issuing a profusion of how-to guides about manners. *The Habits of Good Society: A Handbook for Ladies and Gentlemen* covered every subject, from carving a roast to proposing marriage. Other popular etiquette manuals included *The Young Lady at Home and in Society* by Mrs. L. C. Tuthill and *The Bazaar Book of Decorum.*

The readers who eagerly consulted these etiquette manuals were dismayed to discover that polite behavior was a full-time job. There were hundreds of complicated rules that covered every possible occasion and circumstance, from the proper way to eat strawberries (pick them up by the stem) to the best way to "cut" an undesirable person (gently and without undue drama). Books in a lady's library were supposed to be separated according to the gender of the author (unless a male author and a female author were married, their works could not stand together). Gentlemen learned that they could wear their hats on the street, or on a steamboat deck, but not at the theater or the opera. And a young lady could drive with a young man in her pony cart without a chaperone, but she was not allowed to ride in his coach alone.

Society also had various secret languages to be mastered by aspirants, and they were usually built around inanimate objects. Well-bred ladies used their parasols and fans to express feelings that would have been decidedly unladylike if spoken. When a young woman wanted to meet a gentleman, she carried her fan, or raised her parasol, with her left hand. If she wanted him to follow her, she held an open fan, or a closed parasol, in her right hand. The wrong signal, or the wrong interpretation of a signal, could lead to confusion and scandal.

Flowers, too, had their own special language. A man had to be very careful to use the right bloom to express the right sentiment. A red rose signified true love, while a yellow rose, however beautiful, communicated jealousy and disenchantment. Florists and their customers had to speak flower fluently, or risk serious misunderstanding.

Even innocent-looking calling cards—the nineteenth-century equivalent of a business card—were fraught with meaning. A custom of the day was the virtual visit: guests left their calling cards at a residence—usually deposited at the door by a coachman—instead of actually entering the house. Each of the four corners of the card held a message, and the caller folded back the one that best expressed the purpose of the visit. The top left corner indicated a routine call, the top right communicated congratulations. The bottom left corner bade adieu when a caller was leaving town, while the bottom right was reserved for condolences. Cards had to be left at specific times of day, during a hostess's preset at-home hours. After a card was left, the recipient had the option to return the favor, if she wanted to pursue the friendship, or to ignore it. If she reciprocated, she probably did so by sending a card with her coachman. In this way, it was possible to carry on an entire relationship with a minimum of face-to-face contact.

The newly rich diligently studied their etiquette books and tried to improve themselves, but the old guard called them "climbers" and "silver gilts," and scorned them for trying to "break into society with a pen and check book." Many of the newcomers were blessed with thick skins as well as deep pockets, so they were not deterred by the snobs or their snubs. A story circulated about a persistent businessman, a banker with money but no social standing, who blackmailed a prominent gentleman into securing him an invitation to an important party. The happy interloper dressed in his best evening clothes and entered the ballroom to enjoy his victory, only to find that he was alone. The gentleman and his well-bred friends stayed home to communicate their disapproval of the climber's ill-mannered behavior, making the point that social acceptance could never be forced.

Society was under siege when an unlikely leader stepped forward and put her dainty foot down. She was Caroline Astor, wife of William Backhouse Astor, and she was prepared to lead her fellow Knickerbockers into battle to keep the barbarians out of their ballrooms.

"The" Mrs. Astor

Caroline Webster Schermerhorn was not beautiful. She was short, plump, and, according to one of her more candid relatives, "really homely." But she was blessed with impeccable bloodlines—her ancestors came to America from Holland in 1636—and her family was so prosperous that in 1845, when Caroline was fifteen, the Schermerhorns warranted their own entry in the bluebook *The Wealth and Biography of the Wealthy Citizens of New York*.

Young Caroline grew up the old-fashioned way, on a very short leash. In Old New York, there were rules that governed how a proper young woman spent her day. In the morning, she could visit the Society Library and stroll in an acceptable neighborhood close to home. Lunch was followed by a drive in a coach and tea, and evenings consisted of private dinners and dances. Faces, and the family histories that went with them, were always familiar, so there was no room for error.

In 1853, Caroline married William Backhouse Astor Jr., grandson of John Jacob Astor. Some people wondered what the newlyweds saw in each other because she was plain and he was handsome. Moreover, the Astor name was still a little nouveau in Knickerbocker terms. But there was great logic to the union: if Caroline had the finer pedigree, William definitely had the bigger bank account. Together, they were a perfect couple. Perfect . . . until the honeymoon ended and they retreated into separate worlds. Caroline devoted herself to raising their children while William spent his time breeding horses and sailing on his yacht.

The social anarchy that followed the Civil War coincided with an important milestone in the Astor household: Caroline and William's eldest daughter, Emily, was about to make her debut. But, unlike in Caroline's day, it was impossible for a mother to ensure that her children met the right people because the wrong people were suddenly turning up everywhere.

Caroline Astor decided that something had to be done about it, and she enlisted the aid of Ward McAllister, an effete, middle-aged, and exceedingly well-mannered lawyer turned society walker. McAllister was famous the world over for his expertise on etiquette and entertaining. He knew the best ways to plan a menu or arrange a seating chart, his invitations were models of politesse, and he was every hostess's first choice to lead a dance. These were not trivial matters to McAllister, who believed that old-fashioned propriety was the cornerstone of civilization. Even his speech was imperious, punctuated with affected, lockjawed expressions such as "doncherknow" and "donchersee."

McAllister joined forces with Mrs. Astor to see to it that the previously unspoken rules of the social elite became codified. The idea was to establish a first line of defense against the troublesome outsiders who were insinuating themselves where they were not wanted. Mrs. Astor and her fussy majordomo instituted a rigid lexicon of who-knows-whom rules. First, McAllister identified a group of socially superior men he called the Patriarchs, twenty-five bona fide gentlemen who, by virtue of birth and/or worth, were indisputably "in society." He gave these men the responsibility of creating the guest list for the Patriarch's Ball, an event that determined New York's ins and outs each year.

McAllister took exclusivity a step further by declaring that Mrs. Astor's ballroom was society's inner sanctum and that there were only four hundred people worthy of entering it. Actually, Mrs. Astor's ballroom, spacious as it was, could not hold more than four hundred, so the number was a practical one. As soon as word of the list got out, it became very important to be included.

The lucky socialites who made the cut were thrilled to be invited to Mrs. Astor's annual ball, which she held on the second or third Monday in January. At the appointed hour of eleven p.m., Mrs. Astor positioned herself in front of her portrait, which had been painted by Charles Émile Carolus-Duran, one of the most popular artists in Paris. She usually wore a gown by Worth and a dazzling display of diamonds that circled her neck, wrists, fingers, and even her wig. Outfitted like a queen, Mrs. Astor greeted her guests as they made their way into her famous ballroom. Throughout these long evenings, spectators marveled at their hostess's impressive posture, not realizing that her heavy jewels and constricting garments—a form of armor—made it impossible for her to slouch.

5

Calculated Moves

E ven a hostess as skilled as Mrs. Astor was exhausted by the constant battle to keep the fashionables in and the undesirables out.
McAllister, who owned a scenic farm on the outskirts of Newport,
advised her to move to the genteel, semicloistered resort during the
summer, pointing out that society would be much easier to manage
on the small, out-of-the-way island, which was practically a gated
community. Mrs. Astor was convinced and, in July 1881, she purchased Beechwood, one of the original Bellevue Avenue cottages.

McAllister always carried on about the pastoral picnics and
square dances he organized in Newport, but Mrs. Astor had no
intention of staging such casual entertainments at her summer
palace. Her parties there would be as sophisticated as the ones
she hosted on Fifth Avenue. That meant building a ballroom for
the Newport Four Hundred.

Mrs. Astor selected Richard Morris Hunt to make this all-
important addition to her cottage. Hunt was an interesting

combination of Old World and New, having been the first American architect to study at the prestigious École des Beaux-Arts in Paris. There, he witnessed Baron Georges-Eugène Haussmann, the architect of modern Paris, transform the dark and medieval city into a dazzling metropolis. Hunt returned to America in 1855 and quickly rose to the top of his profession, designing a French château, an Italian villa, an apartment house, a museum, or a skyscraper with equal skill. He may not have had a particular style, but he had style, and plenty of it.

When Mrs. Astor settled into Beechwood, she encountered one irritating problem. Her nephew and niece, Mr. and Mrs. William Waldorf Astor, also had a house in Newport. The elder Mrs. Astor imperiously decided that she was the family's one and only "Mrs. Astor" and insisted that her mail be addressed to "Mrs. Astor, Newport." The practice led to great confusion because, stubbornly, the younger Mrs. Astor used the exact same address. Of course, each woman received mail meant for the other, until an exasperated William and his wife threw in the linen towel and moved to England, where they, too, could be the "one and only" Astors.

Mrs. Astor's presence in Newport confirmed that the city was a significant social capital and signaled the beginning of a new era of entertaining. Suddenly it became very important for society—and the socially ambitious—to establish a toehold in Newport no matter what the cost. Millionaires were eager to follow in Mrs. Astor's footsteps, but McAllister, the perpetual gatekeeper, was ready with a list of new rules.

It would take at least three seasons for even the wealthiest outsiders to break into Mrs. Astor's Newport, he cautioned, and only if the supplicant were very, very lucky. Realistically, there were only three hours each day that could be spent on productive social climbing. There were thirty-six weekdays in the season, but it rained 20 percent of the time, and inclement days did not count. That left a grand total of ninety hours in which to get the job done. Some aspirants could expect to devote as many as seven summers to the quest. "Few are bidden and many devoured" was the unwritten caveat on Newport's portals. Insiders liked to point out that even Alexander Graham Bell, despite his accomplishments, never rose very high in Newport society, although there is no evidence to suggest that Bell ever noticed he was an outcast.

Even a victory, after summers of hard work and great expense, could be short-lived, for entrée one year was no guarantee of approval the next. "You can launch them into the social sea, but can they float?" McAllister liked to quip. Once accepted, neophytes had to fight to maintain their status, and the experience could be so punishing that it made them mean. They waited for the day when they could snub outsiders, perpetuating the very suffering they had endured. William Makepeace Thackeray, whose novels were brilliant chronicles of social climbing, described the process as "licking the boots of those above (and) kicking the faces of those below."

Some tycoons welcomed the challenge. Ogden Goelet and his brother, Robert Goelet; William K. Vanderbilt and his brother, Cornelius Vanderbilt II; Oliver Belmont; and E. J. Berwind, to name a few of the Newport aspirants, amassed more money than they could spend and, with the encouragement of their ambitious wives, were fully prepared to use it for social advancement. Mary Goelet, who was married to real estate baron Ogden Goelet, wanted to toss her very fashionable (and very expensive) hat into the Newport ring and had the means to do it. The Goelet brothers owned more than $100 million worth of New York City property, an empire that had been built, square foot by square foot, by their notoriously parsimonious father and uncle.

In addition to her hefty bankroll, Mary had strong social connections. She was one of the "marrying Wilsons," as she and her siblings were called, because of their knack for selecting especially wealthy spouses. The Wilsons were southern charmers, but they were not nearly as rich as their mates, which made them appear somewhat opportunistic. Furthermore, there was a slight shadow over the family name because their father, Richard T. Wilson, was said to have been a Rhett Butler–like profiteer during the Civil War, and his ill-gotten money was held against him.

The Wilsons' brilliant unions were the result of skill, not chance, and their ambitious and resourceful mother, Melissa, waged a campaign to launch each of her children into the best families. Belle Wilson landed a British aristocrat, and her brother, Orme, wed one of Mrs. Astor's daughters. So ingenious was one of Mrs. Wilson's stratagems that it earned her the title the Kingmaker. When she heard that the scion of an old New York family was recuperating from an illness in the countryside, she rented the house next door so that her pretty daughter could visit the unsuspecting patient every day. He came out of it with his health . . . and with a Wilson wife.

Grace, the baby, added yet another impressive dynasty to the family collection when she married Cornelius "Neily" Vanderbilt III. He was the grandson of the infamous and irascible steamship and railroad robber baron Commodore Cornelius Vanderbilt. Neily's parents objected vehemently to the union because Grace had been linked to their other son, William Vanderbilt, before he died at age twenty of typhoid. When she quickly and conveniently transferred her affections to their younger son, they suspected that Grace might be after the Vanderbilt money.

Rumors aside, the Wilson family connections and the Goelet family fortune placed Mary Goelet in a very good position. She owned a Fifth Avenue mansion, a yacht, and the highly coveted Box No. 1 in the Diamond Horseshoe of the newly built Metropolitan Opera House. (Families with new money had to erect their own opera house because they were not invited by the old-money families to join the established Academy of Music.) If Mrs. Astor had a house in Newport, Mary had to have one, too, so the Goelets bought a spectacular piece of property on Ochre Point, a bluff overlooking the Atlantic Ocean. Unfortunately, Mary came face-to-face with a formidable rival—Alva Vanderbilt, the wife of multimillionaire William Kissam Vanderbilt—who was busy climbing up the very same social ladder, and who, like Mary, had set her eye on Newport.

Alva

Born in Mobile, Alabama, in 1853, Alva Smith was the original "steel magnolia," refined, determined, and tough. She spent her early childhood in the South and summered in Newport, where the family rented a house on Bellevue Avenue. Alva loved the free and easy lifestyle she enjoyed during her vacations. She was a spirited young tomboy who delighted in rolling down hills and building bridges with her friends.

During the Civil War, Alva and her family moved to Paris, where she attended a boarding school and learned to appreciate French art, history, and culture. But, like many moneyed Southerners, the Smiths experienced severe financial woes after the war; they were forced to return to America, and they settled in New York City. At first, Alva did not notice that her father was increasingly concerned about money, but as she matured, she opened her eyes to the disturbing realities of her family's situation. Her father's income was reduced to the point where he thought he might have to take in boarders. Then her mother died.

Alva was keenly aware that she and her sisters had not been prepared to support themselves, so she decided that it was her responsibility to rescue them all by marrying well. William K. Vanderbilt, the handsome grandson of Commodore Vanderbilt, appeared to be the answer to her prayers, and she married him in the spring of 1875. Her father was too sick to attend the wedding, but he gave Alva his blessing, thanking her for taking a great burden off his mind. He died shortly thereafter, knowing that his daughter would be able to look after the rest of the family.

After the marriage, Willie K. made two important discoveries about himself: he had a talent for making money and a taste for fast women. Alva, like many unhappy wives, turned a blind eye to her husband's chronic infidelity, and kept herself busy with their three children, Consuelo, William Jr., and Harold. Soon she found that the best way to ignore William's peccadilloes was to become involved in the long, absorbing, and fabulously expensive process of building a house. One of Alva's earliest memories was of playing in her father's library, building houses out of books. She enjoyed every stage of the process—the planning, the construction, even making choices about a seemingly infinite number of details.

Alva was born to be a builder, and she found a friend and mentor in architect Richard Morris Hunt. They shared a love of European culture, history, and architecture, and he encouraged her to collaborate with him on the designs for her homes in New York and on Long Island. In 1881, Hunt built the Château de Blois, Alva's sprawling, medieval-style mansion on Fifth Avenue. It was a $3 million showplace, outfitted with turrets, a limestone facade, a Moorish billiard room, and a two-story paneled dining room. Ward McAllister was so impressed by the over-the-top château that he declared the William K. Vanderbilts worthy, and invited them to one of his Patriarch balls.

Despite McAllister's blessing, Alva faced one potentially insurmountable problem: Caroline Astor had not given the Vanderbilts her personal seal of approval. In polite society, an established matron had to make the first move before a junior socialite could claim her as an acquaintance. Until Mrs. Astor left her calling card at the Vanderbilts' door, Alva could not include her on any guest list, nor expect to be invited to the Astors.

Alva provoked a resolution when she announced that she would host a costume ball at her new home in honor of her titled friend the Viscountess Mandeville. Alva invited sixteen hundred of New York's crème de la crème to 660 Fifth Avenue on March 26, 1883. It was unlikely that anyone would refuse the triply enticing opportunity to dress up, mingle with royalty, and view the most talked-about new residence in the city. Alva's guest list was enormous, but one name was conspicuously absent: Astor.

Carrie, Mrs. Astor's youngest daughter, was inconsolable when she did not receive an invitation to the Vanderbilt ball, which all her friends were attending. In fact, they were practicing a special dance for the evening, a quadrille, or a German, as these carefully choreographed dances were called, and Carrie wanted to be part of it. The unhappy teenager huffed and puffed until she persuaded her mother to dispatch her coveted calling card to Alva's front door. This simple gesture signified the highest form of acceptance. Alva was free to invite Carrie and her mother to her ball, and the Astors would then be obliged to return the favor when they entertained. Alva Vanderbilt had officially arrived.

6

The Cottage Wars

The Vanderbilt ball confirmed that Alva was an important member of New York society, but Newport remained unvanquished territory. There was only one effective, albeit expensive, way to make a big splash in that city and that was to engage in the sort of real estate one-upsmanship that, in some circles, was actually called Vanderbuilding. The object was to outbuild, or Vanderbuild, one's neighbor (and, in some cases, as with the Vanderbilts and the Goelets, to outbuild one's very own brother) by erecting the largest and the most ostentatious summer home. Building a showplace in Newport became a rich man's sport. This was especially true in 1888, the year when production began on some of the city's most opulent houses, the year that marked the start of Newport's cottage wars.

Newport already had its share of jaw-dropping estates. In the 1870s, Charles McKim and Stanford White, the pioneering architects behind the firm McKim, Mead, White, created some of

Ochre Court, the Goelet family's enormous French chateau.

Newport's finest residences and buildings, including the Casino, the resort's popular tennis and social club on Bellevue Avenue. They popularized a signature shingle style—the use of natural-looking wood shingles to cover an entire building, including the exterior walls and roof. The look was perfectly suited to Newport's unspoiled landscape, and the shingles made new houses look gently weathered and aristocratically old, in a manner that would much later come to be known as shabby chic.

But words such as "gentle," "weathered," or, for that matter, "shingle" were not in the vocabulary of Newport newcomers like Mary Goelet. The natural beauty of Ochre Point was unmatched, but the Goelets were more interested in man-made splendor, so they commissioned Richard Morris Hunt to design their house, Ochre Court, in the style of a French château. But if Mary thought that her castle—however massive, magnificent, or expensive—could depose Alva from her top-dog position, she was mistaken.

Much to Mary Goelet's dismay, the William K. Vanderbilts retaliated by hatching plans for their own dream house in Newport. William presented his wife with a blank check to cover the cost of a cottage and the attendant trimmings. The gift, on the occasion of her thirty-fifth birthday, was ostensibly a sign of her husband's boundless love, but insiders whispered that the money materialized after Alva found William in a compromising relationship with yet another woman. However the Vanderbilts' summer retreat came into being, it was a fine consolation prize for either infidelity or approaching middle age. In August 1888, Alva re-teamed with Hunt to create Marble House.

Newport was a boom town for the next several years, with construction sites popping up everywhere. An exhausted Hunt, who was getting on in years, shuttled the short distance—a little over a mile—between Ochre Court and Marble House, supervising crews of workers, and also had several other projects in the city at the same time. One of these was an unconventional bachelor pad he was building on Bellevue Avenue for Oliver Belmont, a member of the banking family. A dashing sportsman, Belmont was so fond of his horses that he instructed Hunt to set aside the entire first floor of Belcourt, his brand-new, sixty-room castle, as a stable for his pampered steeds. He was not as solicitous of humans. Belmont instructed Hunt to allot space for only one bedroom in his baronial mansion, the best way to discourage pesky houseguests.

At Ochre Court, Hunt's team erected a gigantic building on a narrow, thirteen-acre lot. The outside of Mary Goelet's palace was made of blue Indiana limestone. Inside, electric lights

Belcourt, Oliver Belmont's sixty-room bachelor pad, which he shared with his beloved horses.

illuminated a massive, hand-carved stone stairway, arched windows, and a soaring, three-story ceiling. One of the windows, an impressive stained glass creation, was a masterpiece salvaged from a fifteenth-century German church. By the time the Goelets closed their checkbook, they had spent $4.5 million (over $100 million today) on the "perfect" beach house.

Hunt's plans for Marble House were on the same grand scale. The project was so hush-hush that the site was surrounded by a large fence to block the view of curious spectators, and was patrolled by private detectives. French and Italian artisans, many of whom did not speak English, spent four long years working on a veritable Tower of Babel as they fashioned five hundred thousand cubic feet of fine marble into a neo-classical palace.

The whole time, Alva and Hunt fought spiritedly over the details. "Damn it, Mrs. Vanderbilt," Hunt stormed, "who is building this house?" "Damn it, Mr. Hunt, who is going to live in it?" was Alva's tart reply. Despite their disagreements, Alva worshipped Hunt and considered the homes he built for her masterpieces. Alva's lavish birthday present had sixteen-foot-high bronze gates inside the house, a gilded ballroom, a grand staircase, and room upon room decorated in the opulent Baroque style of France's Sun King. Alva trumped Mary Goelet by spending $11 million ($260 million today) on her beach cottage.

The contest continued when Alva's brother-in-law, Cornelius Vanderbilt II, engaged the ever-popular Hunt to build The Breakers, a four-story, seventy-room Renaissance palazzo. Cornelius and his wife, Alice, had bought an existing house called The Breakers, but

Alva Vanderbilt's Marble House, the palace she created with Newport's most in-demand architect, Richard Morris Hunt.

it burned to the ground in 1892. They decided to build a new version of their lost vacation home, but this cottage would be a showplace. It also would be completely fireproof. The kitchen was separated from the rest of the house by thick doors, and the furnaces were placed in outbuildings, where they could do no harm.

The Vanderbilts were very competitive about construction. If the Cornelius II's had their way, The Breakers, not Marble House, would be *the* Vanderbilt residence in town. The *New York Times* considered the story so newsworthy that it offered regular updates about "The Progress of the Work on Mr. Cornelius Vanderbilt's New Residence." The awed journalist who scored an early look raved about the palazzo's two-story dining room with Italian marble walls, onyx pillars, and intricate ceiling frescoes. With its superb carvings, paintings, expensive furnishings, tapestries, and extravagant touches such as bathroom taps that offered a choice of saltwater or rainwater, The Breakers, the *Times* proclaimed, "outrank[s] any private residence in the world." It was one of Richard Morris Hunt's last and greatest creations. He died suddenly in Newport in July 1895, shortly after the house was finished.

The Cornelius Vanderbilt II's won the race to build Newport's biggest and most grandiose cottage, but at a price. Fortunately, it was a price they could afford. When property taxes were assessed in 1895, Cornelius Vanderbilt II had the distinction of being the highest-taxed individual in all of Newport. Thanks to The Breakers, his tax bill for the year was $10,324.50. Not surprisingly, given how many millions she spent, Alva Vanderbilt was the runner-up on the tax rolls. The Ogden Goelets, despite their efforts to beat out the competition, trailed in third place.

A few years later, in 1899, a self-made coal magnate named E. J. Berwind hired architect Horace Trumbauer to build another oversized Bellevue Avenue cottage. Unlike Richard Morris Hunt, Trumbauer never studied in Paris but learned on the job, working his way up the ranks of a Philadelphia architectural firm, yet

Cornelius Vanderbilt II's multimillion-dollar cottage, The Breakers, was so opulent it inspired the word "Vanderbuilding" to describe Gilded Age real estate one-upmanship in Newport.

Trumbauer's houses were imbued with Old World grace and grandeur. Whatever he may have lacked in European polish he made up for in confidence. "If money bothers you, then I'm not your architect," Trumbauer arrogantly told a prospective client. He built big, so his patrons had to have deep, open pockets to support his vision.

Spending money never bothered E. J. Berwind. The millionaire and his wife were inspired by palaces they saw while on a rich man's trek across Europe and, upon their return, they spared no expense to build The Elms, a house that paid homage to the Château d'Asnières, an estate outside of Paris. They set their marble cottage on a fourteen-acre lot and surrounded it with formal gardens to showcase their recently acquired collection of European statuary. The house's Louis XIV facade featured three magnificent glass and wrought iron doors that were engineered to open simultaneously. Inside the house, there were forty-seven rooms, including a dazzling white and cream Louis XV ballroom. The bedrooms on the second floor were decorated in the styles of Louis XV and Louis XVI. The Berwinds were enthusiastic about *everything* Louis and thought nothing of juxtaposing 150 years of disparate monarchial motifs under one roof. They liked to say that they were the brains behind the designs for The Elms and boasted that they supervised every little detail of its construction.

Paul Bourget, a French writer who traveled in titled circles in France and England, visited Newport and found much to criticize about the city's newly minted aristocracy and their dwellings. An eloquent freeloader, Bourget was happy to be a pampered guest in Newport even as he expressed negative feelings about the showy millionaire lifestyle. The houses were too big, the lawns too small, and the interiors too stuffed, he complained. "It revolts you or it ravishes you accordingly, as you are nearer to socialism or snobbery." Fascinated by the motivation behind such extravagance, Bourget wisely concluded, "When they set themselves to spending money, they spend too much in order to have the sensation of having spent enough."

The cottage wars launched Newport's Gilded Age, a term coined by writers Mark Twain and Charles Dudley Warner in their 1873 novel *The Gilded Age: A Tale of Today*. In their book, Twain and his collaborator satirized greed, corruption, and social climbing in post–Civil War America. The title was inspired by lines from Shakespeare's play *King John*, where a wise character observes, "To gild refined gold, to paint the lily . . . is wasteful and ridiculous excess." But the Vanderbilts, the Goelets, and their newly rich friends liked excess. In fact, they thought a gilded lily was even more beautiful than nature's simpler, unadorned version. In the seventeenth century, wealthy people wore solid gold buttons on their clothing to display their worth. In nineteenth-century Newport, they gilded their enormous houses.

Mamie

Marion Graves Anthon Fish, better known as Mamie, or Mrs. Stuyvesant Fish, was a forcefully eccentric society woman who always spoke her mind. She was plain, she could barely read or write, and her raucous laugh was described as "horselike." But Mamie was sharp, spirited, and irreverent, and when she was around, there was never a dull moment.

She and her husband, a true Knickerbocker, were childhood sweethearts. Stuyvesant Fish could trace his ancestors all the way back to the *Mayflower*, and his father, Hamilton Fish, was secretary of state under President Grant. Like many of his peers, Fish tried working in the banking business, but he was happier—and ultimately more successful—in the fast-growing world of railroads. Fish joined the Illinois Central Railroad as a director and worked his way up to president, a position he held for twenty years.

Mamie was the first to admit that the Fish assets were unimpressive, especially by Newport standards. "We are only moderately well off: we have but a few million dollars," she'd say. Luckily, as Ward McAllister pointed out, "a man with a million dollars can be as happy nowadays as though he were rich." The couple certainly seemed rich. In New York they lived in an Italianate town house designed by Stanford White. Their place was so up to the minute that it had its own Otis elevator.

In Newport, they built Crossways, an imposing white colonial manor overlooking the ocean. Unlike the ersatz palazzos and châteaus that lined Bellevue Avenue, Crossways was American through and through. The house was designed by Newporter Dudley Newton; erected by Newporter R. W. Curry; and furnished by Vernon, a company based in Newport. Even Crossways' location was unusual for Newport. It was built in the undeveloped part of town, on the Ocean Drive near Bailey's Beach.

Unlike many society couples, the Stuyvesant Fish (when referring to this notable couple, the plural of "Fish" was "Fish") adored each other. Playful in a Ma and Pa Kettle way, they enjoyed a lively repartee. One day, Mr. Fish noticed that Mamie was suffering from a cough. A solicitous husband, he asked if there were something he could get her for her throat. "That diamond and pearl necklace in the window of Tiffany's" was Mamie's quick—albeit hoarse—retort. Her wish was Stuyvesant Fish's command, and by the time Mamie recovered from her cold, she owned the necklace.

Like a good wife, Mamie was equally indulgent of Fish's desires, although his requests were far less extravagant than hers. All he wanted was to dine on his favorite meal of corned beef and cabbage once a week. Mamie had their chef prepare it just the way Fish liked it—boiled—ignoring the disapproval of their haughty French maid. Mademoiselle protested that the smell got in her hair, and she refused to eat anything but bread and butter whenever the nasty dish was served.

Mamie welcomed disapproval; in fact, she thrived on it. She insulted her friends and snubbed her enemies, hoping to make social life a little livelier. One day, she entered a ladies' luncheon remarking, "Here you all are, older faces and younger clothes." When Alva Vanderbilt, a pal and confidante, accused Mamie of telling everyone that she looked like a frog, her friend assured her, "No, no . . . not a frog! A toad, my pet, a toad!" Her barbs were so sharp and clever that most people considered it a badge of honor to be her victim.

But not everyone was so forgiving of Mamie's caustic humor. According to local legend, there was a time when the Fish estate was marred by unusual topiary hedges belonging to a disgruntled neighbor. The victim of too many of Mamie's insults, the neighbor had his hedges sculpted into leafy soldiers holding raised bayonets. As a finishing touch, their "guns" pointed directly at Crossways.

7

Upstairs and Downstairs

Economist Thorstein Veblen must have been thinking of Newport in 1899 when he coined the term "conspicuous consumption" to describe the practice of spending money to attain status. Even though he grew up on a farm in Minnesota and was a teacher by profession, Veblen understood the fin-de-siècle obsession with being—or appearing to be—rich. His book *The Theory of the Leisure Class*, a satirical analysis of society, class, consumers, and consumerism, explained that for Gilded-agers, the houses they built, the clothes they wore, and the goods they purchased were symbols of their net worth. Even their choice of a pet was meaningful: a domesticated dog whose only purpose was to adore (and adorn) his master was a four-legged status symbol.

Servants were status symbols, too, suggested Veblen. They may have been extravagances in some households (in the 1870s and the 1880s, upper- and middle-class Americans spent as much as a third of their income to employ domestics to do all the jobs they didn't want to do), but in a Newport cottage, they were a necessity because they made the luxurious lifestyle possible. The houses in Newport were so big, and the social schedules of their owners so demanding, that it took a fleet of servants to get an ultrafashionable family through the summer season. In 1895, there were 2,287 servants working in Newport, almost 10 percent of the city's permanent population.

At every cottage, the housekeeper and the butler held the top positions in the household chain of command. The housekeeper was "probably the hardest-worked woman in Christendom," according to *Millionaire Households and Their Domestic Economy*, a popular book about household management. She supervised the servants, oversaw purchases, settled accounts, and acted as a liaison between the lady of the house and the other employees.

One of the housekeeper's most unusual jobs was keeping track of the family linen. Imported sheets, embroidered tablecloths and napkins, and delicate, lace-trimmed personal items were very valuable, sometimes costing as much as or more than a servant's yearly salary. The housekeeper had to log each item in her notebook as it went to the in-house laundry to be washed and pressed, and cross it off her list when it came back, carefully returning it to its proper drawer or closet.

The butler was also a formidable presence in the house. Tradition demanded that he be large, imposing, and have perfect diction. Another important skill for a butler was the ability to feign disinterest in absolutely everything. No matter how many family dramas or indiscretions he witnessed, his expression had to remain impassive. His duties were varied—he maintained the wine cellar, made sure the table was set properly, and kept track of the family's china and silver. At dinner, he wore a dress coat and stood behind his mistress's chair, anticipating her needs. Essentially he was the perfect surrogate husband. He looked dignified. He was always home. And his answer to every request was an obliging, "Yes, ma'am."

The status of the person who prepared meals for a Newport family depended on whether the position was held by a woman or a man. Women were "cooks" who did their jobs without fanfare. But men, especially imports from France or Italy, were called "chefs," and they received more respect—and higher salaries—than any women performing the same job. A talented chef could make a hostess look good and attract guests to her table. Alva Vanderbilt convinced her husband to pay $10,000 a year to Chef Rammeau, a French culinary superstar. His cuisine was so impressive that few people turned down an invitation to dine at Marble House.

Other male servants on staff included the assistant butler and assorted housemen and footmen. Strapping Swedes and Norwegians made the most impressive-looking footmen. If they were not available, local lads with shapely legs could do the job. Having a good physique became important when Pierre Lorillard, a tobacco baron and Europhile who summered in Newport, revived the Continental custom of dressing male servants in livery. The idea was embraced by the cottager community. Footmen were required to wear white stockings, knee breeches, and the family colors. The Astor servants dressed in blue, while the Vanderbilt men were resplendent in maroon. In some houses, men also had to whiten their hair. "Will you powder?" applicants were asked at job interviews. If the answer was yes, they were taught how to coif themselves in the manner of an eighteenth-century dandy, an affectation that earned them a little extra money for their trouble.

Americans were often puzzled by the notion of footmen. Aside from answering the front door and running a few errands, footmen seemed to exist to support the illusion that a rich man's house was his castle. One day, Stuyvesant Fish came home to find his wife's retinue of gorgeously dressed footmen standing at attention in his front hall. "Well, I have been working hard for nearly twelve hours to help support these gentlemen of leisure," he quipped.

The social secretary was another highly placed staff member in the millionaire's household. Her position was unique because she was the hard-working alter ego of the lady of the house. She maintained the calendar, answered the mail, put together guest lists, dealt with caterers and florists, and navigated tricky social situations. She was expected to know everything, from the best night of the season to host a summer ball to the latest gossip, including who wouldn't sit next to whom at a dinner party.

The first professional social secretary was Maria de Barril, an aristocrat turned amanuensis, whose tony background set the bar very high for her successors. De Barril was born into a wealthy South American family with strong ties to Newport. She was a privileged society insider until the stock market crash of 1893 obliterated the de Barril fortune and left her penniless. Plucky Maria was not one to curse fate. She realized that the skills she had mastered as a socialite could be put to good use. She offered to manage the social lives of women who did not have the time— or, in some cases, the expertise or connections—to take care of themselves.

Miss de Barril's endeavor was an instant success. One of the reasons for her popularity was that she was extremely selective. Prospective clients had to come to her for a consultation. If she didn't like what she saw, she rejected them. She boasted that she investigated *the* Mrs. Astor before agreeing to work for her. When word got out that de Barril was a bigger snob than her clients, she was in constant demand.

Miss de Barril was a familiar sight in Newport. She wore ostrich-feathered hats and eye-catching gowns as she rode imperiously in a carriage that shuttled her to appointments. She was always busy supervising the details of someone else's important party. Her ornate penmanship was so recognizable that desperate women scrutinized their mail in the hope of finding a cream-colored envelope addressed in her distinctive backhand, the sure sign of an invitation to an A-list event.

The lady of the house also leaned heavily on her personal maid, who was expected to be a hairdresser, a makeup artist, and a fashion stylist all rolled into one. The personal maid was the first person to greet her employer in the morning and the last to see her at night. A maid even had to accompany her lady to social functions in case she had to attend to a wardrobe malfunction. Cottages had special anterooms where visiting servants cooled their heels, waiting to be summoned. The maid's night was just as long if she stayed home. She had to wait up to help her mistress disrobe and attend to the wardrobe selection for the next day.

The governess, preferably French or English, cared for the children. The upstairs maid worked upstairs, while the downstairs maid and the parlor maid cleaned the public rooms on the first floor. The laundress ruled her own steamy basement kingdom, where mountains of clothing and linens were processed each week. Even the servants had laundry, which was handled by the least experienced laundress on the staff, or farmed out to a local washerwoman. Laundresses had to be strong enough to lift vats of hot water and piles of sodden clothes and to beat and rub stains by hand. But these women also had to be skilled enough to process the expensive fabrics used in haute couture designs. Decorations and trimmings had to be removed from these garments every time they were cleaned, and sewn back on before they could be worn again. Ironing was an art in itself, with different irons designated for different jobs, including special ones for sleeves and ruffles.

The chauffeur, the gardener, and the engineer (and the people who worked for them) rounded out the cottage's staff. A skeleton crew consisted of at least a dozen servants. Generally, salaries for these domestics were low. At the top end, the housekeeper, the butler, and the social secretary made $720 to $1200 annually, while the lowly parlor maids, kitchen workers, and laundresses earned a mere $300 to $400 a year, although they probably worked harder than anyone else.

Even though servants were living and breathing symbols of conspicuous consumption, they were supposed to be invisible. In most Newport homes, the kitchen, wine cellar, laundry, heating system, generators, and other utilitarian facilities were tucked away in the basement, far from sight. Above ground, the staff used a concealed network of stairs and hallways when they carried laundry, delivered breakfast trays, and toted brooms and scrub brushes around the house. Their backstage world stretched from the kitchen to the rafters. In this way, cottagers maintained the illusion that an enormous house ran itself. At Marble House, the door used by the butler to enter and exit the dining room was so cleverly concealed that guests found his comings and goings positively supernatural.

At night, servants retired to small, functional bedrooms, usually on the top floor. At The Elms, Horace Trumbaeur pulled off a neat architectural trick by hiding the servants' quarters—the entire third story of the house—behind a decorative stone balustrade. The wall looked beautiful from the outside, but it blocked the servants' view, preventing them from catching even a glimpse of the house's spectacular vista of the Newport harbor.

The relationship between servant and employer was complex, with concerns and complaints on both sides. Experienced servants preferred experienced employers, families who had grown up with domestic help and knew how to treat them. A master and a mistress with an "English" attitude—a formal and impersonal air—created the best working environment because they, too, knew their place. Parvenus who tried to befriend their servants because they didn't know better were subjects of derision. Servants wanted to be treated humanely, but they had no desire to be either comrade or confidant.

There was one upside to working for new money: higher wages. "Are you shoddy, or old family?" a servant asked a prospective employer. In the early nineteenth century, "shoddy" was the name given to a fabric that looked like wool but was made of rags. Later in the century, the same word was used to describe people who looked like aristocrats but had more money than breeding. The consensus among servants was that "Shoddy pays the best!" Sometimes a tour of duty with a vulgar new family could be more profitable than a job with a tightfisted old one.

Occasionally, servants revolted when their employers asked too much of them. Morton, Mamie Fish's headman, was an impressive figure who knew all the intricacies of butlery. He was famous for his claret cup, a wine punch that was very popular at parties. Unfortunately, Morton enjoyed drinking his concoction as much as Mamie and her guests did, and when Morton was in his cups, all hell broke loose.

One day, Mamie brought home an unexpected visitor for lunch. Fortified by spirits, Morton blasted his mistress for taking advantage of the people who worked for her. Mamie was horrified by his impudence and fired him on the spot. Morton retaliated by removing the family's ornate gold service from the safe and methodically dismantling every single piece of it. Since Morton was the only member of the Fish household who knew how to put it back together, the situation was dire. Tiffany, the company that made the set, had to rush an expert to Crossways to reassemble the Fish cutlery in time for the next party.

Butlers were expected to be solid and dependable, so Morton's crime was particularly egregious. Chefs, on the other hand, were considered artists and were supposed to be temperamental. On one occasion, police rushed to answer an emergency call from Ogden Goelet's Ochre Court only to find the highly excitable French chef gleefully using his freshly sharpened cleaver to shatter his employer's fine china. He was in the throes of a nervous breakdown because he couldn't stand the family's profligate ways. "Les Américains sont des peegs!" he shouted in a combination of French and broken English. Luckily, one of the officers spoke a few words of French. His simple "Bonjour" managed to calm the hysterical chef before he hurt himself or the Goelets.

The Berwinds faced an unprecedented situation downstairs at The Elms when the entire household staff staged a dramatic palace coup. Dooley, the spirited head butler, rallied his coworkers to join him in a protest against their punishing eighteen-hour, seven-day workweek. Mr. Berwind ignored their petition for shorter shifts and better working conditions (he was equally unwilling to negotiate with the mineworkers in his employ), prompting the servants to organize a strike. An angry Dooley stuck his nose in the air and led a parade of irate domestics to the Newport train station, where they departed for New York.

The Berwinds had no trouble securing replacements for their runaway servants, but the new staff also found the working conditions intolerable and left en masse. The next group of servants must have come sans references. They were rowdy, tough, and undependable. A quarrel broke out in the pantry while dinner was being prepared, and one servant stabbed another with a carving knife. By the time the police arrived, the victim had been horribly disfigured and was in danger of losing his eyesight. Other cottagers experienced similar insurrections, prompting the *New York Times* to run a special report about Newport called "Trouble with Servants."

Most servants did not dismantle the cutlery, break dishes, or go on strike when they were feeling abused or underpaid.

There were less extreme ways for a clever servant to pick up extra income in Newport. The best-known secret of every millionaire's household was the commission, or kickback. The butler, the housekeeper, the chef or the cook, the coachman or the chauffer, and any other staff members who oversaw purchases, were willing to turn a blind eye to inflated bills if they received a cut from the vendors who submitted them. Sometimes the transaction involved goods—a new coat for the housekeeper from the family's tailor, or a special bottle of port for the butler courtesy of the wine salesman. It was the cost of doing business, and the servants knew their employers could afford to pay extra.

Another lucrative business for servants was selling information to gossip columnists. Newport's scandals were reported— and often fabricated—by Colonel Eugene Mann in a popular tabloid newspaper of the time called *Town Topics*. Mann's spies were everywhere, in the local telegraph office, in front of shop windows, and on staff in Bellevue Avenue mansions. Unscrupulous domestics who had a bird's-eye view of their employer's private life reported choice items to Mann and his representatives every Monday morning. They sold stories about shotgun marriages, closet alcoholics ("Miss Van Alen suffers from some kind of throat trouble—she cannot go more than half an hour without a drink," *Town Topics* reported), drug addiction, and other improprieties and indiscretions. Every Thursday, publication day for *Town Topics*, society folk turned to Mann's "Saunterings" column for the latest gossip, not realizing that some of the most tantalizing tidbits came from within their own households.

Mrs. Astor's servants came up with a novel way to feather their nest. Cautious cottagers maintained a caretaker during the winter months to watch over their empty houses. One winter, Mrs. Astor entrusted her gardener and his wife, who lived in a small lodge near the main house at Beechwood, to handle off-season emergencies and ward off criminals and vagrants. But instead of protecting the property, the enterprising gardener turned the Astor estate into a boardinghouse. Unbeknownst to Mrs. Astor, her summer palace was home to carpenters, bricklayers, masons, and other common workfolk who needed a place to flop. Transient laborers slept in her beds, ate in her dining room, and made merry in her famous ballroom. The gardener pocketed the rent, thinking his absent employer would never be the wiser.

The *Chicago Tribune* gleefully reported Mrs. Astor's utter horror at this "paralyzing discovery." There was a "taint" on the estate, the item suggested. "Beachwood [sic] cannot hold up its head in the stately manner which has been its wont. A house which has been harboring carpenters, plasterers, and hod carriers cannot boast that exclusiveness which is the ambition of the Four Hundred." The only possible solution, according to the newspaper, was "a thorough fumigation and disinfection."

Money aside, servants had a tendency to be exclusive and territorial, just like their employers. The social secretary did not offer to dust the furniture. The butler never filled in for the chauffeur. And the personal maid did not lend a hand in the laundry on a busy day. Servants even had a tendency to marry among themselves. The ideal couple resulted when a butler and a housekeeper found happiness together. The social ladder, and the business of maintaining one's position on it, was as important downstairs in the kitchen as it was upstairs in the ballroom.

Tessie

Most wealthy women never expressed much interest in the domestic arts. But Theresa "Tessie" Fair Oelrichs, the owner of a beautiful Bellevue Avenue cottage called Rosecliff, routinely snapped on white cotton gloves and policed her servants while they did their chores. "Bury me with a scrub-brush and a bar of Sapolio," she liked to say, emphasizing her passion for soap and water. No one could clean a marble foyer as well as Tessie. She was Newport's most exacting chatelaine, so suspicious of the people who worked for her that she kept running files on her domestics, labeling them "good," "bad," and "rotten."

Tessie's passion for cleaning began during her rags-to-riches childhood. She was the daughter of James Graham Fair, the proverbial father who struck it rich. Fair emigrated from Ireland to America in 1843, grew up on a farm in Illinois, and headed west at age eighteen to search for the fabled pot of gold at the end of the rainbow. Crafty and ambitious, he earned the nickname Slippery Jim for his machinations in the mining world. Ultimately it was silver, not gold, that made Fair a very rich man. He and three Irish partners took over Nevada's legendary Comstock Lode, a mine that yielded $100 million worth of silver in six years. Newly rich, the Fair family moved from a mining camp to the best San Francisco residence money could buy. But Jim Fair was no fan of high society. He preferred loose women to the uppity "nabobs" on San Francisco's Nob Hill.

In 1883, Theresa Rooney Fair, Tessie's mother, divorced her philandering husband. Thanks to a Solomon-like move on the part of the court, she won custody of the Fair daughters, Tessie and Birdie, while Jim Fair was awarded the couple's sons, James and Charles. Mrs. Fair used the family fortune to groom her girls for social success. In the summer of 1889, she brought them to Newport for their first season. Tessie's launch was the triumph her mother hoped it would be, and Tessie and Birdie, heiresses ripe for the picking, were accepted into an exciting world of money and privilege.

In 1890, Tessie married Hermann Oelrichs, an amiable bachelor of German descent who worked for the North German Lloyd steamship line. The bride's mother celebrated the occasion by hosting one of San Francisco's most extravagant weddings, an event that scored four pages of coverage in the *San Francisco Chronicle*. Hundreds of guests came, but Jim Fair was not invited. Just to prove that he was not the sort of father to hold a grudge, Fair sent the newlyweds a generous wedding gift: a check for $1 million.

Immediately after the wedding, Tessie purchased Rosecliff, a Newport estate named for its magnificent assortment of roses, including the American Beauty, a popular new hybrid of the time. She also bought the land adjacent to Rosecliff so that her property would stretch from Bellevue Avenue to the Cliff Walk. In 1899, Tessie commissioned architect Stanford White to design a house in the style of the Grand Trianon at Versailles. At its center was an enormous ballroom with two walls of windows, one facing the estate's gardens and the other the ocean. The house's most stunning—and symbolic—architectural detail was its heart-shaped staircase. But it was a rare occasion when Tessie passed through the exquisite marble and wrought-iron heart with her husband by her side.

Hermann was not an attentive spouse. He preferred San Francisco to Newport and, when in town, was more likely to spend time at the beach than with his wife. Tessie found consolation in the management of her beautiful house, but her compulsion to clean caused her to suffer a terrible domestic accident. During one of her white-glove inspections a carpenter's tack flew into her face and blinded her in one eye.

8

Members Only

Newport was a paradise for its wealthy summer colonists, but there was one annoying problem that just wouldn't go away. Tourists were overrunning the city and, much to the chagrin of the Astors, the Vanderbilts, and their ilk, ogling the rich had become their favorite sport. Eager excursionists paid tour guides to recount tall, and not so tall, tales about the famous denizens of Bellevue Avenue, and horrified cottagers could hear those guides shouting into their bullhorns as they passed their properties.

Colonists turned up their noses at the notion of these ill-mannered strangers spending the night in their Newport. They viewed the very hotels that had attracted their ancestors as magnets for riffraff and transients. When the Ocean House burned down in 1898, summer residents vehemently blocked a plan to build a new hotel on its site. Thanks to their opposition, most of Newport's hotels fell into disrepair, closed, and disappeared. Tourists could come, but they couldn't stay.

The cottagers used hedges, gates, and an off-putting air of exclusivity to maintain distance from the day trippers. But upper-crust Newport discovered that its most effective weapon in the ongoing war against outsiders was the private club. There was a club for every activity, and each had its own members and its own set of rules. The defining club in Newport was the Spouting Rock Beach Association, otherwise known as Bailey's Beach. Cottagers had been swimming at Bailey's Beach since the 1850s, when Alfred Smith invited them to install private bathhouses there. Conditions were simple, even primitive—but the landscape was beautiful and the company was convivial.

In 1890, Bailey's regulars took a long, hard look at their secluded little cove and decided it was ramshackle. The bathhouses, scattered every which way along a small strip of shore, were old and unsightly. The beach desperately needed a cleanup and a renovation. Bailey's management removed the old bathhouses and constructed an attractive triangular-shaped pavilion with a sloping Queen Anne roof. The new building contained a hundred bathhouses, each offering an ocean view. Old and new families in the Bailey's Beach community, including the Goelets, the Vanderbilts, and the Belmonts, purchased units, some at a cost of $3,000. The bathhouses were private, but the beach itself was open to the public.

In 1896, the wealthy bathhouse owners banded together to form a syndicate—the Spouting Rock Beach Association—for the sole purpose of purchasing Bailey's Beach from the estate of Alfred Smith. The *Newport Mercury* speculated that "this already beautiful site will be so improved as to make it second to no bathing place in America." But beautification was not the syndicate's main motive; it was fear.

They wanted to build a new and impenetrable Bailey's Beach that would be a retreat from prying eyes. "Only the swellest of the swell" would be able to pass through the "walls of exclusiveness surrounding the place," reported the *New York Times*. That was good news to club members who had no desire to swim at a public beach, where they might encounter "domestics and negroes—some of whom one would prefer not to meet in the water, even though one may be thoroughly Democratic in principle," said one member at the time.

The "Bailey's Beach Question" divided the community. Some old Newporters were outraged by the privatization of the beach and called it illegal. They claimed that the city's charter, issued by King Charles II, guaranteed everyone unobstructed access to the shore. "Bailey's Beach or Bust!" they protested. But the Spouting Rock Beach Association held firm. While nonmembers were free to congregate in an area off to the side known as "Rejects Beach," or the "Common Beach," they were not welcome to enter Bailey's pavilion or bathhouses. Just in case an impudent outsider decided to test the boundaries, the association put up a wall and hired five men to keep "all uninterested parties" from trespassing.

The club's coveted bathhouses were spartan compared to the gold and marble palaces its members called home. But shareholders thrilled at the sight of their initials on one of the beach's small, nondescript wooden buildings. These letters signified acceptance to one of the richest and most select organizations in the world.

During the season, members came to the beach from eleven to one every day. They swam, played tennis on the green lawn, and socialized. Samuel A. Young, the beach manager, proudly wore a jacket trimmed in gold and guarded the door. Bathers called him Old Sam and depended on him to watch over their valuables while they went swimming. He often held more than $300,000 in jewels and money in his pockets, "and there has never been so much as a pin lost," he bragged. The hardest task that ever came his way was when he was asked to fill in for a ladies' maid. One of Bailey's most beautiful young bathers asked him to hook up the waist of her dress. "I did the best I could. It was a long and vexing job," was his only comment.

Old Sam's staff, burly men in white uniforms, groomed the sand every morning, although they fought a losing battle against the brown seaweed that washed ashore. Women protected themselves from the sun by carrying gaily colored parasols and dressing in bathing costumes that covered their bodies from head to toe. The club's bylaws stated that ladies were supposed to wear stockings at all times, although young Elsie Clews, daughter of New York financier and Newport regular Henry Clews, flaunted her independence by being the first woman to bare her shapely legs, a bold move that drew harsh words from traditionalists and admiring looks from young men.

Some of Newport's gentlemen were genuine eccentrics. They viewed the beach as a private place where they could let their hair down because they were among friends. James Van Alen, for example, enjoyed playing the role of the dapper Anglophile. He had been married to Emily Astor (she died in childbirth) and liked to emphasize his aristocratic status by peppering his speech with Old English expressions. Words such as "gadzooks!" and "zounds!" made him sound like a character in a drawing room farce. Van Alen was always a humorous sight in the water because he wore a monocle and a straw hat while he swam.

Hermann Oelrichs also was a colorful figure at Bailey's. A large man with a huge appetite, he packed a lunch pail and reading material before setting out for a long, relaxing float in the ocean. Oelrichs stayed in the water for hours, probably enjoying the time away from his wife, and occasionally drifted so far from the beach that the coast guard considered him a hazard to boats.

Newport boasted so many private clubs that a cottager could spend the entire day going from one to another. The Reading Room on Bellevue Avenue was a men's club where very little time was spent reading. It was founded in 1854 by gentlemen in search of a place where men could be men. Mercifully, from the members' point of view, the Reading Room was off-limits to women. All those wives, daughters, mothers, sisters, and mistresses who turned Newport into a social circus every summer were barred. Gentlemen relaxed on the porch or stayed inside, where they indulged in manly vices such as drinking alcohol, smoking cigars, and cussing. Nice women refused to walk in front of the Reading Room's veranda because they feared they would be the victims of whistles and catcalls.

The Newport Casino was a social club on Bellevue Avenue that became the heart and soul of the city each summer. It was founded in 1881 by James Gordon Bennett, the controversial publisher of the *New York Herald*, after he had a falling out with his confreres at the Reading Room. Bennett had sponsored his friend Captain Henry "Sugar" Candy as a summer subscriber to the Reading Room in 1879. He underestimated the reaction of the other members when he encouraged Candy, a polo player, to ride his horse up the front stairs of the club. It was an innocent prank, but Bennett was severely chastised for his friend's rude behavior. Never one to take criticism lightly, Bennett vowed to open a more liberal club.

He purchased a vacant lot on Bellevue Avenue, invited his friends to become stockholders, and hired architect Charles McKim to design a shingled complex that Newporters would use for "games and sports of every kind and description, and for the development and improvement of literary and social intercourse and physical and mental cultivation." McKim's twenty-six-year-old coworker Stanford White designed the casino's interior and spacious courtyard.

Contrary to its name, the Newport Casino was not a place for gambling. It was a social and sporting club for summer residents and "cultured citizens of the town," who gathered there for lawn tennis, bowling, musical and theatrical programs, and other activities. Shareholders paid annual dues to enjoy the extra privileges of membership, including private rooms for billiards, cards, reading, and dining. Nonmembers could purchase admission for the day, or tickets to concerts and plays. Bennett hoped the casino would bridge the gap between the cottagers and the townspeople. It was a noble sentiment, but the casino crowd divided into two distinct groups: the wealthy fashionables and the ordinary people who came to watch their comings and goings.

Members checked in at the casino as soon as they arrived in Newport each summer. Ladies donned their finest ensembles and strolled around the grassy courtyards, their equally fashionable pooches in tow. They mingled with friends, watched (and sometimes played) sports, and listened to the melodious strains of the casino orchestra, including J. M. Lander, Berger's Hungarians, Henri Conrad's Society Orchestra, and John C. Mullaly and His Merrie, Merrie Men. Newporters were passionate about tennis, so the casino's precarious grandstand (once owned by a traveling circus and nicknamed the typewriter because it resembled a giant keyboard) held rows of enthusiastic spectators who followed the sport.

During a typical season, the casino hosted morning, afternoon, and evening concerts. Every Thursday night, from nine thirty to twelve thirty, guests danced in the casino theater. The Flower Show took place in late July. The National Lawn Tennis Tournament drew crowds the last week of August, and the Newport Horse Show, held in September, was the season's grand finale. The casino hosted so many events that it published an official annual program. Merchants from Newport and New York filled the book with advertisements hawking everything from oil paintings to corsets, knowing they would be read by an affluent audience.

The Newport Country Club was founded in 1893. True sportsmen enjoyed the challenge of the brand-new game of golf that had been recently imported from Scotland, not to mention the rare beauty of the club's course, which boasted breathtaking views of the ocean. But, society people who attended the first golf demonstration in Newport did not experience love at first sight. Unimpressed, they complained that the ball was too small and the pace too slow.

One year later, the same disinterested Newporters changed their minds and golf became the new craze. Men and women lined up to play the course at the Newport Country Club and architect

Whitney Warren, a budding golf enthusiast himself, was commissioned to build a clubhouse. It included locker rooms, a café, dining rooms, and a broad piazza for balls and other entertainments. Society tried to make the country club its new headquarters, thinking its restricted atmosphere would be preferable to the openness of the casino. But members discovered that there were times when spectators served a purpose. Privacy at the beach was one thing. But it was no fun to parade in the latest fashions without some kind of audience, so they resumed their daily visits to the casino.

There were other clubs with athletic themes. For a select few, there was the Gooseberry Island Fishing Club, an organization of fourteen male members who gathered on an islet to celebrate the lost art of nude bathing. They also entertained women with relaxed morals (not their wives) at long, sybaritic luncheons. The Graves Point Fishing Club was probably the most exclusive of the Newport clubs because founder J. Pierpont Morgan was the principal—indeed, the only—member. Even though he usually spent no more than five days a year fishing in Newport, Morgan maintained a clubhouse and a staff. It was estimated that his hobby cost him $1,000 a day.

Yachting was another expensive pastime for the moneyed Newport sportsman. The New York Yacht Club came to Newport each summer to enjoy the city's superior sailing conditions, and it was considered a worthy pursuit because it promoted nautical skill, discipline, and the hardiness that comes from living at sea. Not that millionaires roughed it on their yachts. James Gordon Bennett's steam yacht, *Namouna*, had many sumptuous rooms appointed in brass and mahogany. In fact, the engine room was as clean and luxurious as the parlor. William K. Vanderbilt traveled the globe in his steam yacht, *Alva*, one of the largest vessels in the world. He preferred it to Marble House, probably because it was a floating palace without the real Alva, who spent very little time on it. Yacht owners liked to say that if a man had to ask the price of a vessel, he couldn't afford it.

Finally, there was the Clambake Club, a rustic dining establishment on Easton's Point, a dramatic promontory overlooking the ocean. Newport cottagers rarely patronized restaurants. Every house had its chef, and there were so many at-home luncheons, teas, and dinners that there was little time for extracurricular dining. But the Clambake Club, as its name implied, was dedicated to a venerable Newport tradition: the clambake. The classic clambake was a multicourse meal consisting of clams, lobster, fish, potatoes, corn on the cob, and other down-home delicacies, prepared in a special pit. The Clambake Club was founded by a group of men "who hungered for the succulent clam and its accessories and not, mind you, served in the villas of the rich, but in the open and in the simplest manner." *Ex litori clamavi* was the club's whimsical motto, a bowl of steamers and a lobster its insignia. Every summer, members staged "bakes" at various locations on the island. In 1897, the club incorporated and established a permanent home on Easton's Point.

The menu at the club expanded to include meals of all kinds, which were prepared by a Maryland cook and his helper. Their uncomplicated, flavorful dishes provided a welcome contrast to the rich cuisine produced by pretentious French chefs at the cottages. The Clambake Club was the gastronomic version of Bailey's Beach. "This little hostelry, to the general public, is practically a mystery and a forbidden place," wrote *Town & Country* magazine. Gradually the club invited women to partake in the clambake festivities, and ultimately they were admitted as members.

In a resort city where houses were given lovely escapist names such as Idle Hour and Rest Haven, there was surprisingly little free time. Clubbing, whether at the casino, the country club, Bailey's Beach, the Reading Room, or the Clambake Club, guaranteed that cottagers could keep busy and move about town in happy, familiar groups. One definition of the word "club" is "a formal association of people with similar interests." But a club is also "a heavy stick suitable for use as a weapon." The Newport club was both: a safe haven, yes, but also the cottagers' best defense against the rising tide of interlopers demanding admission.

9

Ladies First

If menfolk retreated to the clubby, masculine environment of the Reading Room or the tranquility of the fishing lodge, it was because the women in their lives permitted them to do so. Newport was ruled by its women. Most husbands left the resort at the end of the weekend to go to their offices in New York, Boston, Philadelphia, and other cities, and their exodus left a seraglio of rich, pampered wives and daughters looking for ways to pass the time.

A typical morning began (not too early) with a visit from a personal maid. Armed with a breakfast tray and beauty products—creams for the body, bleaches and rose tints for the face; and rinses and dyes for the hair—mademoiselle prepared her mistress for the day ahead. Redheads such as Alva Vanderbilt and Tessie Oelrichs faced a grueling beauty ordeal every month because it took two whole days to keep an aging redhead red. A closely guarded formula from Paris required several messy applications.

First the hair was dyed black, then green, and then finally the desired hue. No woman dared be seen in this condition, so practitioners were prisoners of their dressing rooms during the long, unsightly process.

The right clothes played a critical part in creating the right image, and it was the maid's job to present a selection of outfits for madame's approval. One Newport hostess boasted that she set aside $10,000 each season for her wardrobe mistakes. Every activity—and there were many in the course of a day—called for a change of clothing. There was a costume for the beach, the tennis court, the yacht, the coach or automobile, and various meals and entertainments. "Different dresses for every occasion, eighty or ninety in a season, worn once or twice and put aside," complained one weary socialite.

The finished product was a beautifully bedecked woman who spent most of her time engaged in complex and calculated social maneuvers. Mornings were spent at the casino, where eager spectators gathered to gawk at the latest fashions. By midday, the ultrafashionables retired to Bailey's Beach, where the uniform was an uncomfortable bathing costume. Tennis and golf required players to wear casual—almost flirty—dresses that were short and wide-skirted for easy movement.

In the late afternoon, usually at three o'clock, the full-dress pageant resumed with a parade of coaches along Bellevue Avenue. Young women outfitted in gay pastel dresses with matching parasols contrived to sit up front with the driver so they could spread their skirts and pose prettily. They knew how charming this appeared to male passersby.

Evenings were given over to the "right" dinners and balls. In her memoir *Who Tells Me True*, Tessie's niece Blanche Oelrichs (using the nom de plume Michael Strange) recalled that grown women in Newport behaved as if their lives were over if a coveted invitation did not come. Acceptance was that important.

One day, Blanche found a beautiful young lady—a vision in pink taffeta and lace—crumpled on her doorstep. She was weeping because Blanche's mother had not been able to secure her an invitation to an important party.

The truth was that, busy as they were, the ladies of Newport were constantly battling boredom. Their frenzied pastimes—dressing up, coaching, paying calls, playing sports or cards (an expensive proposition for the unskilled or the unlucky), and indulging in innocent or not-so-innocent flirtations—got them through the season. Adultery was so widespread in Newport circles that there was a sliding scale of misbehavior. A young gentleman who wanted to dodge a married woman was advised to tell her, "Madame, I have no time for a liaison, but I am willing to oblige you, if you promise our adultery is not to be of a serious nature."

But some women were not content with Newport's social routines and rituals. The ambitious ones shared a tantalizing fantasy—they wanted to be the next Mrs. Astor. *The* Mrs. Astor, who was getting on in years, was well aware that there were plenty of eager understudies, not so patiently waiting for her to retire. "Many women will rise up to take my place," she once predicted in a rare interview. She was still entertaining, although guests noted that her famous ballrooms were looking a little worn. Moreover, there was no longer a Ward McAllister in attendance.

McAllister had fallen out of favor in the early 1890s when he wrote a book titled *Society as I Have Found It*. He was too much of a gentleman to actually name names in his tell-almost-all about the rich, but the book compromised his social standing. He died suddenly in 1895, and Caroline Astor, the woman he admired above all others, did not attend his funeral. McAllister managed to have the last word after his death. He bequeathed a copy of his book to the New York Society library, and, inside, handwritten in bright red ink, were the identities he had politely concealed when the book was published.

The most likely candidate to oust Mrs. Astor was Alva Vanderbilt, who, in 1898, recruited Tessie Oelrichs and Mamie Fish to join her in founding the Newport Social Strategy Board. Working together as a triumvirate, they set out to eliminate the old-fashioned pomp and circumstance that had become synonymous with Mrs. Astor's style of Newport entertaining. These women were eminently qualified for the job. Each had a "good" husband, a great house, superior organizational skills, and plenty of money

Since the opening of Marble House in 1892, Alva Vanderbilt's life had taken many dramatic—and unexpected—turns. There was always an undercurrent of gossip about her frequent outings with Oliver Belmont, the handsome bachelor who lived across the avenue, but in 1893, those rumors turned into bold-faced headlines. Belmont joined the Vanderbilts for a cruise on their yacht, and when the cruise ended, so did the Vanderbilt marriage. The unhappy couple announced that they were filing for divorce.

According to the conventions of the time, blame was assigned to the husband; the divorce petition said the rift had been caused by Vanderbilt's affair with a French courtesan, but it was rumored that both husband and wife were playing with fire. Willie K. had been running around with other women for his entire marriage, yet his infidelities never sparked anything but the gift of a large check to his wife. This time something was different. Rumor had it that Alva was the guilty one, and that Willie K. had found a very embarrassed Oliver Belmont hiding in her bedroom closet.

When the story became public, some newspapers, including the *Chicago Daily Tribune*, came out on the side of the Vanderbilt husband. In an article titled "Misery of an Unsupported

Woman," Alva's accusations of cruelty, desertion, and nonsupport prompted ridicule instead of sympathy. The *Tribune* suggested that cruelty in Alva's set meant that a husband sneered at his wife's hat, or some such minor infraction. As for desertion, Willie K. was probably justified in going elsewhere for what the newspaper euphemistically called "comforts which he could not find at home." But it was Alva's complaints of nonsupport that sparked the most vituperative backlash against her. She said it would be a hardship to live on $200,000 a year, at a time when most working women considered themselves lucky to make an annual salary of $500.

The breakup of her marriage, and the bad press that went with it, posed a serious threat to Alva's position in society. Her advisers tried to talk her out of the divorce, warning that she would have to stand alone if she took this radical step. She noticed that old friends snubbed her at church, and she suspected more insults were on the way. But Alva was not afraid of scandal. In fact, she was proud of asserting her independence. "I always do everything first," she boasted. She may have been the first of her set to ask for a divorce, but she was not the first to want one. Other society women would follow in her footsteps, she thought confidently. They always did.

While Alva waited for her peers to catch up with her bold behavior, she hatched a plan to bullet-proof her family's social standing: She decided that her teenage daughter, Consuelo, would marry Edwin William Spencer-Churchill, the Duke of Marlborough. He was a prize catch for a "dollar princess," as marriageable American heiresses were called. It was irrelevant to Alva that Consuelo was in love with Winthrop Rutherford, a handsome (if somewhat impecunious) bachelor from a good Knickerbocker family. The duke needed the Vanderbilt money—Consuelo's dowry of $2.5 million—and the Vanderbilts needed the duke's unimpeachable social status. The marriage was a business transaction, not a love match. There were bound to be broken hearts along the way.

Consuelo was desperate to break the engagement, but Alva outsmarted her by feigning a heart attack and threatening dire consequences if her daughter refused to go through with the wedding. A miserable Consuelo became the Duchess of Marlborough and moved to England to settle into an unhappy life with her titled husband, an unpleasant man who never looked beyond her bank account.

But there would be no marital compromises for Alva, not this time. She wed Oliver Belmont in 1896. "Up until the time of my second marriage I had never lived. I had existed," she proclaimed. Marble House was part of her divorce settlement from Willie K., but Alva preferred living in her new husband's cottage. Belcourt became the happy couple's summer residence, where they slept over the stables. The word "stable" was a misnomer in this instance. Belmont's beloved horses lived in expensive stalls on Belcourt's first floor. Like their owners, the horses were surrounded by valuables and outfitted with monogrammed blankets and linens.

Across the street at Rosecliff, Tessie Oelrichs discovered that, in typical poor-little-rich-girl style, her enormous bank account could not buy her happiness. For all her money, she couldn't control anything that was important to her, neither her weight nor her husband's wayward affections. In a time when tiny, wasp waists were the fashion, Tessie suffered from a hormone imbalance that caused her to gain weight rapidly. She was constantly at war with her body, starving herself to compensate for a sudden onslaught of pounds. She tried to appear slim and girlish by squeezing herself into punishing corsets that had to be tightened by her strongest (and most discreet) male servants.

Gossip columnists actually kept track of Tessie's weight fluctuations. "Mrs. Hermann Oelrichs . . . is not as stout as she was last Winter, and her slighter figure is very becoming to her," observed a reporter who penned "Some Tea Table Confidences" for the *New York Times*. But Hermann Oelrichs never appreciated his wife's constant efforts to be attractive. He spent most of his time in San Francisco, overseeing the family's financial interests.

Not that Tessie was incapable of taking care of her own money. Like her mother, she knew how to pinch a penny. Tessie was so protective of the Fair fortune that when her brother Charlie and his wife died in a car accident, she cleverly decided that her sister-in-law, not her brother, had been the first to go. That meant her dead sister-in-law's share of the estate would be inherited by the equally dead Charlie Fair. Next in line were his heirs, including Tessie. This was her way of making sure that the Fair estate stayed with the Fairs. The case was so complicated that it took two full years for the courts to determine which unlucky Fair died first. Tessie won.

Mamie Fish, the third member of the Newport Social Strategy Board, was an unlikely candidate for the role because she was always breaking—then rewriting—the stuffy rules of society. Mamie decided that Newport dinners, often lasting three to four hours, were interminably long, so a meal at her house was a speedy affair. One night, her staff managed to serve an eight-course feast, including oysters, whitebait in a potato basket, salad, soup, little birds with sculpted vegetables, ice cream, bonbons, fruit, and more, in a record-breaking thirty minutes. Guests complained that they had to hold down their plates to slip in a hasty bite before a nervous servant whisked it away. One audacious guest tried to finish his fish course while Mamie stared him down. When he held fast to his food she snapped, "No wonder you're so fat!"

Instead of serving wine, Mamie plied her guests with champagne. "They're as dull as dishwater until they get a little of that," she complained. But her trick of serving bubbly did not always elevate her own spirits. There were nights when Mamie regretted being a hostess. On one occasion she had to be talked out of instructing the band to play "Home Sweet Home," the song that usually indicated a party was over, as her guests were coming in the door.

Though Mamie was famous for being a rebel, she demanded a certain level of politesse from the people she admitted to her inner circle. She maintained a list of words and phrases that offended her. The unsuspecting guest who said "Pleased to meet you" instead of the more formal "How do you do," "Pardon me" instead of "I beg your pardon," or "I presume" instead of "I suppose" would not receive a second invitation to Crossways.

With these three unusual women—the rebel, the perfectionist, and the loose cannon—at its helm, the Newport Social Strategy Board debuted in 1898 with a festive dinner picnic staged at Gray Craig, the Belmonts' farm in nearby Middletown. Alva, Tessie, and Mamie worked for two weeks planning every detail. Guests expected a typical excursion to a country estate—the kind of rustic affair that had been Ward McAllister's specialty. Instead they were treated to a merry-go-round, a shooting gallery, fortune tellers, staged fights between cowboys and Indians, an African juggler, a brass band, a vaudeville show, and a spectacular display of fireworks. The party was called "one of the most unique social functions" in the city's history, and the triumvirate triumphed.

Cottagers eagerly awaited news of the next entertainment from the fun-loving Social Strategy Board, and a barn dance at Crossways was their reward. Mamie encouraged her guests to dress as dairy maids and farmers. They donned calico and muslin and rode in hay wagons to a barn decorated with rakes and sickles. A farmhand in overalls clanged a cowbell to announce dinner, live chickens mingled with the guests on the dance floor, and robber barons disguised as French chefs performed the quadrille, a fancier version of a square dance.

Crossways, residence of the fun-loving Stuyvesant Fish, was the setting for many of Newport's most outrageous parties.

Mamie's wealthy friends had such a good time pretending to be simple country folk that she offered them another opportunity to be hayseeds the following season. This time, guests were invited to attend a Harvest Ball at Crossways. The entrance was flanked by twelve-foot jack-o'-lanterns, and the grounds blazed with electric lights illuminating thousands of sunflowers and poppies. Mamie sat on a throne made of farm implements, and her guests deposited chickens, ducks, pigs, and cats at her feet. Ladies who were used to wearing silk and velvet dressed in peasant outfits and walked around carrying baskets of live animals.

Sometimes servants were bewildered by the odd appearance of their employers at these affairs. At one costume party, a large dowager wearing the shabby garb of a poor laborer swanned over to the footman who was announcing the guests and identified herself as a "Norman peasant." To her surprise (and everyone else's great amusement) he turned to the crowd and solemnly introduced her as "an enormous pheasant."

Edith

Edith "Pussy" Jones was the daughter of George Frederic Jones and his wife, Lucretia Stevens Rhinelander Jones, a solid Knickerbocker couple with town and country homes in New York and Newport. They had just enough of an income to liberate Mr. Jones from having to work for a living. In fact, this Jones family, and their leisure-class lifestyle, is thought to have inspired the saying "Keeping up with the Joneses," a term that described competitive spending.

Despite her insider status, young Edith always felt a little out of place in Newport. She participated in all the social rituals—even the debutante's "coming out"—to please her parents. But she wanted to be a writer, and it pained her to set aside her poetry and stories to go through the motions of being a dutiful young socialite.

Edith was engaged briefly to a young man named Henry "Harry" Stevens, but her prospective mother-in-law, a notorious social climber, was opposed to the union because she wanted to control her son's substantial inheritance and was afraid that a smart girl such as Edith would get in her way. *Town Topics* reported that the breakup was caused by "an alleged preponderance of intellectuality on the part of the intended bride," which meant Edith was deemed too intelligent to be a good wife.

Three years later, Edith overcame her bad press and married Edward Wharton. The newlyweds lived in Newport for a time, but Edith still found it oppressive because there were rules for everything. Even coaching had a strict protocol. Lesser socialites had to surrender the right of way to more established matrons, and drivers were expected to recognize a coach's passengers and behave accordingly. One afternoon, Edith's driver cut ahead of a dowager's coach, and Edith immediately received a tongue-lashing from its offended occupant. The outraged woman—Edith's mother—made no allowances for the fact that the transgressor was her own daughter.

In Newport, Edith had ample opportunity to observe careerist hostesses in action. Years later, when she fulfilled her dream of becoming a writer, she depicted them in her novels, including *Age of Innocence, The Buccaneers*, and most notably, *The House of Mirth*. In that book, Edith introduced the character Judy Trenor, a rich and socially ambitious woman who "seemed to exist only as a hostess." She wrote that Trenor "knew no more personal emotion than that of hatred for the woman who presumed to give bigger dinners or have more amusing house-parties than herself." Edith Wharton knew all too well that these women lived in a world where social achievement was the definitive unit of measure.

10

Fast Times

Newport's delight in the triumvirate's supersize parties proved that socialites were children at heart. They liked to play dress-up; they had short attention spans; and they loved excess in every form. Consequently, keeping them entertained was a very demanding job. "I know of no profession, art, or trade that women are working in today as taxing on mental resources as being a leader of society," complained Alva. Fortunately, help was on the way in the form of a spirited new ringleader for the social circus.

Harry Lehr was a handsome young man who wanted the best things in life but couldn't afford them. His pedigree (he was born and raised in Baltimore) was nothing to speak of, and his profession—he was a wine salesman—was never going to make him rich. Yet Harry entered Newport society at the highest of levels because he had an outrageous sense of humor, a more distinctive attribute than fine breeding or a big bank account.

Harry Lehr, ringleader of Newport's Gilded Age social circus, and Mrs. John Jacob Astor, sitting pretty in a carriage decorated with flowers.

"Haven't you heard Harry Lehr's laugh?" asked one society columnist. "That shows you have not been within a hundred miles of Newport this season. . . . He simply laughed himself into the bosom of the ultra-exclusives."

The most influential tastemakers in Newport, first Mrs. Astor, then Alva, Tessie, and Mamie, welcomed the charismatic bachelor as their playmate because he was a lively companion and a candid confidant. He played the piano, danced ballet, told funny stories, poured afternoon tea, designed chic costumes for his hostesses, and spoke French. Best of all, he loved to plan parties, and the wilder they were, the better.

Unlike Ward McAllister, who was a stuffed shirt, Harry liked to shake things up. He planned one memorable ball when the gentlemen dressed up as cats and handed out live mice to their terrified dance partners. On another occasion, he played a practical joke on A-list Newporters by inviting them to a private audience with a visiting "king," who turned out to be Harry in disguise. Harry was so irreverently charming that he could get away with anything.

His celebrity status prompted merchants to give him everything, including the clothes on his back, free of charge. If he needed pocket money, Harry simply advised Alva, Tessie, or Mamie to stock their cellars with one of his fine wines. No one begrudged darling Harry his little commission.

His detractors called him "the human poodle" because he was the pampered lapdog of these very rich women. In another time, they would have categorized him as the "gay best friend." Harry had the shapeliest legs at Bailey's Beach, a "faultless pair of shoulders," and "a throat which might have been the envy of many women." He seized every opportunity to dress in women's clothes at pageants and costume parties, and he wore silver bracelets on his wrist and ankle. It seems that his friends were either too naive to notice—or too sophisticated to care—that Harry Lehr was more interested in being a lady than a ladies' man.

Harry came out to one person (his incredulous bride) when the Social Strategy Board urged him to marry a wealthy young widow named Elizabeth Drexel. Immediately after the ceremony, Harry visited his wife's bedroom to make a shocking announcement: "I do not love you, I can never love you," he told her. "Do not come near me except when we are in public, or you will force me to repeat to you the brutal truth that you are actually repulsive to me." Harry had no interest in Elizabeth, or any other woman. For the duration of their twenty-eight-year marriage, the Lehrs feigned affection outside of the house and ignored each other the rest of the time.

It turned out that Harry, or King Lehr, as he was often called, had a terrible effect on Newport's social scene because he encouraged hostesses to go too far. On one occasion, Harry and Mamie invited friends to a dinner in honor of Prince del Drago, a visiting dignitary from Corsica. They gathered at Arleigh, the cottage the Lehrs had rented for the summer, eager to rub elbows with a new "royal." At the appointed hour, the guest of honor swaggered, or rather, swung, into the room. Prince del Drago was, in fact, a monkey attired in full evening dress. He behaved well enough—for a monkey—until someone gave him a little too much champagne and he started swinging from the chandelier and throwing things at the human guests.

The story leaked to the press and turned into a tale of monkey abuse. Journalists and preachers (who seemed most offended by the idea that the simian was served alcohol) denounced the naughty Newporters for their depravity. Both Harry and Mamie tried to deny that it ever happened. "That monkey story is a wicked falsehood," protested Harry when the scandal broke.

The infamous "dog's dinner" was another headline-grabbing spectacle. It was a birthday party for Elizabeth Lehr's Pomeranian, Mighty Atom. Seven dogs and their mistresses received engraved invitations to the unusual event. The birthday "boy" presided at a table decorated with red dahlias, and his canine "friends" were served stewed liver and rice, fricassee of bones, and shredded dog biscuits. There was also a birthday cake with three candles. One happy dachshund ate so much that he passed out and had to be carried home. The other dogs enjoyed a lively after-dinner game of hide-and-seek with several cats that were let loose for the occasion.

There was a spy in the Lehrs' yard that day—a reporter posing as a gentleman holding a poodle on a leash. After he was chased away by an angry Harry Lehr, the writer filed an inflammatory story about the affair. A private dinner for eight dogs turned into a bacchanalia for a hundred. The public found the over-the-top banquet for pampered pets another example of wretched excess in Newport.

Harry and Mamie were not the only Newporters to come under fire. Mr. and Mrs. Pembroke Jones became targets when they hosted two wildly extravagant balls. Their cottage was not large enough to accommodate their enormous guest list, so the Joneses erected a temporary ballroom on the lawn . . . twice. When the parties ended, the temporary rooms and all of their expensive trimmings came down, as if they had never existed.

The party coverage included a description of a special entertainment the Joneses staged for their guests. "Negroes in a Watermelon," proclaimed the bizarre headline in the *New York Times*. According to the story, a young boy dragged a five-and-a-half-foot watermelon into the ballroom. He then "carved dat watermelon," removing a large slice. Out came "two picaninnies who executed a clever cakewalk," to the delight of the crowd. The Joneses were referred to as "Mr. and Mrs. Croesus" because their parties probably cost in the vicinity of $200,000.

No less a critic than Henry James, who had spent happy summers in Newport in his youth, was appalled by the "gilding" of the city. He remembered when Newport reminded him of "a little bare, white, open hand," charming, inviting, and delicate. He returned to find that same hand vulgar and unattractively stuffed with gold. James despised the marble monstrosities and their socially ambitious occupants. The houses were "white elephants," he said, "all cry and no wool."

James chose the term "white elephants" carefully. He was referring to a tradition in ancient Siam whereby a monarch expressed his displeasure with a subject by bestowing upon him the gift of one of these fabled animals. White elephants required so much upkeep that the unfortunate recipient was certain to go bankrupt trying to meet its needs. James predicted the same fate for Newport. He wrote his lament in 1904, joining the growing backlash against the city and its profligate big spenders.

Another critic wrote that the smart set in Newport "devoted themselves to pleasure regardless of expense." But Colonel Waring, a wit who lived in Newport and observed the social circus firsthand, disagreed. He said that his rich neighbors "devoted themselves to expense regardless of pleasure."

Excess extended to other areas, and Newporters suddenly developed a reputation for recklessness. They loved anything that moved, and embraced the new sport of "motoring" with the same passion they once showed for horseback riding and coaching. Many a society matron, including Mamie, wrecked at least one new car while learning to drive, but would be indignant when police officers stopped them for speeding. Newport's first families blocked any form of public transportation in their community because they didn't want an onslaught of riffraff. Yet they believed their own automobiles should not be subject to any rules.

The city's young bucks were particularly irresponsible on the road. Alva's son, William K. Vanderbilt Jr., was criticized repeatedly for racing his "lightning machine" through town, and Tessie Oelrichs's young Hermann was horsewhipped by the president of the New York Stock Exchange for speeding on Bellevue Avenue. But seventeen-year-old Vinson Walsh was Newport's most dangerous driver. The police appealed to millionaire Thomas Walsh to talk some sense into his son. But he claimed he was "powerless," confessing that he was always frightened when Vinson was at the wheel.

One day in 1905, Vinson attended a party at Crossways and got annoyed when a fortune teller refused to give him a reading. Mamie pressed the seer for details and was told that the young gentleman was going to die in a few hours. Rubbish, thought Mamie, especially after lunching with Vinson at the Clambake Club the next day. But destiny would not be denied. After lunch, Vinson carelessly drove his car off a bridge and was instantly killed. The speeding car became a metaphor for Newport itself. The city and its summer people were moving too fast and breaking all the rules in their race to nowhere. A crash was inevitable.

There was desperation brewing beneath the surfaces of Newport high life, and it was starting to boil over. Harry Lehr certainly had his share of problems, and now Tessie's always troubled marriage was officially on the rocks. Hermann insisted on a separation, leaving lonely Tessie with no way to pass her time besides staging increasingly elaborate entertainments.

Finally, Mamie Fish, with Harry Lehr egging her on, went into a tailspin, and behavior that had once seemed amusingly eccentric became downright odd. Tales of her misadventures abounded. Once, she and Harry disrupted an auction by making rude noises, and on another occasion the duo showed up at the Newport Casino with an oversized rag doll, carrying it around as if it were a human being.

Even when her own well-being depended on it, Mamie seemed incapable of exercising self-control. In 1906, she had a disastrous run-in with railroad baron E. H. Harriman, a newcomer to Newport who sought acceptance by Mamie and her set. Harriman had business dealings with Stuyvesant Fish, so it would have been hospitable (and very easy) for Mamie to open all the necessary doors. Instead, she willfully blocked the couple's entrée and even made unflattering comments about them in mixed company. Mrs. Harriman tearfully repeated Mamie's insults to her husband, who promised he would "make these people suffer."

Harriman retaliated by mounting a successful campaign to oust Stuyvesant Fish from his long-standing post at the Illinois Central Railroad. Some maintained that the feud was just business: Harriman wanted to control the company, and that meant getting rid of its president. Others said that Mamie's social snub had been more lethal than any boardroom contretemps. There were even rumors that Mamie had a drinking problem.

A year later, Mamie waged an embarrassing custody battle over Prince Wilhelm, the second son of the crown prince of Sweden. Wilhelm was a boyish twenty-two-year-old lieutenant in the Swedish Navy who was accustomed to spending his time with sailors. He came to Newport because it was an important naval station, and the grandiose complexities of its social life were complete mysteries to him.

Mamie and her friends were a little disappointed because the prince seemed ill at ease at the events they staged in his honor. They never understood that the dutiful lieutenant's early departures were the result of his having to take his turn at night watch on his ship. The high point of Wilhelm's visit to Newport was a party organized by the city's patriotic Swedish servants. The girls were young and pretty and loved to dance, and the prince spent the evening waltzing with one of Mamie's parlor maids. He then sailed out of town without a backward glance, and Mamie's enemies cattily observed that she was no longer the hostess she used to be.

The Mrs. Astor, who had been the first grande dame to welcome Harry Lehr, made no secret of her disapproval of the social strategists' antics. She was appalled by the extravaganzas that passed for parties, and came right out and said that they "belonged under a circus tent rather than in a gentlewoman's house." She was clearly referring to Alva, Tessie, and Mamie when she condemned certain hostesses with the words "Their sole object is notoriety, a thing that no lady ever seeks." "Mrs. Astor is an old woman" was Mamie's only retort.

Mrs. Astor was an old woman, and eventually she stopped entertaining. A recluse in ill health, she sat with her social secretary, Maria de Barril, as she had in the old days, compiling guest lists and agonizing over seating arrangements. But the parties never took place. Mrs. Astor's mind had deteriorated to the point where she no longer lived in the present. She dressed in outdated finery and greeted imaginary guests. The legendary hostess's sad decline inspired Edith Wharton to write the short story "After Holbein." In it, Mrs. Jaspar, a woman very much like Caroline Astor, surrenders to dementia while maintaining the social rituals that were once so important in her.

The Mrs. Astor died of heart failure in 1908, and a genteel way of life died with her. The *New York Times* devoted an entire page to the remarkable woman, crediting her with having "almost absolute power to make or mar the social destiny of those who sought her patronage." Her obituary even recounted the story of her social tug-of-war with Alva Vanderbilt in 1883. It also confirmed that society was not what it used to be. Mrs. Astor, for all her airs, was a kind and decent woman with high standards, a compliment that could not be paid to the ostentatious socialites who followed in her footsteps.

A cloud hung over Newport following the public outcry against its hostesses and, for a time, it seemed as if they could do nothing right. "No more monkey dinners," blasted one disapproving critic. Journalists scrutinized the summer folks' activities, seizing every opportunity to portray them as selfish, careless snobs who behaved as if the city were their private playground.

By 1908, Alva, Tessie, Mamie, and even Harry Lehr were fed up with the smear campaign. They packed up and went to Europe, wisely waiting for the backlash to die down. Tessie insisted that she was leaving Newport forever and actually put Rosecliff on the market, while Mamie, who had been injured in one of those speeding car accidents, said she was thinking of selling Crossways.

Alva moved to Europe to recover from the sudden death of Oliver Belmont. She wanted to spend time with Consuelo, whose loveless marriage to the Duke of Marlborough had yielded two obligatory children, the famous "heir and a spare," and then ended in a very public separation. Mother and daughter drew closer and developed a passion for the controversial women's rights movement. Alva daringly marched alongside suffragettes in England, although her friends wondered if she would have the stamina—or the appropriate shoes—to keep up the pace.

Back in Newport, a concerned group of cottagers decided it was a good time to reform the summer colony. They embraced a healthier lifestyle, advocating plenty of outdoor exercise and early curfews, and they replaced Alva, Tessie, and Mamie's showy affairs with simple picnics and sedate dinners. They also cut down on their drinking. Less alcohol was consumed during the 1908 season than at any other time in Newport's history, which may have been the real reason for the city's new sobriety.

Even though reporters no longer had the Social Strategy Board to kick around, newspapers continued to search for stories about bad behavior in Newport. In 1911, the *Washington Post* gleefully covered a very public feud that was playing out among the Bailey's Beach set. The Clews and the Cushings, two of Newport's oldest and most respected families, lived next door to each other on one of the most spectacular promontories on Ocean Drive. The Clews' house, The Rocks, was a rambling structure overlooking Bailey's Beach, while the Cushings' house, The Ledges, was a large white Colonial on the very edge of the Atlantic. The two families seemed to have a great deal in common—money, social standing, and a love of art. Henry Clews Jr., son of stockbroker Henry Clews, was a sculptor

The Rocks, home of financier Henry Clews.

who spent most of his time in Paris enjoying la vie de bohème. Howard Gardener Cushing, whose ancestors had made their fortune in the China trade, was a painter who was developing a respectable following in Boston and New York.

The trouble began when Clews Jr. sent his three-year-old son, nicknamed Bamboo, to summer with his grandparents at The Rocks. Young Bamboo whined, cried, and screamed under Howard Cushing's window while he was trying to paint. The next three summers were torture for the Cushings because

Bamboo was a frequent houseguest and the Clews refused to discipline him. By the time little Bamboo was six, he was making three times as much noise. The Cushings had no choice but to take matters into their own hands.

Grafton Cushing, Howard's older brother, armed himself with a hoe and a spade and started to build a large fence between the two properties. "What is that horrid, big nasty thing you're building?" Clews Jr. asked. Outraged to learn that his neighbor intended to establish a barrier little Bamboo could not cross, Clews plotted his own revenge. He would use the fence as a canvas and paint a giant French château, complete with smiling, large-bosomed milkmaids, cows, and other barnyard animals. The *Washington Post* was so amused by the story that it commissioned an artist's rendering of the "spite fence" as it might have looked after Clews painted it. The Supreme Court of Rhode Island prevented the Cushings from actually building their fence, and thereafter there was a perpetual frost between the two families.

More tabloid fodder was provided by Harriet Gardiner Coogan, daughter of one of America's oldest families, whose greatest desire was to be a popular hostess in Newport. Her goal was not out of the question because her parents owned $3 million worth of Manhattan real estate, including the Polo Grounds. But Harriet had a serious handicap: she was married to James Coogan, a Bowery merchant and aspiring politician, and, worst of all from society's point of view, a Democrat.

Coogan ran for mayor of New York in 1888, his campaign fueled by his wife's fortune. He lost that election, but with the help of Tammany Hall influence peddler Richard Croker, became Manhattan's first borough president a year later. While in office, Coogan mounted an exemplary campaign to break into Newport society. He purchased Whitehall, an estate designed by Stanford White and described as "one of the most attractive of the

When Newport artists Howard Gardiner Cushing and Henry Clews Jr. became embroiled in a bitter dispute, the *Washington Post* ran an illustration of the "spite fence" they threatened to build to separate their properties.

smaller summer residences in Newport." The word "smaller" must have grated on Coogan, who liked to live large. He immediately ordered extensive renovations, hoping to make his new house more impressive.

Columnists who covered the Newport beat routinely reported the Coogans' annual arrival and departure, but their names never appeared on any guest lists. There was a rumor that Mamie Fish disliked them. Sometimes hostesses banded together to exclude a "detrimental," a person who did not blend well socially, and the Coogans seemed to fall into that category. As one writer put it, "Newporters continued to yank in the welcome mat when the Coogans called." One of the reasons for the big chill was that most cottagers were Republicans who disapproved of Tammany Hall, an institution that was synonymous with patronage and political corruption.

Undaunted, Harriet Coogan invited Newporters to a coming-out party for her daughter Jessie. Three hundred invitations went out, and the Coogans were delighted when it seemed as if everyone would attend. The happy hostess and her daughter ordered extravagant gowns for the occasion and imported chefs, waiters, and musicians from New York City. There was a full moon on the night of the event, and Whitehall never looked more beautiful. Footmen waited at the door, and Mr. and Mrs. Coogan and their children excitedly prepared to greet their guests at the stroke of ten o'clock.

There are two versions of what happened next. In one account, the guests descended upon the house en masse and left minutes later—a sure sign that attendance was a perfunctory duty call. In the alternate version, the Coogans stood in their front hall until the appointed hour came—and went—without a single guest showing up.

In both stories, the angry Coogans dismissed the musicians and servants, closed the doors to the house, and fled the scene of their humiliation, leaving Newport forever. "Whitehall can rot on its foundations before I or any of my family ever return," vowed Harriet as she walked out the door, abandoning everything, from the lavish food that had been laid out on tables, to the nightclothes on the beds. There was an open copy of *Burke's Peerage*, the definitive guide to British royalty, on her night table, a reminder of her sad, and ultimately futile, obsession with society.

There may have been such a party, and it may have convinced the Coogans to give up their campaign to penetrate Newport. But there was also a practical reason why they left town. In November 1911, Whitehall was ravaged by a fire that caused

more than $40,000 worth of damage, leaving the house unin-
habitable. The Coogans had been responsible homeowners,
so Newporters assumed they would make repairs and return
the following summer. But Whitehall remained a burned-out
shell, and its once-manicured lawn was taken over by weeds. As
time passed, people forgot whether there was any truth to the
story about the disastrous party, and the wreckage of Whitehall
became a monument to Harriet Coogan's social failure.

Another sensational story that year involved Colonel John
Jacob Astor IV, Caroline Astor's forty-seven-year-old son. Astor,
one of the wealthiest men in the world (with a net worth of
about $87 million), had been trapped in a loveless marriage to
Ava Willing, a beautiful but spoiled socialite who cheated on
him. "They lived a cat and dog life up there and we all knew
it," was the way a candid neighbor described their tempestuous
marriage. The Astors divorced, and the colonel found true love
with eighteen-year-old Madeleine Force. They set their wedding
date for September 1911, only to discover that no legitimate
minister would marry a divorced man. The millionaire offered
a thousand good reasons (in the form of cold cash) to anyone
who would indulge his request, but the answer was still no.

Finally, Astor found a liberal-minded clergyman to offici-
ate. There was a great public outcry because some saw this as
another indication of relaxed morals in Newport. But Astor
explained that he was such a great fan of marriage, he wanted
to try it again.

The newlyweds traveled to Europe for an extended honeymoon, and then headed home because Madeleine was pregnant. The Astors booked passage on the world's newest ocean
liner, the RMS *Titanic*, and were joined by another Newport
family, the Wideners. George Widener, a wealthy Philadelphia
businessman, was in the early stages of planning his Bellevue
Avenue cottage, Miramar, with Horace Trumbauer. Widener,

his wife, Eleanor, and their son, Harry, had spent two months in Europe and were looking forward to the luxurious trip home.

Widener and Astor were on top of the world until April 15, 1912, when the "unsinkable" *Titanic* sank. At first warning, Widener carefully placed his wife in a lifeboat, as Astor did with his bride. Both men—and Widener's son—perished. Their deaths should have cast a shadow over the upcoming Newport season, but ironically the city was livelier than ever. Families were so fearful of crossing the Atlantic that they canceled their trips and stayed home. There was not a room, private or public, to be had in all of Newport. Moreover, in the face of tragedy, people wanted to be entertained. Mamie was back in Newport and ready to accommodate her friends with a brand-new ballroom at Crossways.

In August, the Fish hosted a Louis XVI Fantasy Ball for four hundred guests. There were two ballrooms (the old and the new), three bands, a procession of page boys, frolicking nymphs, Russian dancers, hundreds of butterflies, and thousands of flowers. Guests swore that the butterflies were real, not suspecting they were the work of a clever illusionist who tricked the eye with lights and wires. A costumed Mamie and her guests partied just as they had in 1904. After so many dreary seasons, they were happy to be back in the world of sweet excess.

11

A Very Good Year

In 1913, nine years after Henry James predicted a tragic fall for the rich in Newport, the city was in fine form and its summer residents were thriving. America wanted a homegrown aristocracy, and the Newport cottagers were the closest thing to it. They were forgiven their past transgressions, and the resort reclaimed its position as the country's unofficial kingdom by the sea.

The town fathers were committed to making Newport look its best, so they commissioned Frederick Law Olmsted Jr., a successful landscape architect and son of the dean of American landscape architects, to evaluate the city's strengths and weaknesses. Olmsted concluded that Newport possessed several qualities that made it unique among cities, but he was most impressed by its scenery. He advised that Newport's exceptional vistas of the ocean and its sumptuous cottages and gardens had to be protected at all costs.

"Have you ever seen the gardens of Newport?" asked reporter Mary A. Stillman in the *Newport Journal*. "No cottage is too old

or too small to have its little garden plot brilliant with bloom, and every poor man is rich at least in flowers." Roses, temperamental flowers in less hospitable locations, always flourished in Newport, as did lilies, gladioli, dahlias, hydrangea, hollyhocks, and almost every other type of flower. The ever-present fog provided a constant blanket of moisture that encouraged nature to go wild. And for those times when nature wasn't up to the job, there was the greenhouse.

Every cottage had one, along with a master gardener who performed Garden of Eden–like miracles. Exotic plants such as orchids, hibiscus, and palms, and tropical fruits such as nectarines, grapes, melons, and assorted berries were available on demand. The Ochre Court greenhouse provided life support for owner Ogden Goelet when illness and stress caused his digestive system to fail and he had to exist on a diet of hothouse grapes, which, fortunately, he had in unlimited supply.

Newporters proudly participated in the city's Horticultural Exhibition every year, and inevitably the summer residents who owned the largest greenhouses walked off with the big prizes. It was not unusual for Mrs. Astor to win a blue ribbon for growing the most beautiful gardenias, coal king E. J. Berwind to be honored for his grapes and nectarines, and Alfred G. Vanderbilt to score prizes for his tomatoes, cauliflowers, and onions. These green-thumbed millionaires were tactfully called society gardeners, although they spent little to no time with their hands in the soil. It was not their expertise, but their money, that turned Newport into a bower.

Newport wasn't just pretty in 1913, it also was fun. Easton's Beach, with its boardwalk and flashy amusement-park rides, was a mecca for tourists. Thrill-seekers lined up at the roller coaster, while young children (or the faint of heart) rode the tamer carousel, with its quaintly decorated wooden horses. Some tourists bypassed the resort's man-made attractions altogether and headed straight for the beach, where a bathing suit and a changing room could be rented for just a few cents.

The palatial cottages continued to attract oglers, and everyone was intrigued by a new building that was going up on the grounds of Marble House, where Alva Belmont had an ambitious architectural project in the works. Ever loyal to Richard Morris Hunt, Alva hired his sons, architects Richard and Joseph Hunt, to create an authentic Chinese teahouse on her back lawn.

Cliff Walkers could appreciate the building's ornamental tile roof and arched windows, but the splendidly decorated interior was reserved for Alva's guests. William Andrew Mackay, a local muralist, experimented with more than a thousand different shades before settling on Chinese yellow, deep violet blue, and seven other vibrant colors that re-created the brilliant hues of the Ming period. He also conducted extensive tests on varnishes to determine their durability. Fog, rain, and even sunshine could destroy a beautiful finish, and this very special building was meant to last.

There was one small practical problem with Alva's authentic teahouse: there was no place to make tea—at least not the kind of tea Newport ladies expected. Her solution was to design a special train that could be assembled in minutes. Collapsible tracks linked the kitchen to the teahouse, and small cars, some with heating compartments, carried food and beverage straight from the chef to Alva's guests. Sometimes a very uncomfortable-looking butler squeezed himself into one of the trains' toy-size seats to serve delicacies from a tray. After the refreshments were delivered, the temporary railroad could be taken apart and stored.

Her catering problem solved, Alva's next crisis involved two dozen beautiful ducks who were supposed to sit decorously in a little Oriental pool that had been built especially for them. Alva noticed that the birds had a defiant look about them, so she covered their pool with wire mesh to give them a chance to get used to their surroundings. The moment the mesh was removed, the ducks ran excitedly across the lawn and escaped onto Bellevue Avenue.

They were captured by frantic servants and returned to their pond to learn proper behavior. But the next time they were released, they ran off in the opposite direction, heading straight for the Cliff Walk. One by one, they jumped off the edge into the water. "Our last view of them was when they had got well over the cliffs and were fast putting out to sea," recalled Alva's granddaughter.

The ducks were not the only rebels at Marble House. Alva invited an army of suffragettes to attend a historic summit meeting at her cottage. Newporters were dumbfounded by the sight of hundreds of "Man-hating college women with screwed-back hair and thin-lipped, determined faces" marching alongside "giggling shop girls," as one horrified observer described the visiting feminists. Mamie and Tessie forced themselves to attend the gathering, although their sympathies were not with their less-well-heeled "sisters." The suffragettes were not typical Marble House guests, but the newly liberated Alva delighted in shocking her neighbors.

She wasn't the only one causing raised eyebrows on Bellevue Avenue. Just a few blocks away, a real estate revolution was in the works. Bruen Villa, a sizable estate consisting of two main houses, a gardener's cottage, outbuildings, and a large parcel of land, was placed on the auction block after its elderly owner died. George D. Haskell of Boston was the lucky buyer, but he had no intention of moving in. His plan was to carve the estate into smaller lots—an early form of subdivision—and sell them at a profit. He renamed the property Bellevue Terrace and scheduled another auction.

A brass band, raffle tickets, and the promise of prizes attracted hundreds of gawkers along with a few prospective buyers. Newporters were appalled by Haskell's radical intention and the carnival atmosphere of the event, and the sales were slow. But one of the smaller lots sold quickly and quietly to Miss Julia Sullivan, a woman who ran a small variety store on Thames Street. There were more Sullivans in Newport than Vanderbilts, and most of them could trace their ancestry all the way back to Ireland. But, unless they were servants, the Sullivans were not the kind of people who were usually found on Bellevue Avenue.

None of the cottagers bothered to ask why Julia Sullivan bought a gardener's cottage nestled among the most palatial residences in town, nor did they imagine that the Irish shopkeeper might one day be their neighbor. They were too busy enjoying the gayest summer in recent memory. First, Mamie Fish announced that she was inviting a select several hundred guests to a Mother Goose Ball in August. Then Mrs. Arthur Curtiss James said that she would host a party, which she called the Masque of the Blue Garden, a week later. One—and only one—of these two women would emerge as the hostess of the season, and the cottagers were dying to find out who it would be.

Commodore Arthur Curtiss James had an immense fortune that came from railroad stock and copper mines. He and his wife, Harriet, were frequent visitors to Newport and the owners of a large and expensively appointed yacht called the *Aloha*. The couple decided they wanted a manor to go along with their floating palace, so they purchased Beacon Hill, a large estate on the northern side of the island. The Jameses had spent four years building, renovating, and planting their 125-acre property, and now they were ready to unveil it with a party that would give Mamie Fish a run for her money.

Mamie was the more established hostess, so she had first choice of a date. She selected Friday, August 1, the apex of the season. Mamie hated false formality, especially at parties. "Where's the corpse?" she'd ask when an evening was stuffy or pretentious. "My entertainments are like screen doors," she bragged. "Everybody can see through them and everybody can get out of them. That's why people are crazy to come to my house." The Mother Goose theme would appeal to the fun-loving child in everyone. Women who wanted to look pretty could don tiaras and dress as princesses, while a guest with a sense of humor might come as Red Riding Hood, Little Jack Horner, or any number of whimsical nursery rhyme characters. Two hundred New York dressmakers created fanciful ensembles for their best clients. Guests who did not plan ahead could rent from costumers who came from New York and Boston with a broad selection of ready-made outfits.

Mamie brought in a party planner, a caterer, and a florist, and it was her social secretary's job to make sure everyone worked together. Lighting experts illuminated everything from fountains and pumpkins to the glass eyes of toy cats, and decorated the garden with thousands of tiny bulbs that blinked on and off like lightning bugs. The evening might look as if it cost hundreds of thousands of dollars—and many Newport hostesses spent that much on an event. But Mamie was ingenious at finding high talent for a low price. Sometimes she badgered vendors into giving her substantial discounts because her patronage made them more desirable to other hostesses.

Evenings of this sort offered two kinds of entertainment: a theatrical production choreographed by a professional, and an amateur dance performed by debutantes and their escorts. Mamie hired Caroline Crawford, an innovative dance teacher from New York City, to stage a Mother Goose show. Crawford was the force behind a well-received production of Maurice Maeterlinck's classic play *The Blue Bird*. One of its most talked-about numbers featured dancers dressed as a loaf of bread and four small loaves. Mamie wanted Miss Crawford to do something equally creative with Mother Goose and her nursery rhyme gaggle.

Tessie Oelrichs kicked off the evening with an extravagant pre-ball dinner at Rosecliff. In keeping with Mamie's theme, the centerpieces were whimsical recreations of nursery rhymes. On one table, Jack and Jill fell down their hill, and on another, Little Red Riding Hood recoiled from the Big Bad Wolf. Later the revelers gathered at Crossways, where they were greeted by Mamie, who seemed a little irritated that Tessie's event threatened to upstage her own. Decked out in diamonds, rhinestones, and electric lights, Mamie held court over several Mary, Mary, Quite Contraries and a number of Little Bo-Peeps, including Mrs. Robert Goelet, who dragged around a trained lamb on a leash.

Cinderella was there, along with the Snow Queen, Snow White, the Queen of Hearts, and a variety of princesses. Mrs. T. Suffren Tailer was a convincing Little Miss Muffet because she carried a bowl of curds and whey and her very own spider. One observer estimated that the guests had spent about $60,000 on their costumes. That figure seemed small compared to the $12 million worth of jewelry in the room. Police and plainclothesmen were everywhere (there had been many robberies that summer), and their sole objective was to thwart any would-be jewel thieves.

Miss Crawford's dance show was a big success. Mother Goose stood before the crowd and introduced the characters from her rhymes, who stepped out of a giant book and danced prettily around a maypole. Fairies whirled, pages marched, and a witch stirred a cauldron. A poem was read in Mother Goose's honor, celebrating her love of nonsense. At the end of the performance, hundreds of red balloons were released and a midnight supper was served.

During the festivities, Mamie noticed several young women behaving suspiciously. They rushed out of the ballroom at the end of each dance and, when they returned, they fox-trotted, dipped, and twirled with unseemly abandon. Stuyvesant Fish was so concerned that he followed one of the dancers outside, apprehensive about what he might find. Alcohol? Drugs? An illicit tryst? No, the young lady in question was checking her pedometer.

The latest craze to hit Newport was "dancing by the mile," whereby competitive young women attached pedometers to their garters to see who could tally the most miles in the course of the season. "Good morning. How many miles did you dance last night?" was a typical greeting among debutantes. Experienced girls knew to kick and shake their legs while dancing—hence the expression "shake a leg"—to clock twenty or so miles in one evening. At the Mother Goose Ball, the pedometers were kept busy until three o'clock in the morning, when Mamie, ignoring the pleas of a pretty Snow White and a dark-eyed Spanish dancer, instructed the orchestra to play "Home Sweet Home."

Some guests crossed the street to Bailey's Beach to enjoy "daybreak swimming," another Newport fad. The evening was a crazy combination of innocence and decadence, old-fashioned fun and Newport's signature brand of excess. The Mother Goose theme invoked childhood, yet it was childhood reimagined by adults who had been spoiled rotten. Mamie enabled her friends to return to the nursery, but they did so dressed in costly clothes and dripping in diamonds.

The next day, society columnists praised Mamie and her party. "Scores Triumph of a Generation . . . Mrs. Fish at the pinnacle of fame as hostess," wrote one admirer. Whenever Mamie's name appeared in the newspaper, supplicants sent letters to the Fish household, pleading for financial help. Usually they claimed to need money for an operation, or some other worthy cause, but one woman took a different approach. "If you have all that money to spend on champagne and nymphs," she wrote, "I should like you to send me a seven-passenger automobile. Perhaps you could send us one of your last year's cars." Mamie was so impressed by the novelty—and audacity—of the request that she wished she had a spare car to send.

Mamie's fame was short-lived because the James event, scheduled for Friday, August 22, became the new hot topic. Joseph Lindon Smith, a respected artist, was brought in to stage a medieval pageant called the Masque of the Blue Garden, and when Mrs. James said "Blue Garden," she meant blue garden. Olmsted Bros. designed most of Beacon Hill's landscaping, and there were many beautiful plantings on the large estate. But the Blue Garden was planned by John Greatorex, a horticultural specialist who lived on the premises. It was a magical place, filled with clematis, delphinium, heliotrope, hydrangeas, Siberian iris, lobelia, pansies, veronica, and other blue blooms, with a few touches of white—roses, lilies, and alyssum—for contrast. The area was long and perfectly proportioned, with Corinthian columns, a blue-tiled lily pond, and symmetrical beds of flowers that had to be replanted several times in the course of the summer to maintain a constant blue. This was the backdrop for Smith's entertainment.

Smith labored for months on his script, an elaborate fable involving ancient gods, goddesses, nymphs, and other mythical creatures. A masque was a particular kind of entertainment that originated in sixteenth-century Europe and consisted of pantomime, dancing, recitations, and song. Smith sketched plans for the staging, lighting, and costumes, always mindful of the fact that the garden was the main attraction.

An outdoor event was risky because rain could spoil everything, but luckily the weather cooperated. Commodore James escorted his guests to the Blue Garden, where there were stadium seats built especially for the occasion. They waited expectantly until Harriet James appeared in the distance. Outfitted in a heavy blue medieval dress, she walked slowly to the strains of Wagner and solemnly welcomed her guests to "the dedication of my blue garden." Smith, playing the master of ceremonies, summoned the cast of fifty-four actors, along with the entire crew of James's yacht. Illuminated by dramatic electric lighting, they spent the next forty-five minutes marching, leaping, and twirling through the garden. Mamie Fish watched impassively. The show was a little pompous for her taste, precisely the kind of "entertainment" that might prompt her "Where's the corpse?" barb.

Things got a little livelier when Florence Noyes made her entrance. She was a famous modern dancer who was called the high priestess of rhythmic expression. Like Isadora Duncan, Noyes was a free spirit who dressed in Greek robes and taught earnest young women to move with passion and poise. She was carried in on a large conch shell, wearing one of her flowing (and revealing) costumes, and leaped from the shell into the water. She "danced with reckless grace," her dripping white draperies clinging to her impressive body and becoming transparent. Suddenly the gentlemen in the audience sat up a little straighter and appeared very interested in the stories of Ceres, Neptune, Amphitrite, and the other dancing deities. "This beats anything I've ever seen," said one appreciative young man as he watched a scantily clad Noyes shimmy in the water. The pageant ended to great applause, and the guests headed back to the main house at Beacon Hill for a dinner of wild boar and other medieval treats.

The gossip columnists in attendance watched Mamie Fish's every move, hoping to spy a reaction. Everyone congratulated Commodore and Mrs. James, calling the masque "the triumph of the season." Mamie's nose was definitely out of joint. A few weeks earlier, her party was "the triumph of a generation." But memories were short in Newport. She and Tessie Oelrichs slipped away from the crowd and disappeared into the garden for a heart-to-heart talk. An eavesdropper overheard Mamie

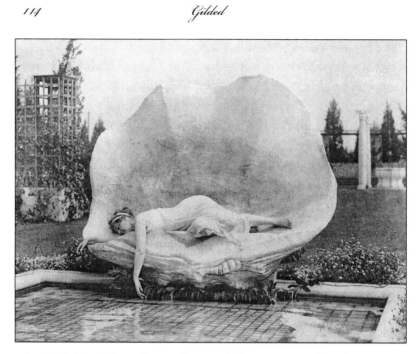

Scantily clad exotic dancer Florence Noyes made the young men in the audience sit up and take notice when she performed at the Masque of the Blue Garden.

telling her friend not "to croak too sadly" because she was planning another party to trump the James success.

A reporter summed up the fickle colony's sentiment this way: "Newport is busy comparing the two biggest entertainments of the almost dead season. And naturally the rather tawdry affair given at Crossways suffers at the hands of Mrs. Fish's dearest enemies . . . today, Mrs. James may have anything she wants, even to the leadership of the Circus Set." This year, the social baton had passed to Harriet James, but there was always next year.

Beatrice

Nineteen thirteen was a turning point for Beatrice Turner, a young woman who summered with her parents at Cliffside, a large Victorian house overlooking Newport's Cliff Walk. She was an aspiring artist who dreamed of studying at the Academy of Fine Arts in Philadelphia, but her very proper father insisted that she stay home. "Paint me a picture of yourself," he suggested as an alternative. She did, and when he saw it, Mr. Turner's reaction was far from fatherly. He composed a poem expressing his unnatural feelings about his daughter's forbidden beauty:

When looking at thy form divine,
Perfect in each curve and line,
And gazing at thy silken hair
And looking in thy orbits rare,
A misnomer 'twas in naming thee
Aught else but Venus.

And he watched her very, very closely, especially when young men were around.

When Mr. Turner died suddenly in the fall of 1913, it seemed that Beatrice would pursue art school, a social life, and freedom. Instead, Beatrice retreated into a strange and private world. She insisted on painting a portrait of her father before he was buried and used his embalmed corpse as her model. After the funeral, there was more odd behavior. Beatrice had Cliffside painted black, dressed in old-fashioned clothes, and settled into quiet, repressed spinsterhood.

At least that's how she appeared to outsiders. But inside her black house, with brush in hand, Beatrice was a different woman. She painted hundreds of self-portraits chronicling an alternate life that showed Beatrice dressed in a gown and flirting with imaginary admirers; Beatrice staring into a mirror; and, shockingly, Beatrice nude. Beatrice's art revealed the woman she wanted to be, but she hid her paintings—and her true self—from Newport and the rest of the world.

12

That Sinking Feeling

The world was changing, in Newport and everywhere else. For one thing, a fortune wasn't what it used to be. On March 1, 1914, anyone with an income of more than $3,000 had to pay America's brand new personal income tax: 1 percent on the lowest amount, and up to 7 percent on $500,000 and over. Most Americans—some 99 percent of the population—did not make enough money to be considered taxable. But rich Newporters did, and they were well aware that the newly ratified Sixteenth Amendment, authorizing taxation, was going to have a dramatic impact on their privileged lives.

Before the tax, millionaires happily kept every cent they made, and that was how they were able to afford $11 million cottages, European antiques, and a fleet of servants. They were reluctant to surrender even a small percentage of their hard-earned—and hard-spent—money to the government. In financial circles, the chase was on for tax loopholes, legitimate ways to dodge the dreaded tax. One funny loophole was created by the very officials who wrote the tax law. They specified that the tax was to be applied to lawful income, implying that unlawful income was not taxable. Congress wisely deleted the word from its 1916 revision, which led to the downfall of many a tax-evading bootlegger during Prohibition.

The war in Europe was another looming problem. On June 28, 1914—just before the Newport season was about to begin— Archduke Francis Ferdinand and his wife, Duchess Sophie, were assassinated in Sarajevo. Austria-Hungary's declaration of war on Serbia was upsetting to the normally carefree colonists because some families, including the Goelets, had daughters who were married to foreigners. Others, including James Van Alen and assorted Vanderbilts and Oelrichs, were traveling in Europe and couldn't get home. At first, hostesses threw themselves into their usual this-will-be-the-gayest-season-ever preparations. Mamie Fish, for example, announced a floral-themed party for August, and florists were already hard at work cornering the market on expensive blooms.

The mood in Newport took a downward turn when a group of financiers rushed to New York via yacht because they were concerned about the effects of war on the stock market. Mamie canceled her ball because it was suddenly inappropriate to celebrate, and joined forces with Alva Belmont and Harriet James to sponsor a charity bazaar for the war effort. Other hostesses followed their lead with fundraisers of their own. As it turned out, fund-raisers were just parties with a conscience; yes, they served a higher purpose of making money for good causes, but guests still had the opportunity to dress up and have a good time.

One unanticipated consequence of the war was that foreign-born servants packed up their belongings and returned to their native countries. Suddenly it was a liability to have had a French chef or a German chauffeur, and cottagers found themselves woefully understaffed. Even though the nation's unemployment rate was soaring, Americans turned up their noses at the prospect of working as domestics, and it would prove difficult to keep a large household running without proper help.

Mamie Fish contemplated the world's economic and political problems from her perch as a social leader and formulated her own unique solutions. "I, for one, believe that people who have money should spend it this year," she announced in an interview. Instead of cutting back, she said, the rich had a responsibility to keep caterers and dressmakers as busy as possible. According to Mamie, an unemployed butler, pastry chef, or florist was as sad a sight as an unemployed steelworker.

Mamie also blasted Americans for their reluctance to work as domestics. Why, she wanted to know, did young women prefer to work in a department store when they could make more money as a lady's maid? She suspected that they were ashamed to be "in service," and she was shocked by their snobbery. Mamie would never look down on a servant. In fact, she was sure that she could be a maid if she had to be. "I could go out and do any kind of work without losing personality," she boasted.

Mamie's "let them eat cake" observations actually made some sense. The trickle-down effect she described would boost the economy, even if it trickled down from hostess, to party planner, to caterer, to waiter. And, as she suggested, the unemployed needed to be more realistic and open-minded about work. A job—even as a maid or a footman—was still a job. Mamie, who could barely read, was hailed as a "forceful and fearless woman" who was "intellectually very able."

Even when she got older, Mamie retained her wicked sense of humor. She had fallen out of touch with Harry Lehr, who spent most of his time in Europe. But when Mamie heard that her old friend had suffered a nervous breakdown and was failing, she invited him to visit her in Newport. She told poor Harry not to think twice about his deteriorating mental condition. "You know quite well, sweet lamb, that you won't need any mind to go with the people here."

In May 1915, Mamie died of a cerebral hemorrhage. Her admirers praised her for being thoroughly American, from her Colonial house to her larger-than-life, independent spirit. Subsequently, the Stuyvesant Fish suffered public humiliation at the hands of an indiscreet employee who spilled the beans for a popular roman à clef entitled *Confessions of a Social Secretary*. In the book, which was ghostwritten by journalist Corinne Lowe, a social secretary described her tour of duty with a famous society matron. The matron, though called "Mrs. Cuttle," was clearly Mamie.

All of her secrets were revealed—her wardrobe allowance of $20,000 a year and the $10,000 per month she spent on household expenses. *Confessions* also exposed the rude behavior of Mamie's friends and houseguests (they wiped their pens on her sheets and undertipped the servants); the politics behind her party invitations (grab any single man who had the right clothes and manners); and most revelatory, her odd, manic-depressive behavior. According to the informer, there were times when Mamie's bold highjinks seemed to mask boredom, desperation, and even madness. An angry Stuyvesant Fish engaged a private detective and discovered that the culprit was a trusted housekeeper who had betrayed her employer for a little cold cash.

Confessions of a Social Secretary did not actually condemn Mamie and her friends, but it set them up for disapproval by exposing their frivolity. The book was so popular that it was serialized in the widely read *Saturday Evening Post*. Mamie and other famous socialites were the celebrities of their day, and the public loved peeking into their lives the same way they would follow the activities of movie stars in years to come.

Alva Belmont attended the funeral of her old friend Mamie and, at age sixty-two, found herself in a contemplative mood. Her involvement in the fight for women's rights was a full-time job, but Alva wanted to create a personal legacy, so she hired Sara Bard Field, a poet and fellow suffragist, to ghostwrite her autobiography.

Field was so committed to the suffragette crusade that she traveled cross-country in an old car to gather more than five hundred thousand signatures in support of the cause. And she was as passionate as she was political. Field was unhappily married to a Baptist minister when she met Charles Erskine Wood, a forward-thinking lawyer from Portland, Oregon, who represented controversial clients such as birth control advocate Margaret Sanger and lawyer and civil libertarian Clarence Darrow. Wood and Field were kindred spirits who quickly fell in love. Field divorced her husband, but Wood had a Catholic wife who refused to let him go, so the modern-minded lovers contented themselves with a long-term affair instead of marriage.

During the summer of 1917, Field traveled to Newport to work with Alva on their writing project. She moved into a suite of rooms at Marble House, where, to her horror, she discovered that she had been assigned a personal maid who was supposed to bathe and dress her and style her hair. "It would take me a week writing all day to describe that house. . . . Well, you know how the rich live," Field wrote to Wood. Eventually she persuaded Alva that she would work more efficiently if she lived elsewhere. She moved into a nearby rooming house, and every morning Alva's chauffer drove her the short distance to Marble House.

Their interview sessions took place in Alva's Chinese teahouse. Conversations were lively because Alva was not embarrassed to talk about herself, and Field was not too timid to ask tough, personal questions. Topics included Alva's southern childhood, her years in Paris, and her rocky marriage to William K. Vanderbilt, who, Alva confided, brought mistresses home to humiliate her. Field was encouraged by Alva's candor because she figured that a tell-all that actually told all would sell many, many copies.

But Field's initial enthusiasm waned when she was forced to spend time in the larger world of moneyed Newport. Alva invited her to tea at the Arthur Curtiss James home, where they were greeted by Harriet and her liveried footmen. The tea table was sumptuous, yet Field had no appetite. "Such rich food while the millions starve" was her reaction. The conversation turned serious for a moment, as Mrs. James tried to interest Newport socialites and the wives of high-ranking navy officers in the plight of soldiers who were passing through Newport on their way to war. The men did not have a change of underwear, a situation Mrs. James hoped to correct, but the other ladies did not share her concern.

"Come mighty Revolution" Field thought as she listened to these women prattle. She considered them "mindless creatures of inherited wealth or pirated riches" and felt more at home with the young servicemen who filled the streets of the city. She longed to ask them why they were willing to go to war and die for "those rich fools upon the cliffs and Belleview [sic] ave."

As the summer progressed, both Newport and Alva lost their charm for Field. She realized that Alva was the kind of suffragette who cared more about the cause than she cared about any individual woman. Although she paid her servants well, she was often abusive. One day, Alva smacked her maid with a hairbrush for some imagined offense. Field was also shocked to learn that Alva had forced her daughter to marry a man she didn't love—highly questionable behavior for someone who professed to believe in women's rights. Field speculated that Alva's avowed feminism was a way for her to express her inner rage against men—that she wanted to get even for a lifetime of oppression, starting with her disastrous marriage to Vanderbilt.

Field endured Alva's idiosyncrasies and the discomfort of an unusually hot summer for the sake of the book. She was devastated when Alva announced that she had lost interest in finishing the manuscript, or in having it published. Alva was concerned about the reaction of her children, she said. But William K. Vanderbilt was a rich and powerful man, and it is possible that he threatened to suppress publication of his ex-wife's memoir.

Another energetic and outspoken critic of Newport was Francis O. French. Unlike Sara Field, who was always an outsider, French was an insider who had become an outsider. He was born in Newport, and his pedigree was impeccable. His father, Amos Tuck French, was a banker who served as governor of New York's exclusive Knickerbocker Club. His mother, the former Pauline Leroy, came from a long line of society matrons. French and his siblings, including Pauline, Julia, Stuyvie (short for Stuyvesant), and Ned, spent every summer at Mapleshade, their family's beautiful Newport cottage, and his earliest memories were of servants and velvet lawns. He studied with his equally privileged pals at St. George's Preparatory School in nearby Middletown, and then at Harvard. Newport's first families considered young French an A-list bachelor. He danced in Mrs. Stuyvesant Fish's ballroom at Crossways and bowed to the Swedish prince at Mrs. Berwind's reception at The Elms.

When he graduated from Harvard, French felt like a master of the universe, confident of the golden opportunities ahead. A few years later, he found himself disheartened by a series of go-nowhere, entry-level jobs at businesses owned by his father's cronies. His income was meager, not nearly enough to support the costly lifestyle he had enjoyed in Newport, and French was suddenly confronted by a sobering reality: downward mobility. His family's luxurious standard of living was not his birthright.

He had to make his own way in the world, and it was now a different world.

French might have survived on the social circuit as an "extra man" because bachelors were always in demand, but he wanted a more stable position and decided to look for a wife. His father advised him that "with all the girls there are about, it is so easy to choose one not for money, but with money." French dutifully proposed to Eleanor Burrill, the quintessential "rich girl who was supposed to be as easy to love as a poor girl." After the wedding, he discovered that Eleanor's parents wanted the very best for their daughter, but they expected him to pay for it. "Starting out" meant staffing a house with a cook, a maid, a laundress, and a handyman.

In time, the couple had a daughter, Ellen, and their expenses increased. French realized that he was paying his staff more than he made in salary. But his wife and her meddling parents scoffed at his feeble attempts to economize. What good was it to cut down on the milk delivery when there were servants to pay? During the Great War, French looked longingly at recruiting posters. They may have said, "Join the navy and see the world," but to French, enlistment meant "Join the navy and leave your in-laws!" He did just that, but the war—and his new-found freedom—ended just one year later.

Upon his return from Europe, French philosophized that Eleanor, her family, and even his family were all victims of what he liked to call the "Newport idea." For these people, spending, snobbery, and social ambition clouded the most basic human emotions, even love. "The most important thing in the world was to keep up with the smart, rich people who constituted society," he complained.

French was finding it difficult to be that person. He longed for a simpler, more practical life. In fact, after the birth of the Frenches' second daughter, Virginia, he suggested moving to an apartment in the Bronx. But Eleanor wanted no part of his discount dream. She divorced him and proved her allegiance to the "Newport idea" by living on Park Avenue in the winter and summering in Newport. As for the newly enlightened Francis O. French, when he had trouble finding a desk job, he became a New York City taxi driver. He routinely waited outside the city's fashionable clubs, hoping to pick up an old acquaintance as a fare.

One day, the fabulously wealthy Robert Goelet jumped into his cab and was shocked to see a Newporter behind the wheel. "Why, Frank French, what are you doing this for?" he challenged. French explained that he was trying to make an honest living. Goelet seemed embarrassed and offered a fifteen-cent tip—a paltry amount for one of New York's richest landlords. French found that most of his "friends" and acquaintances from Newport had difficulty accepting his defiant—and very public—flight from society. They simply did not like change, and suddenly, it seemed, everyone was rocking the boat.

The world, with its wars and financial woes, was becoming less and less idyllic, even in Newport. Private clubs, such as Bailey's Beach, the Newport Country Club, and the Reading Room, were fine escapes from such disagreeable realities. And for a privileged few, it was possible to take the concept of a club to a new level. Arthur Curtiss James, Tommy Tailer, and Thomas Brayton used their vast resources to build their own little worlds within the resort's exclusive borders.

James and his wife had been enchanted by quaint little mountain villages they saw in Europe and were inspired to create one in Newport. They brought together architects, demolition experts, carpenters, stonemasons, horticulturists, gardeners, workmen, and artist Joseph Linden Smith (the mastermind behind the Masque of the Blue Garden), to build Surprise Valley Farm, or the Swiss Village, as it was called, on the grounds of Beacon Hill. There was a cow barn, a piggery, a henhouse, a smoke-house, a carpenter shop, and cottages for the Jameses' staff. With its turret, curved bridge, winding stairs, and medieval-style windows, the village appeared absolutely authentic, and the clever use of ivy, moss, and lichen made it look "aged" from the start. "The Old World would have been a hundred years making it," pointed out one of the master carpenters. But James's $60 million fortune bought instant antiquity and instant gratification.

Mrs. James liked to entertain her friends in a pergola with a flower-thatched roof, her version of Marie Antoinette's Petit Trianon. Like the famous French queen, Harriet James could play at being a simple country lady in her expensive and care-fully constructed pastoral setting. On the James farm, the pigs and the pigsty were washed several times a day, and unsightly cow and horse droppings were swept out of sight.

The Swiss Village may have looked decorative, especially after Smith added gaily painted signs depicting the various ani-mals and a mural of Mr. and Mrs. James dressed in medieval garb, but its whimsical surface disguised a working farm with state-of-the-art facilities. The cow barn had a maternity hospital for its prized Guernseys, and the dairy produced large quanti-ties of milk, cream, butter (stamped with the James crest and rolled in parchment paper), and cheese. These farm products were never sold; James distributed them free of charge to the people who worked for him.

High-level employees such as the butler, the farm superin-tendent, the head gardeners, and the men who supervised the herds of cows and sheep were given their own houses on the sprawling property. The estate paid for their coal, telephone, and electricity, and a driver transported their children to and from school every day. Even when times were bad in the outside world, Beacon Hill was an oasis of privilege and plenty.

James's generosity extended to sightseers, who were allowed to drive through the Swiss Village during the summer, although they had to stay in their cars and be mindful of the animals. A sign warned:

> You enter here to see the Farm,
> Please drive at snail pace lest you harm
> The pigs, the motors, maids and men,
> A cow, a duck, a dog, a hen—
> All these, and more you'll meet to-day
> So slowly drive along the way.
> —The Farm Committee

For the thousands of tourists who passed through the gates, the Swiss Village was the closest they would come to seeing Europe, and the fanciful creation was an early version of a Disneyland attraction.

T. Suffren Tailer, another rich gentleman who summered in Newport, had a different kind of fantasy, but one that was equally ambitious. Tailer was a successful banker who never met a sport he didn't like. When he became dissatisfied with the conditions at the Newport Country Club, he decided to build his own golf course—not a mere putting green or practice hole, but an all-out, nine-hole masterpiece. He purchased a twenty-six-acre site in Newport and hired leading golf architects Charles MacDonald and Seth Raynor to bring his dream to life. The finished course, which Tailer named Ocean Links, was beautiful to behold and challenging to play. Tailer had ambitions for his son, Tommy, to become a championship golfer, so he saw to it that Ocean Links was the best possible training ground.

Master gardener George Mendonca trims a leafy giraffe, maintaining the intricate topiary menagerie his father-in-law, Joseph Carriera, started on the Brayton farm.

In 1926, the *New Yorker* ran an admiring description of Ocean Links, calling T. Suffern Tailer's private course "the feature of Newport golf life." The club was so exclusive that guests were sent engraved invitations. No one refused because, as the *New Yorker* pointed out, "the course duplicated the nine most perfect golf holes in the world." It was also the only golf club with just one official member: Tailer himself. Ocean Links became a destination for the best players of the day, many of whom competed in the course's annual Golden Mashie Tournament.

As Tailer hoped, Tommy grew up to be a formidable golfer. Unlike his father, however, he did not have a sentimental attachment to Ocean Links. When T. Suffern Tailer died suddenly in 1928, he left funds to maintain his prized course. But Tommy was happy to play at the Newport Country Club, so the course was closed and ultimately forgotten.

On a different part of the island, in nearby Portsmouth, textile industrialist Thomas Brayton purchased a seven-acre farm overlooking Narragansett Bay. It was a simple, unspoiled place, with a white-clapboard farmhouse, rolling fields, and an orchard—a perfect summer retreat for Brayton and his two children, Alice and Edward. Brayton hired Joseph Carriera, a Portuguese gardener from the Azores, to oversee his property. Carriera did a fine job with the farm's flowers and vegetables, but he was an absolute magician with its shrubs. He had seen interesting topiaries (bushes carefully sculpted to look like animals and objects) in his native land and, with Brayton's encouragement, Carriera used his clippers to create extraordinary figures in the garden, including a camel and a giraffe.

It wasn't as simple as it sounded: Carriera had to study a young shrub and imagine it growing into a particular shape. Then he spent the next ten to fifteen years training its branches and leaves to "sit" until his vision was realized. Gradually, a shapely green animal emerged. Carriera filled the Braytons' garden with his whimsical creations. Since the farm was on an out-of-the-way country road in Portsmouth, few locals realized it housed a wondrous, leafy menagerie and was a magical private retreat for Brayton and his family.

13

The Binds That Tie

While some cottagers were busy pursuing extravagant forms of solitude, others were searching for company. In matters of courtship, an "our crowd" mentality had always prevailed among Newport's rich. The same families who summered there in the gilded days—the Vanderbilts, the Oelrichs, the Astors, the Goelets, the Frenches, the Van Alens, the Clews, and the Cushings—returned year after year with their children and grandchildren. Their offspring played together and bowed and curtsied to each other at dancing school. Inevitably, somebody would fall in love. Some of these romances occurred naturally, when boy met girl at the beach club, on the tennis court, or at a debutante ball. Ultimately, marriages were made, and if the union failed, the couple divorced, stepped to the left, and partnered with new mates from the same insular social set. One observer actually blamed the quadrille, the dance that was popular in the heyday of Newport entertaining, for this attitude. Cottagers were so accustomed to changing partners in an orderly fashion on the dance floor that they were overly skilled at doing it in real life.

Mr. Dooley, a popular character in a nationally syndicated newspaper column, commented on these strange and often comic Newport mating rituals. "'Tis there th' millionaire meets his wife that was an' inthrajooces her to his wife that is to be if she can break away fr'm her husband that oughtn't to've been," he observed. Marriage, divorce, and remarriage had reached epidemic proportions in Newport, and everyone from preachers in the pulpit to reporters at pulp newspapers was talking about it.

Before Alva Vanderbilt made divorce a socially acceptable solution to an unhappy marriage, many discontented spouses routinely kept mistresses or lovers on the side. When a Newport matron was asked about her relationship with her husband, she answered, "Yes, I am his wife, but I have an assistant down the street." She actually sounded grateful for the "help." The legendary, oft-married stunner Rita De Acosta Stokes Lydig had only one concern when she learned that her handsome young husband had a mistress in Paris, and it wasn't that he was seeing another woman. Someone told her that her rival was unfashionable, so Lydig quickly arranged for her to go to a proper dressmaker. Infidelity was one thing, but Lydig refused to let a shabby mistress reflect badly on her.

Divorce made the exercise of switching partners easier, and some Newporters seemed engaged in an ongoing game of "musical" marriages. Sometimes these divorces and remarriages rearranged the social landscape. The various Vanderbilt-Belmont mergers were perfect examples of creative couplings in Newport. Alva Smith married William K. Vanderbilt and then divorced him. Oliver Belmont married Sara Whiting, then divorced her. The newly liberated Alva and Oliver married, and Sara Whiting Belmont went on to marry George Rives, also a respected figure in Newport. Ironically, Alva and Sara were best friends when they were young, before their ex-wife connection.

These men and women barely had to leave Bellevue Avenue to find suitable mates.

Henry Clews Jr., the artist with the boisterous son Bamboo, found his second wife in his own backyard, or, more accurately, in the Newport art studio attached to his backyard, when he fell in love with his beautiful pupil, Elsie Whelan Goelet. She was married to Mrs. Ogden Goelet's son, Robert. Elsie filed for divorce in the Newport court, accusing Goelet of "gross misbehavior and wickedness repugnant to and in violation of the marriage covenant" and subsequently married her art teacher.

Their union made it difficult for members of the Clews family to socialize with the Goelets or the Wilsons, since Robert Goelet's mother was Mary Wilson Goelet. Furthermore, his aunts were Grace Wilson Vanderbilt and Carrie Astor Wilson, so both the Vanderbilts and the Astors were involved. It was a wise social secretary who knew how to navigate these treacherous waters when putting together a guest list for a party: either feuding clans could not be invited to the same place at the same time, or all differences had to be set aside because a feud would involve too many people.

On the very same day when Elsie Whelan Goelet petitioned for divorce, Mrs. Pauline French, Frank French's mother, asked the Newport court to end her marriage to Amos Tuck French. He, too, was accused of "gross misbehavior and wickedness repugnant to and in violation of the marriage covenant." The French family, in fact, was becoming famous for its divorces and was dubbed "The Family Where Marriage Is Always a Failure" in one sensational newspaper headline.

Samuel Tuck French, Frank's stuffy father, voiced disapproval when his sister, Elsie French Vanderbilt, divorced her husband, Alfred Gwynne Vanderbilt. Then he abandoned his wife of twenty-eight years, who, in turn, filed for divorce. Their split followed their daughter Julia's elopement with Jack Geraghty, an automobile salesman (who most people assumed was the family chauffeur). After the couple's dramatic elopement (appropriately, in a car), Julia and Jack lived like church mice in a small rented house in Newport. They barely had enough money for a Thanksgiving turkey, and eventually poverty stopped being romantic for Julia. The hands that were more comfortable swinging a tennis racket "wearied of peeling potatoes and washing dishes," according to one reporter, and the unhappy couple split.

The trend continued with Julia's sister, Pauline French. She seemed to be the exemplary daughter when she married Samuel Wagstaff, a likable young man from a fine family. Similarly, Frank French's merger with Eleanor Burrill was a socially correct move. But both marriages ended in divorce. Their brother, Ned French, bucked convention by running away with a voluptuous telephone operator from rural New Hampshire, only to discover that love, or, more appropriately, lust, did not conquer all. When Ned's disapproving family cut off his allowance, he called off the marriage.

The Frenches had the dubious distinction of racking up more elopements, hasty marriages, separations, and divorces than any society family in Newport. Although Frank's daughters were children when the article about the "divorcing Frenches" was written, the piece suggested that little Ellen and Virginia would "grow up to assume their share of the family's apparently inevitable heritage of unhappy marriages."

Some headline-grabbing divorces in Newport involved outsiders rather than members of the social establishment. This was the case with the Battle of the Budlongs, a suit that had all the drama (and comedy) of a long-running serial. Milton and Jessie Budlong moved to Newport with a big bank account and an ambitious social agenda. Budlong had made enough money in the automobile business to purchase The Reef, a sprawling estate on the ocean. His wife expected their fortune to open all the right doors, so she was a little miffed when their money did not automatically buy acceptance. But all was not lost. Tommy Tailer, who was in the process of building Ocean Links at the time, approached his eager new neighbors with a plan.

Tailer, who had sold The Reef to Budlong, needed some of the land back to complete his golf course. The Budlongs needed someone to help them break into society. Tailer agreed to sponsor the newcomers, prompting Jessie Budlong to spend a small fortune on her dress-to-impress Newport wardrobe. Problems started when Tailer had second thoughts about the agreement. Instead of promoting the Budlongs, he snubbed the pushy couple, even refusing to invite them to play on his private course. Jessie reacted badly, and Milton decided that he was fed up with his wife's relentless social climbing. In January 1925 she sued him for a separation, and he countersued.

Both Budlongs engaged in the very sort of colorful mudslinging that endeared them to the press. Jessie Budlong accused her husband of extreme cruelty, neglect to provide, and gross misbehavior. He retaliated by recounting tales of her extravagance and anti-Semitism. He spent more than $1,200 for opera tickets the previous year, he complained, and Jessie had said in public that she would find another "rich Jew" to pay for her clothes if Budlong refused. The staff in Newport was another bone of contention between them. Budlong thought The Reef had more servants than anyone needed. He was shocked to learn that several of those domestics who appeared to be useless were actually detectives hired by Mrs. Budlong to spy on his every move.

For the next five years, America devoured every scandalous detail of Jessie's hunger strike and Milton's accusations of extreme cruelty. She locked Milton out of the house and forced him to beg the servants for clean clothes; then he tried to prevent her from seeing their children. The soap opera came to a close in 1928, when Milton was granted a divorce and custody of seventeen-year-old John and thirteen-year-old Milton Jr. The judge was solicitous of Mr. Budlong, ruling that Mrs. Budlong had caused her spouse great "pain of mind." Jessie appealed to a higher court, but lost.

As the Budlongs faded from the headlines, Newport became the setting for another colorful marital melodrama. This one featured an heiress, Louise Van Alen, and not one but two Russian princes. The Van Alen family tree was made of solid gold. On her father's side, Louise was a direct descendant of *the* Mrs. Astor, and Louise's mother, Daisy Post Van Alen, was related to the Vanderbilts. The family lived at Wakehurst, a magnificent Newport estate that had been modeled after Wakehurst Place in England. The first James Van Alen (the Anglophile who wore a hat and monocle at Bailey's Beach) bought the architectural plans of the original house so that his American reproduction could be accurate in its every detail.

The Van Alens lived formally in their castle, with a retinue of liveried servants and innumerable rules dictating polite behavior. Mrs. Van Alen, a widow, insisted that her dinner guests be absolutely punctual. Her invitees were so terrified of offending her that they lined up their cars on the street leading into Wakehurst a few minutes before the appointed dinner hour. That way, they could enter the house precisely when expected. Women had to wear long gowns because Mrs. Van Alen scorned the newly popular cocktail attire.

Her daughter Louise, on the other hand, was a modern young woman with a relaxed sense of decorum. When she brought home a husband-to-be, he was not the son of a Newport first family. Instead, her Prince Charming was a charming prince—albeit one with dubious ancestry. "Prince" Alexis Mdivani claimed to be a Russian royal from the province of Georgia, although his name was nowhere to be found in the almanac of Russian royalty. After the Revolution, it was difficult to prove such things, and it seemed as if every expatriate Russian had served the czar and "lost everything" when fleeing the homeland. Mdivani's own father, Zakharias Mdivani, made light of the idea by joking that he was the only man to inherit a princely title from his children.

American women decided that the Mdivanis looked like royalty and acted like royalty, so the truth about their background was unimportant. Alexis and his brothers, David and Serge, became the "marrying Mdivanis" because, like the "marrying Wilsons," they habitually (and serially) wed wealthy partners. Movie star Mae Murray snapped up "Prince" David to be her fourth husband. Sultry actress Pola Negri tapped "Prince" Serge to be her mate. And young "Prince" Alexis wooed and won Louise Van Alen, despite (or perhaps because of) her mother's horrified protests. Daisy Van Alen seemed to have conveniently forgotten the scandal surrounding her own marriage—the senior Van Alens did not want their son marrying her because she was older than he and perhaps not up to their expectations.

The wedding took place in Newport on May 16, 1931. It was a simple ceremony at Wakehurst, with the bride's family in attendance. The groom listed "gentleman" as his profession on the marriage certificate application, a sign that he was ready and able to be a kept man. The newlyweds went off to Paris, where they lived not so happily ever after.

Their marriage came to a screeching halt when a better catch presented herself. Louise Van Alen was rich, but Woolworth heiress Barbara Hutton was richer. Alexis met Hutton, who was about to inherit more than $30 million in the summer of 1932. Their romance was reported by gossip columnist Cholly Knickerbocker, and Louise, who was disenchanted with married life, obligingly divorced Mdivani, but not before asking Hutton if her intentions were honorable. Louise may have had a few regrets about losing her handsome prince, but her family was ecstatic. News of the breakup "was joyously received in Newport by Louise's mother."

Daisy's happiness was short-lived because there was another Mdivani in her daughter's future. Prince Alexis died in a car accident in 1935 while speeding with a woman not his wife. By that time, Prince David was divorced from Mae Murray, and Prince Serge was exiting his second marriage. The "marrying Mdivanis" were in danger of becoming better known as the "divorcing Mdivanis," but then Serge restored his family's reputation by marrying his ex-sister-in-law, Louise Van Alen Mdivani. Newport society was "flabbergasted," wrote the *New York Daily News*. But in a funny way, Louise and her prince were doing what had come naturally to generations of Newporters— marrying within a tight little circle.

The wedding took place in Palm Beach in February 1936, but the honeymoon came to an abrupt end one month later, when Serge Mdivani was kicked to death by his polo pony as Louise watched helplessly from the sidelines. Her heartbreaks were more tragic than those in any Hollywood weepie. She was the poor little rich girl whose money could not buy her happiness . . . twice.

Given all the Sturm und Drang that plagued upper-crust relationships, it was understandable that some wealthy women preferred to remain single. Newport had its share of well-heeled spinsters who seemed to enjoy their independence. Alice Brayton, who wistfully alluded to a romantic "disappointment" in her past, lived happily with the animal topiaries on her secluded farm. And Edith and Maud Wetmore were lively and quick-witted bachelorettes who led long and full lives. When they were young, they traveled to Europe, where they shopped at Worth, sailed on yachts, and danced and flirted with young gentlemen. In Newport, the sisters lived comfortably at Chateau-sur-Mer, attended by a butler, maids, and liveried servants. Time passed, and somehow the moment for romance came . . . and went.

As they matured, the Wetmore sisters pursued different interests. Edith loved art and culture, while Maud was a staunch Republican and sportswoman who enjoyed driving her automobile. The men in their lives were relatives, friends, domestics, and financial advisers. There may have been no Prince Charmings, but in their absence, there also was no heartbreak.

John Jacob Astor 3d (left), the city's most eligible bachelor, whose engagement to Eileen Gillespie was broken. Announcement by Eileen's parents stunned the social world.

Eileen

Louise Van Alen's game of marital Russian roulette with the Mdivanis, which ended badly, was offset by a fairytale romance between two of high society's finest. In December 1933, America was enchanted by the news that Eileen Gillespie of Newport and New York was engaged to John Jacob Astor VI. The eighteen-year-old debutante came from a solid, happy home with a loving "mummy" and "daddy." The Gillespies had money and blood so blue it went all the way back to Rhode Island's first settler, Roger Williams. They also were also related to John Carter Brown, whose family founded Providence's Brown University.

But the Gillespies were not pretentious people. Unlike many of their neighbors, they did not give their Newport home a fancy name. And whether they were in Newport or New York, they raised their two daughters with great care. There were health-threatening epidemics when Eileen was a child, so she was nine years old before she was allowed to attend school, and she and her sister, Phyllis, were forbidden newspapers until they were sixteen. Dickens was acceptable reading, but risqué authors such as Balzac were strictly taboo. The Gillespie girls were always chaperoned, and their mother cautioned them to remember that "the essence of flirtation is the promise of more."

Eileen was fluent in French and was an outstanding tennis player. In a sense, she was the girl next door, although the "door" in question was attached to a house on Fifth Avenue and a villa in Newport. She was one of the leading debutantes of the season and the very first girl in her set to receive—and accept—a marriage proposal.

John Jacob Astor's name said it all. His mother, young Madeleine Force Astor, was pregnant with him while crossing the Atlantic on the *Titanic*, so he made headlines before he was even born. His elder half brother, Vincent Astor, inherited the bulk of the family fortune, nearly $70 million, while John was the beneficiary of a less bountiful $3 million trust fund. It is likely that their father would have changed his will to properly acknowledge his second son, but he died before having a chance to do so.

Young Astor claimed his inheritance (which had grown to $5 million) on his twenty-first birthday, in 1933, and happily went on a spending spree. His purchases included a yellow Rolls-Royce, nine other cars, and a Newport estate called Chetwood. The newly prosperous young man needed a chatelaine to go with his chattels, so he proposed to Eileen Gillespie.

Eileen sent excited telegrams to her friends, saying she wanted them to be the first to know her good news. Stories about the engagement, accompanied by photographs of the attractive young lovers, ran in newspapers all over the country. News of the Astor-Gillespie romance was escapist entertainment for readers who were enduring hard times. The main "characters," John and Eileen, were young, beautiful, and rich, and instead of trying to make ends meet, they were happy-go-lucky sweethearts. The engagement ring was the proverbial "diamond as big as the Ritz," thirty-two dazzling carats in a classic setting. It was an Astor family heirloom, purchased by *the* Mrs. Astor from the jewel box of France's Empress Eugénie. Depending on whether it was described by the *New York Times* or a tabloid, it was worth $100,000 to $250,000.

On January 3, 1934, America learned that the nuptials would take place in New York City's St. Thomas Church on February 6. Two weeks later, the names of the wedding attendants were announced. Gillespie's sister, Phyllis, would be joined by a bevy of other debutantes, including Eileen's dear friend Ellen Tuck French. "Tucky" French was the now-grown-up daughter of Frank French, the independent-minded gentleman who shocked his Newport friends by working as a cabdriver.

On January 22, only two weeks before the big day, readers opened their newspapers to a shocking headline: "Eileen Gillespie Not to Wed Astor." America's favorite wedding was off, and columnists scrambled for the story behind the breakup. There were reports that the couple had stormed out of a dance because Astor was paying too much attention to another woman. He and Eileen argued bitterly in the lobby of the Savoy Plaza Hotel, according to another source, and Astor used improper language while addressing his fiancée. However it happened, the sweethearts decided not to go ahead with the wedding, and their falling out was even more newsworthy than their engagement. What happened? everyone wondered. And what about the ring?

The Gillespies were very proper people who proceeded carefully. They offered to send Astor the ring in exchange for a letter of apology "for his language to their daughter and a retraction of his threats concerning her and her family." Astor's response was to jump on a boat for Shanghai. He needed a change of scenery and he was "trying to forget" his shattered romance, he said. He was spied in China, gazing "morosely out the window." Meanwhile, Eileen's family closed ranks to protect her from the press. The incident was so unpleasantly public that it was terribly important to stem the tide of unwanted celebrity so that her good name could remain intact.

Astor returned from his trip in early May and immediately resumed his conversations with reporters. His fiancée's parents were to blame, he said, because they interfered with the relationship. He even hinted that there was a possibility of reconciliation. "I was willing to marry her, and if I were to think about it, I might still be willing to marry her," he stated.

But if Astor was still considering marriage, Eileen Gillespie was not necessarily the woman he had in mind. A few weeks later he announced his engagement to another lovely young debutante, Ellen Tuck French—the same Tucky French who was to have been Eileen's bridesmaid. The girls had grown up together, so it was a little surprising when Tucky behaved as if Astor's engagement to her lifelong friend had never happened.

Frank French may have been the only person who wasn't shocked by the news. His daughter had told him about her feelings for Astor back in February, not long after the Astor-Gillespie debacle. Tucky had plenty of time to think about Astor while he was in Europe, and their secret longing for

Five months after John Jacob Astor's supposed heartbreak, he shocked society by marrying Ellen Tuck French, Eileen Gillespie's dear friend and almost-bridesmaid.

each other withstood the separation. Astor pressed her to announce their engagement, but her mother and grandmother were so opposed to the union that they refused to pay for it. Tucky was about to marry one of the wealthiest young men in the world, yet she was as desperate as a chauffeur's daughter, with no resources for a proper wedding. This was a difficult problem for an eighteen-year-old debutante to solve, so she turned to her father for advice.

Luckily, Frank French appreciated rebellious behavior and knew how to manipulate his ex-wife. He arranged to meet Tucky and her mother in Newport and offered to host the wedding at his modest home in Dedham, Massachusetts. Of course, that idea was anathema to a Newport matron, especially one whose daughter was marrying an Astor. Tucky's mother had a quick change of heart and agreed to give the couple her blessing. There would be a ceremony at Trinity Church followed by a reception at Mapleshade. There was some talk of preventing Frank from escorting his daughter down the aisle, but Tucky held firm on that point.

While Tucky planned the wedding, Astor had to settle unfinished business with Eileen. There was still the matter of the Empress Eugénie diamond. He penned a curt note to Eileen, writing, "I willingly withdraw anything I may have said to you in the corridor of the Savoy-Plaza Hotel on Sunday, Jan. 21, 1934, which may have hurt you, and I apologize." Satisfied, the family returned Astor's ring.

Astor placed the tainted diamond in a safe deposit box and presented Tucky with a much smaller ring, which she told her father was "just the right size," and the French-Astor wedding was set for June 30. On that day, Eileen and her family boarded the *Leviathan* in New York City to set sail for Europe. Reporters at the dock unkindly reminded the travelers that Astor's wedding ceremony was scheduled for that afternoon. Mrs. Gillespie told them it was "the luckiest day of my daughter's life."

Eileen held her head high, and when she returned from Europe, she threw herself back into the business of being a popular young woman. The smart set waited for the inevitable moment when Eileen and Tucky would run into each other. Their paths were bound to cross, especially in Newport, where the newlyweds lived practically around the corner from the Gillespies.

One day, the feuding friends showed up at the same tea. "Impy," their hostess, knew in advance and alerted both women. "Grand! I would love to see her," said Eileen, leading Tucky to believe that some kind of reconciliation was in store. Instead, the Astor ex-fiancée publicly snubbed the Astor wife. Tucky was furious. "Gone are my softhearted feelings toward her," she complained to her father, suggesting that she had felt guilty about Eileen before their hostile encounter. "There's a girl that's going to be firmly squelched and put in her place," she added, behaving as if she were the injured party.

But Eileen did not suffer. In time she fell in love with John Jermaine Slocum, a Harvard graduate from Charleston, South Carolina, and they enjoyed a long, happy marriage. The Astors did not fare as well. In 1936, Tucky gave birth to a son, but Astor's attention span was notoriously short, and gradually the couple became estranged. Tucky moved to Reno to get a divorce, attributing the breakup to "extreme mental cruelty" on Astor's part. At the tender age of twenty-six, she received a $1 million settlement and custody of young William Astor. As a journalist had predicted of her when she was a child, Tucky officially joined the ranks of the notorious "divorcing Frenches."

14

There Goes the Neighborhood

The weather in Newport during the summer of 1938 was awful. The city was plagued by tropical rains that left everything—and everyone—soggy and depressed. Cottagers found it difficult to have their annual good time at the beach, or in the ballroom for that matter, because so many days of the relatively short season were gloomy and wet. There was a temporary reprieve in August, when it was clear and sunny, but more bad weather was on the way. Wednesday, September 21, began as an unremarkably inclement day at the beach, with clouds, heavy seas, and rain. But by the early afternoon, Newporters learned that what they were experiencing was no normal storm. The city was in the path of a deadly hurricane, and there was no time to prepare or escape.

Within hours, the New England coast was slammed with ninety-five-mile-per-hour winds and a massive tidal wave. The steeple on Trinity Church, Newport's longstanding symbol of stability and tradition, teetered in the wind while horrified spectators watched.

146

Uprooted trees flew through the air, destroying everything in their path. Boats and cars swirled in turbulent waters as the Thames Street business district was flooded by rain and the rising tide. Little Pamela Cottrell and her siblings were riding home from Miss Collings' Day School, as they did every day, and they had no idea they were in the midst of a hurricane when their car crossed the road by Easton's Beach. A few moments after they passed the shore, a giant wave covered the area, and they narrowly escaped death. Students in nearby Jamestown were not as lucky. Seven drowned when their bus driver tried to lead them to safety. Joseph Mateos, the father of four of the young victims, watched helplessly as his children were carried off by the violent waters.

The one serene place in all of Newport was the dining room at Beaulieu, Grace Wilson Vanderbilt's cottage on Bellevue Avenue. Preparations were under way for a formal dinner that night, and Mrs. Vanderbilt would not allow anything, not even a hurricane, to interfere with her plans. Outside the house, several chimneys, half the roof, and a big piece of the porch surrendered to the winds. Inside, Mrs. Vanderbilt's servants blocked their ears to the noise, swallowed their fears, and nervously attended to their chores. The guests were nervous, too. But no one said no to Mrs. Vanderbilt, so they reluctantly left the safety of their homes, uncertain if they would arrive at Beaulieu in one piece.

They were crazy to even try. All over the island, roads were washed away and people were stranded, some clinging precariously to telephone poles and rocks as they prayed for rescue. The Clambake Club and the bathhouses at Bailey's Beach were battered and destroyed, and the Gooseberry Island Fishing Club—the setting for so many rowdy fraternal outings—disappeared without a trace. Mrs. Vanderbilt had invited thirty guests to Beaulieu, but only twenty-seven brave souls made it to her table. As dinner was

A 1933 map indicates the locations of Newport's magnificent "cottages," its biggest tourist attractions.

served, the hurricane deferred to Newport's most imperious hostess. The wind dropped, the rain stopped, and Mrs. Vanderbilt had the evening she'd planned.

Dozens of people died in the hurricane, and the property damage was incalculable. Miraculously, the steeple at Trinity Church and the famous stone cottages that lined the Cliff Walk, Bellevue Avenue, and Ocean Drive were strong enough to withstand what came to be called the Great Hurricane of 1938. Ironically, these houses—and their owners—were less equipped to survive the oncoming winds of change.

One new development that was utterly unacceptable to cottagers was the rumor that a controversial evangelist planned to establish a retreat for his followers in the heart of fashionable Newport. The situation began innocently enough in January 1939, when an enterprising divorcée named Angela Kaufman purchased the stately old Porter Villa, a wooded estate in the older part of town, not far from the Coogan property. Kaufman intended to turn it into a boutique hotel and nightclub, as she had done with a similar property in Bar Harbor, Maine. She spent $25,000 on renovations, renamed the house The Castles, and applied for a liquor license. Kaufman's application was rejected because her neighbors, including Henry S. Wheeler, the mayor of Newport, did not want a bar so close to where they lived. According to Wheeler, no one would patronize it. "Newporters do their drinking at home," he said.

A furious Kaufman announced that she would leave town and rent The Castles to a tenant. Then she shocked everyone by inviting Father Divine, a flashy Harlem preacher, to move into her Newport manse. Rev. Major Jealous Divine was famous, but his biography was sketchy. His real name was George Baker, and some people thought his parents had been sharecroppers in Georgia in the 1880s, while others believed they were former slaves who lived in Maryland. Divine began his evangelical career as a Baptist preacher called "the Messenger" and gradually built up his own congregation, reaching the height of his popularity in 1931. The fact that he considered himself a deity made him a controversial figure, although some disgruntled followers accused him of decidedly ungodlike acts, such as theft and sexual abuse of followers. Divine was always in the headlines because of one scandal or another.

He was in the process of establishing communal dwellings (called "heavens on earth") for his flock when Kaufman approached him with her real estate offering. "Newport is seething in corruption and politics," she wrote. "I own a castle. Kindly advise me when you will visit here. Can arrange for a gathering fitted for your calling."

Kaufman knew exactly what she was doing when she summoned Father Divine to Newport, and she was not motivated by kindness, charity, or religious fervor. She was staging a "spite" sale. At the time, offering real estate to Father Divine became a popular way to punish an offensive neighbor. An angry man in Sayville, New York, did just that, deliberately (and spitefully) selling his house to Divine so that the value of his neighbor's home would plummet. Howland Spencer, a wealthy socialite who despised FDR and his New Deal politics, sold his Hudson River estate to Divine because it was opposite Roosevelt's country spread and he thought it would annoy the president.

Wherever Father Divine and his supporters went, crowds and chaos followed. His mission staged meetings and banquets for hundreds—and sometimes thousands—of believers. Participants did not always behave, and there were often confrontations with the law. A reporter for *Time* magazine pulled no punches when he wrote, "Many a suburban and rural neighborhood around New York City is haunted by a big black nightmare: the possibility that one day someone with a name like 'Wonderful Peace' or 'Beautiful Sweet' will appear in the district, lay cash on the line for a nice piece of property. Then followers of Harlem's bald, black, mousy Rev. Major J. ('Father') Divine will move in." Thanks to Angela Kaufman, the flamboyant minister and his "angels" were on their way to Newport, and their hostess was counting on the fact that her neighbors would be terrified. In fact, she offered them a last-minute reprieve. If Newporters wanted to buy The Castles for $40,000, she was willing to sell. She lowered her price to $10,000, but instead of offers, she received death threats.

Someone hurled a large rock through Kaufman's window. It carried a note that warned of trouble ahead. "Father Divine will receive a warm reception. 1000 strong K.K.K. A bomb will accompany the next warning. Black God Divine must not come," the assailant wrote. Kaufman responded with her own threat. This was "the calm before the storm," she told the press. "Father Divine moves fast, you know." The situation reached an impasse when The Castles suddenly (and conveniently) became tied up in a property dispute initiated by its former owner, and Father Divine set his sights on a larger piece of "heaven," a Hudson River estate that, coincidentally, also had ties to Newport.

In 1938, Newport dowager Daisy Van Alen inherited a fortune from her eighty-two-year-old uncle, Frederick W. Vanderbilt. She became the owner of his residences (on Fifth Avenue and in Hyde Park), his yachts and cars, his valuable commercial real estate, and his personal possessions. Van Alen's sons, James and William, were also big winners at the reading of Vanderbilt's will, but their sister, Louise Van Alen Mdivani Mdivani was not mentioned. Rumor had it that her marriages annoyed her very proper great-uncle to such a degree that he disinherited her.

Hyde Park, Vanderbilt's seven-hundred-acre Hudson River retreat, was renowned for its Stanford White–designed house and its beautiful gardens and forests. The original owners, starting with George Washington's personal physician, Dr. John Bard, were botanists who imported specimen trees from Europe, Scandinavia, Russia, and other faraway locales. The *New York Times* called it "the finest place on the Hudson between New York and Albany." Hyde Park had the further distinction of being adjacent to land owned by President and Mrs. Roosevelt.

Daisy Van Alen didn't need another trophy house, so she listed Hyde Park with Previews Incorporated, an exclusive Realtor that specialized in large estates. Father Divine and his followers registered interest as soon as they learned that Hyde Park was available. Actually, one of the first people Divine contacted was Eleanor Roosevelt. He admired the Roosevelts, he said, and "would not for a moment wish to embarrass you or your friends in any way." He assured her that he intended to use the estate as a private residence, where he would "receive distinguished guests" and foreign diplomats.

Mrs. Roosevelt issued a speedy—and highly diplomatic—reply, knowing that there was no point in alienating the hugely popular religious leader. Basically, she told him that the president believed it was a free country. In fact, Roosevelt's exact words were "there can be no reason against any citizen of our country buying such property he wishes to acquire." But, she added, her husband had long hoped that the Vanderbilt estate would become an arboretum and public park instead of a private residence.

There was nothing diplomatic about Daisy Van Alen's reaction when she heard that Father Divine was aggressively pursuing her property. Frederick Vanderbilt would have been horrified by the prospect of an African American owning his house, and Daisy felt the same way. She issued statements through her real estate agent promising to be considerate of "neighborhood standards and welfare" when selecting a buyer. Ultimately she preferred to give a large portion of Hyde Park to the government rather than sell it to Father Divine and, as FDR had hoped, the property was turned into a national historic site.

One woman in New York was so thrilled by Daisy Van Alen's successful defeat of Divine that she sent her a telegram. "Congratulations Darling Mrs. Van Alen," it said. "I am so glad to see there is an obstacle for you to stop the selling to that nigger and his devils of the Vanderbilt estate. God protect and deliver us from this evil that is spreading all over our aristocrat white America." Van Alen saved the unusual communiqué in a scrapbook of press breaks and family photos.

15

Enemies and Eyesores

America went to war in 1942, and Newport experienced a boom. With the War College, the Torpedo Station, the Naval Supply Station, and the Naval Hospital all within a few miles of one another, and a constant influx of sailors from all over the country, the city's population exploded. There wasn't a vacant hotel room, apartment, or house to be found. Exclusivity would have been downright unpatriotic at such a time, so cottagers turned their cavernous homes into rooming houses for young naval officers. The Breakers, once the inner sanctum of high society, was designated a public air-raid shelter, and E. D. Morgan's majestic Stanford White estate Brenton Cove was transformed into a bustling message center for servicemen.

Newporters had boundless enthusiasm for the war effort. Suddenly everyone in town was in uniform, including the socialites who staffed the city's volunteer groups. They rolled bandages, drove ambulances, and brightened the spirits of homesick men at the USO. Women who were used to being waited on good-naturedly served doughnuts and sandwiches to sailors and soldiers at military gathering places all over town. Daisy Van Alen raised $80,000 for the Red Cross drive, while civic-minded John Nicholas Brown chaired the Office of Civilian Defense. Thanks to him, Newport was the first city in America to have a comprehensive evacuation plan at the ready. Brown, who inherited so much money at birth that he was called "the world's richest baby," was now Newport's most dedicated father. He saw to it that the Office of Civil Defense prearranged safe, temporary housing for more than six thousand children in the event of an enemy attack. He sent his own sons, Nicholas and Carter, out of town for the duration, but kept his little daughter, Angela, close to home.

Wartime food rationing changed the nature of entertaining in the city that was famous for its extravagant dinner parties. Delicacies such as caviar and terrapin were out because comfort foods, including the all-American hamburger, were more in the spirit of the times. Some cottagers had a little trouble understanding the rationale behind rationing. When Miss Julia Berwind (who inherited The Elms from her brother, E. J. Berwind) placed an expensive order at the supermarket and was asked to show her ration books, she answered in all seriousness, "I thought those were for ordinary people."

Miss Julia may have been a little slow to grasp the concept of rationing food, but she understood the fuel shortage and traded her limousine for a giant tricycle, an odd vehicle that looked as if it had been made for an oversize toddler. Miss Julia's chauffeur wheeled it to his mistress, who hopped on and rode it up and down Bellevue Avenue. Other dowagers saved on gas by taking the bus, and were spied with their fare in one hand and a fashionable Louis Vuitton purse in the other. Despite economic hardships, spirits were high.

There was a dark side, literally, to wartime life. When Germany declared war on the United States, the Atlantic Ocean became an active battle zone. German U-boats routinely patrolled the waters off the East Coast, looking for prey. American ships were easy to spot—and sink—because they were silhouetted against the lights of the cities lining the shore. After the United States lost 348 ships to the Germans in this manner, the government decided to turn out the lights in strategic coastal locations such as Newport.

Blackout drills started in 1941. At the first sound of air-raid sirens, private citizens and businesses were supposed to hurry inside and extinguish all lights. Windows and skylights were covered with special fabric to prevent the slightest beam from shining through. "One single case of disobedience or noncompliance might result in a serious catastrophe," authorities warned. Because it was a navy town, Newport was justifiably concerned about being an enemy target. The situation may have been serious, but there were some comic moments. During one blackout, a zealous air-raid warden rushed off to her rounds, accompanied by her husband. As they checked the island for compliance, the civic-minded couple was frantically waved down by two other wardens. It seemed that in her haste to make sure that everyone else was observing the rules, the woman had forgotten to turn off her own lights. In time, people got used to the blackouts and were able to joke about them. One hostess good-naturedly wrote on an invitation, "Five to black-out, Dancing."

The war distracted Newporters from the inescapable truth that their city was beginning to look shabby. Henry James's prophecy about Newport's white elephants was finally coming to pass. "For Sale" signs were sprouting up on Bellevue Avenue and there were more shuttered estates than showplaces. The city still had its iconic ruin, the Coogan family's Whitehall.

In the early 1940s, Helen Worden, society editor of the *New York Evening World*, visited Newport to cover Tennis Week at the casino. One day, while out on a stroll, she stumbled upon the remains of Whitehall. The house was a dilapidated shell, with smashed windows and peeling paint. The front door was open, so Worden peeked inside, where she saw broken furniture, crumbling walls, and rotting floors.

Later, a neighbor guided her through the house, but they had to move cautiously because there were holes in the floors. Toads, snakes, and other creatures rustled in the corners. Yet she noticed a few traces of Whitehall's former splendor. Remnants of fine satin curtains framed the broken windows, and a closet held the faded remains of Mrs. Coogan's gowns. Yellowed calling cards lay scattered on a tray by the front door.

Worden was fascinated by what she saw. She was familiar with the legend of James and Harriet Coogan's social disgrace in 1911, and their sudden flight from Newport. But she wondered what had happened to the family during the ensuing thirty years. Whitehall was an eyesore, a flophouse for drunks, bums, and juvenile delinquents, and it had become a dumping ground for garbage and abandoned cars. Angry neighbors complained that their property values were plunging, but the city was powerless to intervene. Why was Whitehall still standing?

James Coogan died in 1915, four years after the fire, and Harriet Coogan took control of the family's real estate empire. At first it was understandable that the widow was busy with more pressing matters than a damaged summer cottage. Mrs. Coogan seemed well intentioned, and dutifully paid her annual property taxes, but she refused to authorize a single repair. She seemed to be punishing the house as well as all the Newporters who were forced to watch its disintegration. Her behavior was irrational, but Harriet Coogan seemed to become more eccentric every year.

In 1931, she and her daughter, Jessie, checked into suite 638 at Manhattan's Biltmore Hotel and never checked out. In fact, they rarely exited their rooms during the day, nor did they allow anyone to enter. Even when they ordered meals from room service, they instructed waiters to leave all trays outside the door. And when the hotel was undergoing renovations, Mrs. Coogan refused to let her rooms be touched. Every night, promptly at nine, she donned heavy veils and exited the hotel via the freight elevator to go to her real estate office, where she worked in darkness. A disgruntled tenant complained that the one time he met with Mrs. Coogan, she refused to turn on the lights.

Mrs. Coogan may have been a colorful eccentric in New York, but in Newport she was considered a villain. Whenever the town fathers appealed to her to take care of Whitehall, she dismissed their requests. Schoolchildren formed a Caterpillar Brigade to rid the property of insect nests. Police officers patrolled the estate, frequently rounding up vagrants whose discarded cigarettes would cause fires. WPA workers trimmed the trees and cleared the brush.

In 1941, city officials were so desperate to eliminate the blot on the landscape that they tried to flatter Mrs. Coogan into cooperating by offering to replace the house with Coogan Park, a memorial to the family. She remained silent, but Maud Wetmore had plenty to say about the gesture. "That, of course, must have been a joke!" was her response. The outspoken activist blasted the Town Council for not changing the law that permitted the Coogans to do as they pleased simply because they paid their taxes: homeowners in Newport had to be held responsible for maintaining their property, she insisted.

The legend of the Coogans' social disgrace went national in October 1944 when *Life* magazine ran a photograph of the decaying estate with the caption "a monument to Newport revenge." The house was a sorry sight, with graffiti scrawled across its broken doors. The article told the story of the Coogans' ball and the family's sudden flight from the city that spurned them.

A few weeks later, the Coogan controversy came to a head when the estate was attacked by vandals. Whitehall looked like an honest-to-goodness haunted house, so it was a magnet for pranksters every Halloween. This year, a gang of determined hooligans smashed the massive columns that flanked the front door. When its supports were removed, the rotting house toppled onto itself.

This time Mrs. Coogan had no choice but to send her son, Jay, to survey the damage. He was shocked by what he saw. Whitehall was a wreck and had to be destroyed immediately. When it was razed, Harriet Coogan herself experienced a physical decline, almost as if her revenge had been keeping her alive. She died on December 18, 1947, and the woman who wanted nothing more than to succeed in Newport society would forever be remembered for her legendary social failure. Eventually her property in Newport was sold to the city, but not another word was said about turning it into Coogan Park.

There was another eyesore in Newport in the 1940s, and it was right on Bellevue Avenue. Julia Sullivan, the young Irishwoman who purchased the gardener's residence at the Bruen Villas auction in 1912, moved in with her older brother, Timothy Sullivan. People assumed that the Sullivans intended to sell the property at a quick profit and move somewhere else. But the blue-collar siblings happily made Bellevue Avenue their home. When their little house became uninhabitable, the Sullivans replaced it with a modest two-story wooden structure that looked as if it belonged on a farm. There was no plumbing, electricity, or heat, so Julia usually kept a fire burning in a makeshift outdoor kitchen. Surrounded by the fancy estates of the Wetmores, the Browns, and other cottagers, the Sullivans quietly went about their business. The problem, from their neighbors' point of view, was that Timmy's business happened to be collecting junk, which he proudly displayed in his yard.

Sullivan was a jack-of-all-trades—at different times in his life he had been a clerk, a driver, and an oil salesman. But Timmy the Woodhooker, as Newporters called him, loved walking through town with his pushcart, gathering wood and other debris, and trading stories with his customers. Timmy considered himself a collector, not a junkman, although his "collection" was impossible to classify. Typically, the Sullivan yard contained wrecked baby carriages, old doors, metal trays, mattresses, crockery, broken furniture, flower pots (with and without flowers), and, of course, wood of all shapes and sizes. It looked like a haven for rats, but Julia's seventeen cats did a fine job of scaring them away.

Tourists who came to see the villas on Bellevue Avenue were amused by the Sullivans' ramshackle spread. But many of the summer colonists were appalled by the junk pile in their midst, and as early as 1929, a group of concerned citizens petitioned to have the property condemned. Julia and Timmy cleaned up the yard and repaired the house. They even installed modern plumbing. The city was appeased, and the case was dropped. Most people liked the Sullivans and didn't want to see them lose their home.

After the controversy died down, the Sullivans spent the next seventeen years collecting more junk—the same assortment of wood, broken furniture, and baby carriages—until the new pile was a hundred feet long. Julia made matters worse by cooking on an old iron stove she kept outside and hanging her wash out every Monday, the very day the Wetmore sisters received guests at Chateau-sur-Mer. Embarrassed by all that unsightly laundry, the Wetmores told their friends to call on Saturdays instead. Still steaming over the Coogan eyesore, Maud Wetmore complained that Newport was going to the dogs.

Mrs. Peyton J. Van Rensselaer felt the same way. She was a wealthy widow who famously held court in Palm Beach during the winter. She bought The Hedges, an estate on Howe Avenue in Newport, as her summer palace, but unfortunately it was just a hundred yards from the Sullivan property and offered unobstructed views of Timmy's woodpiles and Julia's outdoor kitchen and laundry. Mrs. Peyton J. Van Rensselaer, whose name made her sound like a caricature of a snobbish matron, was a snobbish matron, and the sight of these common people and their rubbish was more than she could bear. In 1945 she rallied her neighbors to sign a petition demanding that the Sullivans remove the junk from their property. Thirty-nine people, including society stalwarts Julia Berwind, Robert Goelet, and Maude Howe Elliot, joined in the fight. But Grace Vanderbilt took the high road and refused to sign, saying it was none of her business.

Timmy and Julia were not overly concerned about the petition. They had survived the previous battle, and they expected to survive Mrs. Van Rensselaer's attack as well. Julia had no use for the uppity busybody, especially after she tried to tell her how to fix her hair. "Her late husband was a man of profound common sense," Julia observed. "He died on his honeymoon, you know." Timmy maintained his dignity in the face of his neighbors' hostility. Whenever one of his enemies, including Mrs. Van Rensselaer, drove by, he removed his faded cap, bowed from the waist, and wished them a pleasant day.

According to Timmy, the real issue was one of class. "The whole effort is nothing more than snobbishness and spite on the part of wealthier neighbors," he argued. His home was his castle, even if it sat atop a junk pile, and a little junk never hurt anyone. Journalists seized upon the Van Rensselaer–Sullivan clash because it was fun to position it as the story of the haves verses the have-nots. Timmy Sullivan was David up against the Goliath of the Newport elite. "Junkman Has Day in Court to Fight '400,'" read one headline, ignoring the fact that Mrs. Astor's "400" existed in the previous century and had been defunct for nearly fifty years.

Some newspapers called Timmy and Julia "the Fighting Sullivans," invoking the five brave brothers who died on the USS *Juneau* during World War II. There was no connection between the two families, but the implication was that the Newport Sullivans were heroic, salt-of-the-earth members of the proletariat. Mrs. Peyton J. Van Rensselaer, on the other hand, was an unsympathetic, high-strung socialite who wept in court when describing the ordeal of living next door to a junkyard. An artist

Mrs. Van Rensselaer's NEIGHBORS

She Said They Were Nice People and That She'd Like to Send Them to Florida

While Julia Hung Out Washing, Social Newport Fumed.

Mrs. Peyton Van Rensselaer turns up her aristocratic nose at her junk-dealing neighbors, Julia and Timmy Sullivan.

for the magazine *American Weekly* portrayed Mrs. Van Rensselaer stereotypically, replete with lorgnette, fur boa, pearl choker, and ridiculous hat. In his illustration, she held her nose so aloft that her eyes appeared to be closed.

As much as the media liked to play up the fact that Timmy and Julia were simple folk, the siblings were not completely unsophisticated. At one point during Mrs. Van Rennselaer's campaign to beautify the Sullivans and their property, she volunteered financial assistance. "I offered to clothe them, fix up their home and paint it and send them on a trip to Florida if they would clean up that disgusting mess," she said. Timmy and Julia knew better than to accept because she wanted to send them south in the summer. No one goes to Florida in the summer, sniffed the Sullivans.

Finally, the fire marshal ruled that if the Sullivans removed all hazards from the area, including mattresses and other flammable waste, there would be no need for a hearing. Timmy and Julia had won a "John Doe" victory against the bossy upper class. Chairman James T. Kaull of the Board of Review explained that even in scenic Newport, the city's demolition law could not be invoked against unsightliness. "If you live across the street from me and want to paint your house red, white, and blue, it may look like the dickens, but there's nothing I can do about it," he said with a sigh.

Newporters who protested the high-profile eyesores created by the Coogans and the Sullivans could argue that in these instances the culprits were "not our crowd" outsiders. The Coogans, for all their money, were social rejects, and the Sullivans hailed from a completely different class. But Newport in the 1940s had a more serious problem than a few colorful gate-crashers. America's richest resort was rotting from within.

16

Fire Sale

The prevailing threats to Newport's gilded way of life were death and taxes. When the robber barons built their castles, they copied the fancy manners and mores of the European aristocrats they admired. But they did not import the foreigners' practical, if hard-hearted, tradition of primogeniture, the system of inheritance whereby the eldest son in a family, simply by virtue of his birth, is the beneficiary of all the property. His younger (and unluckier) siblings have to fend for themselves, unless they are blessed with a bequest or an advantageous marriage. The rationale for this narrow line of inheritance is that it eliminates "heir-splitting." If three children inherit their father's castle and have to sell it to share the profits, the property leaves the family. An estate had a much better chance of remaining intact in the hands of one heir, which is why so many in England had survived the death of one owner after another.

This custom would have come in handy in Newport. Before the advent of the personal income tax in America, the young

Vanderbilts, Goelets, and other inheritors had an easier time hold-ing on to their property. However, by the 1940s, these same cottages were hot potatoes from an heir's point of view, and they couldn't be dropped fast enough. Who could afford the upkeep on the family's costly white elephant? Even if there were enough money to pay the expenses and taxes on a large house (that was used only two months a year), it was impossible to find servants to maintain the demanding old place. Better to sell it than be saddled with it. Of course, that was easier said than done.

The first iconic cottage to hit the market back in 1933 was Marble House. Alva Belmont's health was failing, and she spent most of her time abroad, so her house had been closed for many years. In 1932 she authorized her son, Harold S. Vanderbilt, to sell the Newport landmark to Frederick H. Prince of Boston. The Princes were a respected yachting family who had rented several cottages in Newport over the years. In fact, one of their summer residences was Mamie Fish's Crossways. They were fine people who fit in beautifully both at the beach and on the boulevard. They congratulated themselves for choosing Marble House because it was beautiful, historic, and a steal. The palace that cost $11 million to build and furnish in 1891 sold for a little over $100,000 forty-one years later. Alva was so ill at the time of closing that she was unable to sign the papers, and had to make a simple mark instead. She died a year later, in 1933. Once the Princes moved in, they must have found Marble House a little formal because Mr. Prince built himself a room under the eaves that simulated a cozy cottage—a real cottage, not the Newport variety.

Tessie Oelrichs's Rosecliff was Newport's next high-profile sale. The mythology surrounding the last member of the Social Strategy Board's final years rivaled the stories about Caroline Astor's mental decline. Tessie's niece, Blanche Oelrichs, said that her ailing aunt was a recluse who wandered the halls of her beautiful house, socializing with imaginary guests. When

Tessie died in 1926, her son, Hermann, inherited Rosecliff but lived there for a time on a scale far less grand than the previous generation. Instead of hosting formal dances and importing the casts of Broadway musicals to perform for his guests, he kept a pool table in the giant ballroom and entertained his friends with card tricks.

In February 1941, Hermann sold Rosecliff and its contents to a New York developer named Abraham Leighter. Leighter was part of a real estate syndicate that intended to offload Rosecliff's furnishings, as well as the house itself, at a public auction. A catalog was prepared describing Rosecliff's valuable inventory, which Henry James once called "the loot of Europe." There were Gobelin tapestries depicting the life of the goddess Diana, and costly collections of sculpture, statuary, paintings, books, silver, antique furniture, china, glassware, linens, and hundreds of other items. The sale was scheduled for July 15, the peak of the summer season. On that day, the public could enter Rosecliff's famous ballroom and buy a piece of Tessie's shattered romantic dream. The house that had been closed to all but the most important members of society was now open to absolutely everyone.

All kinds of people showed up, including members of the summer colony, but they were there to gawk, not to buy. Sales were slow, and the daily totals were lower than anticipated because sleek, modern furniture was more popular than massive baroque pieces. Few private homes could accommodate Tessie's gold and white organ, so it went to a church for $1,700. A buyer who had come all the way from California paid $180 for a Louis XIV console and mirror. The impressively named Jerome Napoleon Bonaparte, a descendant of the emperor, congratulated himself for snagging three French pictures and their frames for only $9.

There was great suspense when it came time to auction the house itself. The navy was interested because it was always on the lookout for facilities for servicemen, and it was easy to turn an oversized Newport villa into an institution. The auctioneer tried to spark a contest. "You are looking at a steal, ladies and gentlemen," he told the crowd, and inspired a very animated Mrs. Anita Niesen to make her winning bid of $21,000. She was the mother of Gertrude Niesen, a popular singer and actress, and she planned on presenting the estate to her daughter as a birthday present. "I bought something I'll never forget as long as I live," was Mrs. Niesen's excited response when the auctioneer brought down his gavel on the sale.

The purchase came from left field. No one was expecting a celebrity to swoop in and buy Rosecliff, and Niesen was a genuine celebrity. Known as the "nightclub thrush," she was a throaty song stylist who drew large audiences onstage and in film. Most recently she had starred in the World War II movie musical *Rookies on Parade*. Niesen was delighted with her gift because, as she explained to a journalist, "our family kind of collects houses." Her jocular father, Monty, who was present for the interview, offered his wholehearted approval of his wife's real estate acquisition. "I haven't seen the joint yet, but I understand it's the most tremendous thing you ever saw."

Rosecliff was tremendous. It had fifty rooms, including a two-story ballroom and corridors lined with bedrooms. A girl could get lost in a house that size, especially a girl like Gertrude Niesen, who grew up in Brooklyn. In August, *Life* magazine visited Niesen at her new digs for an article titled "*Life* Visits a Palace at Newport." The blond diva was photographed posing prettily on Tessie Oelrichs's heart-shape staircase and in other rooms in the house. Wherever she stood, Niesen was dwarfed by her grand surroundings. Actually, the house looked more than a little empty because most of its treasures had been sold.

Amid all this publicity, the cottagers were on the fence as to whether they would accept or reject Niesen, but they saw too little of her to decide one way or the other. Niesen's commitments in Hollywood and New York never permitted her to spend much time at Rosecliff, although she and her mother applied to become legal residents of Newport. When Niesen was ready to close the house for the season, she naively assumed that all she had to do was lock the doors and drive away. Experienced cottage owners knew to employ a caretaker during the winter to protect their empty houses from vandals and mishaps.

Disaster struck that winter, and the colorful version of the story goes as follows: At the end of Niesen's last visit to Rosecliff, she left hastily and neglected to turn off a bathroom faucet. The little trickle ran unchecked until it flooded the house. A more plausible, but far more prosaic, scenario was that Rosecliff's oil burner failed during the winter, causing the pipes to freeze and burst. Either way, water ruined the house's fancy ceilings and floors and turned the famous staircase into an icy Niagara Falls. The incident happened sometime in February 1942, when Rosecliff's water meter reader noticed a dramatic surge in consumption. Plumber Charles H. McManus paid a quick house call and opened the door to find a soggy ruin. He reported that the interior of Rosecliff "looked very much like a building immediately after a serious fire."

Neisen arrived at the scene after hearing the bad news. The house was very cold because wood-burning fireplaces were the only source of heat. Every room had suffered extensive damage. Men worked for days to bail out the water, and when that was accomplished, walls had to be removed before the plumbing and heating pipes could be examined and repaired. Renovations would cost many thousands of dollars. And there was a not-so-small insult added to the injury. Niesen had to pay the city for the water that destroyed her house, and the charge was somewhere in the vicinity of $800.

"Rosecliff Owner May Demolish Villa" reported the *Newport Mercury and Weekly News* as Niesen wrestled with the decision to fix Rosecliff or raze it. While she was thinking, she put off paying her water bill, and the Newport Waterworks filed a lien against Rosecliff for the money owed. The former showplace was threatened with destruction, so Niesen did the only sensible thing. She dumped the property, selling it to Ray Alan Van Clief and his wife for $30,000.

In October 1944, *Life* magazine reported on the sad decline of Newport. "*Life* Visits a Fading Newport" was the headline, and it was accompanied by six pages of photographs depicting bleak landscapes, decaying houses, and overgrown yards. The city looked like a ghost town. A caption beneath a picture of the once-exclusive Newport Country Club said that these days anyone who had two dollars could come on over and play. The city's former splendor had "dimmed," the article suggested. Soon the lights would go out in America's richest resort.

The real estate market was so depressed, and the Newport houses so large, that some owners even had trouble giving their cottages away. Ochre Court was a case in point. Owner Robert Goelet was finding it difficult to hold onto the thirty-five servants required to keep his enormous property up and running. He closed the big house, rented a succession of smaller, more manageable places in town, and discovered that he liked downsizing. When he started looking for a permanent new home, he offered Ochre Court to his daughter, Mary, who was a student at Vassar at the time. Not surprisingly, she turned it down.

Goelet was disappointed, although he acknowledged that a college girl might not have much use for a castle. Then he came up with a clever Plan B. Goelet had heard that the newly formed United Nations was looking for a home. Why not Newport? He proposed that the UN set up headquarters at Ochre Court and suggested that they also use nearby Seaview Terrace, a property the city of Newport had purchased for bottom dollar in a tax sale.

Seaview Terrace was the old Edson Bradley estate. Bradley, who made his fortune in the liquor business, built the first Seaview Terrace in Washington, D.C., then had parts of it moved to Newport, where he built an even bigger version. People called the enormous European-style manor the "$2 million summer house." The description annoyed Bradley, who was convinced that the figure worked against him when his taxes were assessed. He died in 1935, leaving his estate to his widowed daughter, Julia Shipman, and she decided to sell her father's objets d'art and the family manor. The customary assortment of expensive tapestries and paintings found plenty of buyers. But the highest offer on the house was only $25,000, and that came from a Providence man who was rumored to be a gambler, so Shipman turned him down. She then failed to pay the $9,945.30 tax bill, and the estate became the property of the city of Newport.

A few prospective buyers came to look at the house—usually someone who was interested in opening a hotel or a school—and a professional football team considered using it as a summer training camp. Like Whitehall, Seaview Terrace deteriorated and became a burden to the city. The estate was bundled into Robert Goelet's UN proposal because everyone agreed it would be better to give it away than to stand back and watch it fall apart.

In November 1945, a delegation of Rhode Islanders traveled to London to make Newport's official offer. They faced stiff competition from other locales, including Atlantic City, Denver, Boston, San Francisco, Chicago, and the Black Hills of South Dakota. Major Sherman Stoner, an Englishman who was a descendant of Rhode Island founder Roger Williams, argued eloquently that Newport was eager to "play a part in the future sanity and security of the world." The UN listened politely but declined, finally settling on New York City as its location.

Robert Goelet was still stuck with Ochre Court, but his experiences with the UN inspired him to come up with a solution to his housing woes. He donated his oversized villa to the Catholic Diocese of Providence, which planned to turn it into Rhode Island's first Catholic women's college. Mother Mary Matthew said the project was "a dream realized" for her nuns, who longed for a school of their own, and a special architect was brought in to reconfigure the castle as Salve Regina College.

With Ochre Court in good hands (and more importantly, off their hands), the Goelets moved into Champ Soleil, a smaller place on Bellevue Avenue. But their new cottage, a gated Norman château with twenty-two rooms, six marble fireplaces, and pine paneling imported from Paris, was hardly a comedown. The big plus from their point of view was that the new residence required only five servants to keep it going.

17

Self-Preservation

The average Newporter might not have noticed that the city's old houses, and the lifestyle that went with them, were imperiled. The low-priced sale of a neglected cottage, or the demolition of a shabby block by the waterfront, might even be perceived as progress, because postwar America was in the mood for a giant cleanup, and anything large, dark, broken, or antiquated was a target. But the wrecking ball, more dangerous than any hurricane, was heading straight for Newport.

Katherine Urquhart Warren, a socialite with a taste for perfume and pearls, was one of the first people to recognize that there was trouble ahead for Newport. She was married to George Warren Jr., a third-generation Newporter, and they were long-standing members of the summer community. One year, Mrs. Warren demonstrated her sense of humor by dressing for a costume party in clam shells, banana peels, and orange rinds and calling herself "Miss Bailey's Beach."

During the season, the Warrens lived on historic Mill Street, right near the Old Stone Mill, the Redwood Library, and the Newport Art Museum. Surrounded by Colonial buildings and Gilded Age palaces, they were inspired by history every day. Even a drive to the grocery store was a trip through time. The Warrens intended to keep it that way, no matter how many magazines predicted death for a "fading" Newport.

Several of Newport's old dwellings were starting to disappear. The Rocks, the former Clews property, had become part of The Ledges in a fitting finale to the feud between its owners and the dignified Cushings. Also gone were The Reef, the Budlongs' controversial divorce house, and other familiar properties. Katherine Warren's immediate concern was Hunter House, a Colonial residence that had served as headquarters for the commander of the French fleet during the American Revolution. The building had survived war, natural disasters, and the ups and downs of Newport's economy, only to be threatened with demolition by real estate developers. Rumor had it that New York's Metropolitan Museum of Art was hoping to add the house's remarkable antique paneling to its decorative arts collection. In her no-nonsense way, Katherine Warren was going to see about that.

On August 9, 1945, she invited ten Newporters to meet at her home. Her guests were as diverse as the little band of dissidents who founded Newport in 1639, ranging from high-ranking executives, such as Lawrence W. Champlin, treasurer of the Savings Bank of Newport, and Richard C. Adams, president of the Newport Realty Trust, to architect John P. Brown and high school teacher William King Covell. Warren also pulled in an assortment of society big guns, including Mrs. John Carter Brown, Maud and Edith Wetmore, and Maxim Karolik.

The Wetmore sisters, who were now in their seventies, were Newport's most vigilant watchdogs. They were old enough to remember the Gilded Age and spirited enough to have plenty to say about the downward direction their city was taking. "We're at the end of an era, if you please," was Miss Edith's way of summing things up.

Maxim Karolik was equally outspoken, and he had the oddest background of anyone at Mrs. Warren's gathering. He was born in Bessarabia, Russia, and grew up to be a lead tenor at the Petrograd Grand Opera House. The dark and handsome singer came to America in 1924, and performed at New York City's Aeolian Hall, where he was warmly received by music critics. They praised the young man's sincere delivery, although one critic pointed out that "his voice had been forced upward" because he was "reaching" for the high notes. In another "reach," Karolik, still in his twenties, married Martha Codman, a millionaire from Boston in her fifties. Their union catapulted him into the highest echelons of society, but Karolik proved that he was not a philandering playboy like his fellow countrymen the Mdivanis. His love for Codman was sincere, and he used his newfound wealth to fund admirable pursuits.

Karolik developed a passion for early American art and antiques, an overlooked period in the art world at the time. He wanted to become a serious collector and had the means to do so, but he was smart enough to know that a great collection required great advice. Karolik approached the Museum of Fine Arts in Boston with a unique proposition. If their experts would help him to assemble his collection, he would give every last piece of it to the museum. In this way, Karolik could enjoy the thrill of the chase without making any big mistakes. He literally "knocked on doors from New Hampshire to Georgia," searching for paintings, clocks, furniture, and other historic pieces. Owners were charmed by the determined Russian, who amassed an outstanding assortment of art, from portraits painted by Gilbert Stuart and John Singleton Copley, to rare pieces of furniture carved by master woodworkers. As promised, when Karolik finished gathering his treasures, he turned them over to the MFA for the brand-new Karolik wing.

By 1945 he was a self-taught art expert with a practiced eye, and a valuable addition to Katherine Warren's little group.

The pearl-clad matron, the eccentric Russian, the two cantankerous sisters, and their well-intentioned friends called themselves The Preservation Society and set out on their mission to protect historical Newport. They succeeded beyond their expectations. Only one year after their first meeting, the fledgling society rounded up a healthy group of members and raised enough funds to secure a mortgage for the purchase of Hunter House.

Although the years had not been kind to the quaint wooden structure, it was still a fine example of Colonial architecture. But it needed a great deal of work, and fortunately, Ralph Carpenter, a Rhode Island native and summer colonist (who was so handsome and charming he was considered Newport's version of Cary Grant), agreed to oversee its restoration. Carpenter was a successful businessman, who, like his friend Maxim Karolik, had become a self-taught decorative arts expert. As a young man, he spent his Saturdays in antiques stores, learning from the dealers themselves. He bought what he liked, sometimes struggling to pay for it, and when he had more money, he upgraded. One of Carpenter's favorite pastimes was knocking on the doors of old houses just to see what was inside. His attention to detail was so great that he thought nothing of chasing all the way to Scotland for a Newport-made cabinet that would be an authentic addition to Hunter House.

The fledgling Preservation Society proved that it was dedicated and resourceful. But to be truly effective, the group needed a long-range plan. In 1947 they invited Kenneth Chorley, the president of Virginia's popular tourist attraction Colonial Williamsburg, to visit Newport. Colonial Williamsburg was the dream of Dr. W. A. R. Goodwin and John D. Rockefeller, two men who wanted future generations to experience an authentic eighteenth-century American setting. In 1927 they launched an ambitious—some said foolhardy—plan to re-create the city of Williamsburg as it was in its pre-Revolutionary heyday. It was a massive undertaking because the city had changed so much. All traces of modern life had to be eliminated, so approximately six hundred buildings, including banks, a power plant, and a mill, were removed. Ninety eighteenth-century buildings were restored and three hundred were rebuilt to replace ones that had been destroyed. Twenty years later, and at a cost of $25 million, Colonial Williamsburg was a historically correct theme park. Skeptics were silenced when, over time, millions of tourists came and spent a lot of money.

Chorley toured Newport for two days, then offered ideas about what to do with the city's historic sites. Preservationists listened attentively, realizing that the solution to their city's decline was right in front of them. Newport's greatest and most exploitable resource was its own history, which the city had in limitless supply. Chorley encouraged his audience to act quickly to preserve its architectural treasures. "Plan to do this job superlatively well," he stressed. "A superficial restoration will not do." Shabby old houses could not masquerade as attractions, or visitors would be disappointed. Preservation was a full-time business, not a hobby.

Chorley also addressed the elephant in the room—the subject of tourism. He knew that many people were asking themselves, "Do we want all these people swarming all over Newport?" Traditionally, Newport was not very hospitable to outsiders. Chorley gently reminded them, "A lot of your things in Newport belong to other people. They are Americans, too, and Newport is a part of their heritage."

When it came to reinventing Newport, there was a high road and a low road. There were those preservationists who were afraid of the "masses" and wanted to prevent the city from turning into a Coney Island. But, there were others who had their own theories about an economic rescue for the city, and exploitation was the name of their game.

Nathan Fleischer was a ne'er-do-well New York lawyer who moved to Newport to start a new career as a furrier. There was something a little slippery about him, but Fleischer was sharp and had a certain huckster charm. Like Alfred Smith, the enterprising tailor who first promoted Newport real estate, Fleischer believed that Newport was a goldmine of opportunity, and he had a plan to improve the decaying city.

In 1947 he published a peppy booklet titled *Newport: Blueprint for a City That Must Do, Develop, or Die.* According to Fleischer, Newport had lost its standing as one of the most vital cities in America because of its dependency on two crutches: high society and the navy. Both entities, he pointed out, were fickle and likely to abandon the city at any time. Newport had to throw aside those crutches and depend on itself. This meant cultivating its greatest asset—its magnificent harbor and waterfront—as a destination for tourists.

The problem was that the waterfront was the worst neighborhood in town. The streets were narrow and antiquated; there was very little parking; and in most areas, the potentially beautiful water view was blocked by seedy old buildings. Newport needed a makeover, suggested Fleischer, before tourists would come and spend their coveted dollars. He wanted to raze the buildings that obscured the harbor, widen the streets to accommodate both the view and traffic, and offer parking and other amenities in a welcoming tourist facility.

Fleischer was a visionary when it came to imagining a tourist-friendly Newport. But his impulse to improve the city was fueled by a healthy dose of self-interest. When visitors arrived in Newport, they would need a place to stay, and Fleischer was ready to oblige them with Cliff Lawn, a Gilded Age cottage he planned to turn into a hotel.

The thirty-room house, built by the John Winthrop Chanlers in 1873, stood at the entrance of the Cliff Walk. It had been given to Fleischer by a client (he still practiced law) in lieu of a fee, and he was trying to upgrade the property with a commercial driveway and a bar, but the city refused his application for a liquor license.

This was when Fleischer discovered that other Newporters did not share his commitment to growing the tourist trade. Mrs. Warren said that Newport must maintain its "character" and not lower its high standards. Fleischer fought the system by running for mayor in 1948, and again in 1950, but he lost both elections.

While hatching his entrepreneurial plans, Fleischer stumbled upon a business opportunity that was, quite literally, in his own backyard. Just a few hundred feet away from Cliff Lawn was Cliffside, Beatrice Turner's black, and increasingly ramshackle, house. Beatrice died of cancer in August 1948. Her house had been closed to outsiders for so many years that no one was prepared for what was inside. The reclusive artist had turned Cliffside into a museum commemorating her own image. Every wall, closet, and open surface was filled with more than three thousand paintings and sketches, most of them of Beatrice, who spent her entire adulthood creating an alternate life for herself on canvas. Beatrice's real story may have been grim and lonely, but her imagined one was rendered in bright colors. She was a vision of Victorian loveliness in her paintings, dressed in lace-trimmed gowns and flowered hats.

Even though Beatrice had exhibited her art on occasion in Newport, no one wanted her astonishing body of work, so it was destined for the town dump. Somehow, Nathan Fleischer heard about the doomed collection and rescued dozens of paintings from destruction. He wasn't an art lover; he was a clever promoter who was looking for a way to attract customers to his hotel, and Beatrice was the very hook he needed. Fleischer staged a dramatic son et lumière show about her at Cliff Lawn, using her paintings to illustrate her unusual life. He told audiences that the artist suffered from a condition called "egosexia," a pseudo-scientific term he coined to describe her odd compulsion to paint herself. Poor Beatrice, who spent her entire life hiding, was now on display like a carnival attraction.

Fleischer had big plans to take his Beatrice Turner show on the road and asked Basil Rathbone, the distinguished British actor who played Sherlock Holmes on screen, to record the narration. Rathbone turned down the job, and Fleischer ended up recording his own soundtrack, adding depth and drama to his voice by sticking his head—and his tape recorder—in a large, reverberating garbage can. The result was spooky and made Beatrice's story sound vaguely supernatural.

Fleischer did a masterful job of selling Turner to the media. The provocative egosexia slant captured the attention of *Life* and *American Weekly*, publications that portrayed Beatrice as a beautiful heiress who lived in a dream world. Newport figured prominently in the articles. Despite Fleischer's success at marketing, his lurid traveling show bombed, especially in Florida, where his performance was banned because some of the sketches revealed a naked Beatrice. Authorities called the exhibition a high-class peep show, not art.

Fleischer's finances were so shaky that he hired someone to torch Cliff Lawn so he could collect the insurance money. At the last minute, he realized that his policy had lapsed. Fortunately, the arsonist had lost his nerve, so the building was spared. Fleischer stored his Beatrice Turner paintings with a friend and moved back to New York. "Egosexia," and all the psychological baggage that went with it, must have made an impression on him, because he studied psychotherapy at Yeshiva University and performed as a mentalist in the Catskills.

Unlike Fleischer, preservationists wanted to improve Newport, but not too much, and not in a flashy way. There was a correlation between Newport's grandes dames and its deteriorating grand houses. *Holiday* magazine called the city's dowagers "women of incomparable dowdiness . . . a dowdiness so absolute, in fact, as to provoke the observation that only the very richest and poorest of American women can afford to let themselves go so luxuriously." The same could be said of the city, which managed to be grand and shabby at the same time.

In its early years, the staid Preservation Society focused on serious projects. They engaged Harvard archaeologists to excavate the Old Stone Mill, hoping to shed light on its controversial origins, and they compiled a comprehensive survey of Newport's buildings, which was published as *The Architectural Heritage of Newport, Rhode Island*. But these activities were all very "insider" and did not make the city a more desirable destination for visitors.

Then, in 1948, Countess Laszlo Szechenyi, the daughter of Cornelius Vanderbilt II, leased her magnificent home, The Breakers, to the Preservation Society for $1 per year. During the Gilded Age, social climbers spent hundreds of thousands of dollars pursuing an invitation to The Breakers. Thanks to the Preservation Society, no invitation was needed, and anyone could enter for only $1.50.

Twenty-six thousand eager tourists lined up at the door during the first four months. They came to see the walls of Caen stone, the vaulted ceilings, and the European treasures that rivaled the collections of the best museums. But most of all they came to see where—and how—the fabulously wealthy lived. The opening of The Breakers was a revelatory experience for Newport because it suggested that its white elephants had a future as lifestyle museums, something Henry James never imagined when he predicted their demise.

The very same year The Breakers became a tourist destination, the *Newport Social Index*, the hardcover book that contained the names and telephone numbers of all "prominent cottagers and notable members of society," ceased publication. It was replaced by a less impressive (and less exclusive) advertising folder that informally listed relevant names and addresses. The Old Guard was still in residence, but one by one, the barricades were coming down.

18

All That Jazz

Newport was a Sleeping Beauty in the early 1950s and so quiet that cottager Elaine Lorillard lamented, "Oh, it's terribly boring in the summer. There's just nothing to do!" She and her husband, Louis Lorillard, were used to a more exciting lifestyle. They had met in Italy in the 1940s when Elaine, a gifted pianist, was teaching music to war orphans, and Louis was a lieutenant in the army. They married in 1946 and established a routine of wintering in Capri and summering in Newport, where Louis' ancestors had been ensconced for generations. They were Newport aristocracy, to be sure, but as members of the city's younger social set, the couple longed for more stimulating activities than the usual Bellevue Avenue dinners and dances.

In 1953, Elaine Lorillard's passion for music inspired her to organize the first Newport Music Festival, a three-day program of events featuring the New York Philharmonic, with conductor Virgil Thompson and baritone Robert Merrill. It was

René Bouché's sketch of Senator Theodore Francis Green, Mr. and Mrs. John Barry Ryan, and founder Elaine Lorillard (far right) at the Newport Jazz Festival.

a noble—and expensive—enterprise that failed to have the impact the Lorillards wanted. In Elaine's own words, it was a flop. Cottagers were used to attending important cultural events in New York, but they were not keen on having this kind of entertainment on their summer calendar. As Alva Vanderbilt, Mamie Fish, and Tessie Oelrichs discovered in the days of the Social Strategy Board, novelty was key to a successful event in Newport. If the Lorillards wanted to make their community stand up and take notice, they'd have to offer something more exciting than classical music.

Six months later, in February 1954, the Lorillards came up with a better way to shake Newport out of its torpor. Elaine was an aficionada of jazz, and during the music festival, someone suggested to her that it would be interesting to build an event around this popular—and edgy—form of music. The Lorillards loved the idea, and with all the enthusiasm of Judy Garland

and Mickey Rooney in an MGM musical, they set out to "put on a show" in their own backyard. They wisely reached out to George Wein, the owner of a Boston jazz club called Storyville, to help launch the first Newport Jazz Festival the following summer. Their mission was "to encourage America's enjoyment of jazz and to sponsor the study of our country's only original art form." But they also wanted to treat themselves and their fellow Newporters to a rollicking good time.

It was a bold and risky undertaking. Swank Newport was an unlikely setting for a festival celebrating the controversial—and largely underground—sound of jazz, and it was doubtful that the terms "Dixieland revival," "bebop," and "cool jazz," were even in the average cottager's vocabulary. The Lorillards optimistically invited sixty-five friends and neighbors to sign on as sponsors. The only insider who responded with his checkbook was George Henry Warren, Katherine's husband, although prominent outsiders (including composer/conductor Leonard Bernstein, writer Cleveland Amory, and Father Norman O'Conner, Boston's "jazz priest") enthusiastically added their names to the list of supporters.

The Lorillards used their pull to secure the venue—the Newport Casino, typically home to tennis tournaments and to the crowd-pleasing strains of Mullaley's Orchestra during the Gilded Age and to those of popular bandleader Meyer Davis in modern times. Meanwhile, George Wein used his connections in the music world to corral the talent. At the time, the only established music festival was Tanglewood, a classical artists' showcase in the Berkshire Mountains of Massachusetts. The event in Newport would offer jazz musicians an unprecedented opportunity to play at a festival dedicated to their sound. The artists were so excited by the prospect of performing together that Wein was able to assemble a "who's who" of vocalists and instrumentalists, including Dizzy Gillespie, Ella Fitzgerald, Gerry Mulligan, Oscar Peterson, and Billie Holiday.

The festival was scheduled to run for two nights in early August of 1954. The organizers recognized that for many people, jazz was uncharted territory. To make it easier for them to understand the music, they asked Nat Hentoff, the New York editor of *Downbeat*, to write a brief history of jazz, which avant-garde bandleader/pianist Stan Kenton would deliver as a running commentary during the performances. Plans were made to transport the artists to Newport, chairs were set up on the lawn at the casino, and "pre" and "post" parties were organized by the Warrens and the Lorillards. The Warrens planned a black-tie dinner for Friday, the night before the festival's opening, while the Lorillards scheduled a midnight breakfast at their place following the performance on Saturday evening

Lillian Ross, the *New Yorker*'s "footloose correspondent," attended the festival and wrote about her experiences in a piece cleverly titled "You Dig It, Sir?" She was one of the guests at the Warrens' dinner, and noted her host's boundless enthusiasm for his hometown. "Newport is not on the skids, no matter what anybody says," George Warren insisted defensively, responding to the recent rash of negative publicity about the city and its decline. As Ross observed the guests, many of whom were the very people who turned down the Lorillards' invitation to become official patrons of the festival, she was struck by the incongruity of the Old Guard celebrating jazz in Newport. The thought returned to her throughout the weekend, but she was an insightful writer who saw past the socialites' conservatively gowned and tuxedoed surfaces and recognized their hunger for a little excitement. One older, white-haired gentleman confessed to Ross that his wife had perked up considerably when she heard that the classical orchestra of the previous summer had been replaced by nightclub musicians. "You know, this just might be fun," she told him excitedly.

On Saturday morning, Wein had last-minute jitters, especially after he learned that saxophonist Lee Konitz missed the bus to Newport. Meanwhile, the Lorillards fretted about attendance, wondering what would happen if no one came. When thousands of people started pouring into town, they soon realized there was no reason to be concerned. "Cats by the sea," *Time* magazine called the influx of fans. There were "loud-shirted bookie types from Broadway, young intellectuals in need of haircuts, crew-cut Ivy Leaguers, sailors, Harlem girls with extravagant hairdos and high-school girls in shorts." They scrambled for hard-to-find accommodations, filled every restaurant, and spent money with such abandon that Mayor John J. Sullivan happily proclaimed the festival "the greatest thing that's happened in Newport in years."

Seven thousand people gathered at the casino that Saturday night, thrilled by the seductive sounds that emanated from the stage. A full moon hung like a spotlight over the crowd, adding a surrealistic touch to the already enchanted evening. Each performer, from Eddie Condon playing the Dixieland classic "Muskrat Ramble" to Dizzy Gillespie, who was introduced as "one of the great figures in the evolution of jazz," left the audience awestruck and hungry for more. The photographer from *Downbeat* noticed that Gillespie was not his usual ebullient self. Years later, in his autobiography *Myself Among Others*, George Wein confessed that he asked Gillespie to tone down his antics for the staid Newport set, something he regretted almost as soon as the words left his lips. Ella Fitzgerald wowed the crowd with her incomparable vocals, and the concert ended with a twenty-minute jam session that, according to *Time*, "sent the strangest sounds ever heard in Newport floating up to the stars."

One very enthusiastic cottager in attendance that night was James "Jimmy" H. Van Alen, the dapper son of Daisy Van Alen. Mrs. Van Alen, who was still the reigning matron in Newport, was now Mrs. Bruguiere, having married Louis Bruguiere, a fellow Newporter and hence a socially acceptable mate despite being low on funds. Jimmy was a true bon vivant who had three passions in life: tennis, songwriting, and his wife, Candace. When it came to tennis, Van Alen was a pro. He was the president of the Newport Casino, where the game was still played the old-fashioned way, on classic grass courts, and founder of the Tennis Hall of Fame. And he was the creator and champion of the VASS (Van Alen Scoring System), a revolutionary way to score tennis matches so that they were shorter and easier to watch. However, when it came to composing songs, Van Alen was a lovable failure. His lyrics were always highly sentimental and awkwardly rhymed. In one melody he created especially for President Dwight D. Eisenhower (and performed at his inauguration), Van Alen wrote, "Believe us, Mr. President, We're glad its you, not we, who have got the job of keeping our great country safe and free."

Van Alen had a ditty for every occasion, and his beautiful wife, Candy, as Candace was called, was his muse. They met in 1948, when she was working for the *New York Herald Tribune*. Before that, she had been a war correspondent in Europe. Candy was smart and spirited, a talented writer, and an adept socialite. She loved the social scene in Newport and enjoyed entertaining at Avalon, the couple's home on Ocean Drive.

Jimmy was so impressed by the performances at the Jazz Festival that he wanted some of the artists to come to his home for an after party—a classic Newport affair with servants offering champagne and perfectly scrambled eggs. According to George Wein, Van Alen voiced one caveat about the prospective guests: "Please try not to invite too many of the African musicians," he said. Wein claimed he finessed this indelicate situation by not inviting any of the musicians to Avalon. (Fifty years later, Elaine Lorillard defended the Van Alens and said Wein's unflattering account of the couple and their party was untrue.)

The second night of the festival was a hit, just like the first, even though storm clouds replaced the brilliant full moon. Six thousand people pulled their raincoats closer and ignored the wet weather as they listened to Billie Holiday sing about love, loss, and betrayal. By Monday morning, publications all over the country carried news of the Newport Jazz Festival's great triumph. "Newport Rocked by Jazz Festival" was the headline in the *New York Times*, while the *Providence Journal* proclaimed the first Newport Jazz Festival a "sensation."

Not everyone was thrilled with Newport's sudden status as a jazz mecca. Octogenarian Edith Wetmore was horrified by the festival and the déclassé crowds it drew. One day, when introduced to young Pierre Lorillard, she asked if he was related to the infamous Louis Lorillards. Upon learning he was their son, she terrified the boy by ordering him to tell his father that "Miss Wetmore says he's a wicked, wicked man." But the Lorillards ignored any grumbling from the Old Guard and immediately started planning another blockbuster event for the following summer.

Jackie

Jacqueline Lee Bouvier grew up enjoying the pleasant routine of wintering in New York and summering in fashionable East Hampton. But everything changed when her mother, Janet Lee Bouvier, divorced Jackie's father and two years later married a wealthy gentleman named Hugh Dudley Auchincloss Jr. The blue-blood Auchincloss clan, consisting of "Hughdie" and his children, Nina, Yusha, and Thomas, always summered in Newport at Hammersmith Farm, a twenty-eight-room manse with gardens designed by the Olmsted brothers. Jackie and her younger sister, Lee, settled in for long, festive vacations at the farm and became popular new additions to Newport's junior social set.

The Bouvier girls could be found at Bailey's Beach and the other Newport haunts, and they participated in all the classic society rituals. When Jackie turned eighteen, she had a proper coming-out tea dance at Hammersmith Farm and a party for her friends at the Clambake Club. Janet Auchincloss was the chief architect of these occasions, and naturally she assumed that she would control her daughter's wedding. That was before Jackie announced her engagement to John F. Kennedy, the handsome young senator from Massachusetts.

If Jackie and her mother were thinking small and simple, über-patriarch Joe Kennedy saw his son's upcoming nuptials as an opportunity to stage a massive political event. The bride announced that the guests would be restricted to "mostly family," but the father of the groom countered with a list of hundreds of invitees. In fact, Joe had opinions about everything, from the wedding dress to the cake. And he backed up his preferences with the ultimate weapon: his checkbook. A horrified Janet, who did not have limitless resources (after all, Hughdie was not Jackie's father), submitted to Joe Kennedy in the end, but she was not happy. She told her friend Eileen Slocum, "The wedding will be just awful—quite dreadful. There will be one hundred Irish politicians!"

Jack Kennedy was fully aware that his prospective mother-in-law had issues with his family and their tendency to do things their way. During the wedding weekend, Kennedy, accompanied by some of his friends, dropped in at the Newport Country Club to play an impromptu round of golf. He was not dressed properly—old shorts and sneakers were not the usual garb of the Newport golfer—and he breached protocol by not clearing the game through the Auchinclosses first. Kennedy joked to a friend that Janet was "convinced that one of the last strongholds of America's socially elite is being invaded by monsters without pedigrees."

Despite nonstop clashes between the two families, the Bouvier-Kennedy wedding took place in Newport in September 1953 at St. Mary's Catholic Church. The storybook couple drew crowds of eager spectators who vied for the best positions to watch the bride and groom enter and exit the church. After the ceremony, two thousand guests attended the reception at Hammersmith Farm, and it was a lively outdoor affair with a radiant Jackie and Jack as its centerpiece. But in Newport circles, Jackie was the famous one, and Jack, for all his money and accomplishments, was merely her consort.

19

What a Swell Party This Is

Like it or not, there was no denying that the Jazz Festival was a money magnet for Newport. Any event that encouraged people to come and, more importantly, to spend, was good for the city, so The Preservation Society got on the bandwagon and tried to figure out how to turn Newport's longstanding tradition of party-giving into a money- (and publicity-) making proposition. Monique Pannagio, a young Frenchwoman who handled publicity for the society, came up with a brilliant idea for a high-wattage, headline-generating celebration. She was a war bride who met her husband, Leonard Pannagio, when he was a handsome young staff sergeant stationed in Casablanca. The couple settled in Newport, Leonard's hometown, where Monique was delighted to find an abundance of French history. She learned that 1955 marked the 175th anniversary of General Rochambeau's arrival in Newport, and the occasion inspired her to propose an ambitious cultural festival that would put a glamorous, international spin on local history.

Katherine Warren loved the idea and set into motion a ten-day fete that paid homage to the triumphant time when the French fleet came to Newport and changed the course of the Revolutionary War. Descendants of the original French generals, including the Marquis de Rochambeau de Vendôme and Count and Countess Phillipe de Lafayette, were honored guests of the city, and the *Jean-Bart*, a modern-day French warship, floated regally in the harbor. There were parades, exhibitions, tours of historical houses, a beauty pageant (to select "Miss Fleur de Lis"), concerts, fireworks, luncheons, dinners, and finally, the pièce de résistance, a formal ball at The Breakers.

Tourists visited The Breakers during the day, and had been doing so for a few years. But The Breakers Ball was the first time the cottage opened its thirty-foot gates to the public for a real social event, the kind the Vanderbilts might have hosted for their friends back in the 1890s. Not that there were nobodies on the guest list. Mrs. Sheldon Whitehouse, a Newport doyenne, was the chairwoman of the ball, and she enlisted the help of Newport's first families, including the Van Alens, the Cushings, and dozens of others, to make the gala an evening to remember. Eleven hundred guests (minus a few "comps") paid $20 to drink champagne and dance to the music of Meyer Davis, their favorite bandleader. Tiaras glittered and guests were resplendent with necklaces, lorgnettes, and military and naval decorations. Even the servants looked distinguished because they sported The Breakers' maroon livery for the occasion.

But the brightest light in the room that night was actress Grace Kelly, who came with friends from Philadelphia. She was just the right sort of celebrity for Newport—a cool, classic blonde with queenly bearing and a Main Line pedigree. On top of that, she was a distinguished actress who had won an Academy Award earlier in the year for her dramatic performance in *The Country Girl*.

Outfitted in true movie-star style with head-to-toe lace, mink, and diamonds, Kelly dazzled the crowd; "1,100 at Big Newport Ball and They All Wanted to See Kelly" was the headline in the *New York Daily News*.

A few months later, Hollywood producer Sol Siegel confirmed that Kelly was the very embodiment of a Newport aristocrat when he selected her to star in *High Society*, a musical update of the classic 1940 film *The Philadelphia Story*. The film was set in Newport during the Jazz Festival and featured Bing Crosby as C. Dexter Haven, a gentleman jazz musician (who, like Louis Lorillard, introduces the new sound to stodgy Newport), and Grace Kelly as his socialite ex-wife. Frank Sinatra played a singing reporter, while trumpet virtuoso and vocalist Louis Armstrong appeared as himself. Cole Porter's lively musical numbers such as "Well Did You Evah?" and "Now You Has Jazz" cleverly conveyed the cultural clash between blueblood and hep-cat that so amused Lillian Ross during her visit to the first festival.

In fact, the movie was in part based on Ross's *New Yorker* piece, which MGM had optioned and was developing as a property called "Jazz in Newport." When Sol Siegel was looking for an interesting way to update *The Philadelphia Story*, he combined it with the Ross-inspired project. And jazz wasn't the only topical update to the story. In the new version, as the characters sipped champagne and lounged by their pool, they quipped about the declining economy in Newport. Poor Uncle Willie (played by Louis Calhern) had to sell his historic manse to a school to avoid punishing property taxes.

America was enchanted by the romantic antics of the musical socialites in *High Society*. It became one of the top-grossing films of 1956, and "True Love," a romantic ballad, sung by Crosby and Kelly, won the Academy Award for Best Song. Of course, the film's popularity was boosted by Kelly's highly publicized engagement and storybook marriage to Prince Rainier of Monaco. The impressive engagement ring Kelly wears in the film (Bing Crosby called it "a skating rink") was the very one that Prince Rainier had placed on her finger.

Everyone agreed that The Breakers Ball was, to use Cole Porter's words, "a swell party," prompting The Preservation Society to plan a bigger and better one for the summer of 1957. The key to supersizing the event would be finding a sponsor who had the right high-end profile and a bottomless budget. Tiffany and Company, New York City's venerable luxury emporium, turned out to be the ideal match. When presented with the idea, Tiffany chairman Walter Hoving immediately recognized the value of branding an upper-crust event in Newport, where some of his best customers summered. He signed on to support the Tiffany Ball, a black-tie dance to take place at Marble House. The Tiffany name was too important to entrust to outsiders, so Hoving asked Letitia Baldrige, a dynamic young executive at his company, to work with The Preservation Society on the event.

Baldrige was a new phenomenon at Tiffany. Hoving recruited her to be the store's first director of publicity and public relations (and its first woman executive, for that matter) because he wanted to update the company's stodgy image. Baldrige came up with inventive ways to give Tiffany a needed dose of sex appeal. She hired New York's hottest models for photo shoots because she was convinced they made the diamonds look more desirable. She raided the Tiffany archives for old styles that could be updated, such as jeweled headbands and garters, and promoted these extravagant novelties on television talk shows. She organized lively exhibitions, including a blockbuster that cleverly reproduced historic love letters on Tiffany stationary. Baldrige had strong commercial instincts, but she understood the importance of propriety, and never resorted to stunts that might tarnish the Tiffany brand.

She started working on the Tiffany Ball in January, six months before the July 13 event. The Preservation Society may have had

René Bouché's sketch of "the beautiful people" dancing at a Newport ball.

mixed feelings about publicity, but Baldrige campaigned for coverage on every front. "What would Who wear to the ball became a matter of grave importance in the New York Fashion World," she later recalled in her memoir *Of Diamonds and Diplomats*. Her biggest coup was to persuade *Life* magazine to visit Newport and run one of their *"Life* Goes to a Party" photo spreads, the perfect antidote to *"Life* Visits a Fading Newport." *Town and Country* agreed to cover the party, too, and there was such a positive response from the press that Baldrige talked Bailey's Beach into bending its no-reporters rule so that journalists could visit the famous club during the Tiffany Ball weekend. A few of the Old Guard complained that those nasty newspaper people would eavesdrop on them and write down everything they said, but a worldly Newporter assured the old-timers that they need not worry. Nothing they might say would be of the slightest possible interest to the reporters.

In addition to cultivating the press, Baldrige was a pioneer in developing promotional tie-ins. She arranged for ball guests to get a brand-new cigarette, appropriately called Newport, as a party favor. Pierre Lorillard of the Lorillard tobacco family had been a great yachtsman in Newport, and in 1957 his company paid homage to him by launching Newport, a cigarette that evoked Lorillard's enthusiasm for all things nautical—the package was marine blue and sported a spinnaker as its logo. When Lorillard executives set out to advertise their new brand—distinctive in the marketplace because it was mentholated—they promoted it as being fresh and clean, the kind of cigarette that would appeal to affluent young Newporters. Newport's first television commercials capitalized on this idea by showing a handsome young couple on a beach—tan, fit sophisticates who look as if they had just stepped off a sailboat—happily puffing away and singing Newport's praises. "Newport tastes better, tastes fresher, too," they sang. The subliminal message was "Smoke Newport to be Newport."

Two weeks before the ball, it was finally time for Baldrige to set up headquarters on location. She flew to Providence, then shared an air taxi to Newport with America's "it" couple, Jack and Jackie Kennedy. The newlyweds visited Hammersmith Farm every summer, and this year the Tiffany Ball was on their calendar. During the short trip, Kennedy expressed concern about all the press Baldrige had invited. Generally, Newport's inner sanctums were safe havens from reporters. Kennedy, who was being touted as the Democratic candidate for the 1960 presidential race, fretted that he might be photographed with a drink in his hand at the party. A photo like that would be damaging for an aspiring president. A matter-of-fact Baldrige advised him that if he didn't want to be seen with a drink in his hand, he simply shouldn't have one. The Kennedys must have appreciated her no-nonsense advice, because after the election, Baldrige became social secretary and chief of staff for the new first lady.

Baldrige worked closely with The Preservation Society, but she never lost sight of the fact that Tiffany was the big brand at its eponymous ball. The store was promoting vermeil—sterling silver that had been extravagantly coated (or gilded) with gold—so Baldrige arrived in Newport with $12,000 worth of vermeil tureens, candelabra, and serving pieces to decorate the giant buffet table at Marble House. The store also sent along its incomparable 128.5-carat Tiffany Diamond, the largest and finest canary diamond in the world. Tiffany purchased the massive South African gem in 1897 and displayed it, unset, in a midnight-blue niche at the store, where it attracted millions of viewers. In 1956, Tiffany announced that the famous stone could be purchased for $583,000, a price that generously included tax and postage. But no buyer materialized, so Hoving and his team searched for an inventive way to promote the dazzler. They decided it would grace the neck of a lucky Cinderella at the Tiffany Ball. But which lucky Cinderella? That was the question on everyone's mind.

"Diamond, diamond, who's got the diamond?" was Newport society's new guessing game reported the *New York Times*. Even women who lived hundreds of miles away from Newport, and who had no hope of attending the party, campaigned to be the first to wear the fabulous stone, which had been set especially for the occasion in a pendant supported by a chain of large white diamonds. A blue-eyed redhead from New Jersey sent a letter to Tiffany confidently suggesting that her coloring was the perfect backdrop for the diamond. A housewife from Larchmont penned a more eloquent plea, writing, "I have only worn rhinestones all my life, but my husband says I was born for diamonds." Tiffany refused to reveal the identity of the woman Hoving had selected until the night of the party, but it was unlikely to be either the narcissist from New Jersey or the wistful Westchester housewife.

On the day of the ball, Baldrige dutifully unpacked the crates of vermeil and supervised the setting of Marble House's thirty-four-foot-long mahogany table. Then she watched anxiously as storm clouds gathered over Newport. "What's a little rain?" she thought, not realizing that a bigger storm was brewing. When the *Life* photographers arrived and tried to set up their equipment in the ballroom, an irate dowager cornered Baldrige and told her the men had to leave immediately because they were not wearing dinner jackets. No amount of pleading on Baldrige's part could change the woman's mind. In Newport, propriety was much more important than publicity. With her magazine coup about to implode, Baldrige had a last-minute brainstorm. She sent out a frantic SOS to a local navy supply store and came up with four steward's uniforms (black ties and white jackets) that enabled the good-natured photographers to pass muster.

The Tiffany Ball was off to a smashing start. It was the first party at Marble House that wasn't a private affair hosted by a Vanderbilt or a Prince, so many of the guests had never seen the interior of the famous house. They were the ones who oohed and ahhed as they entered. Mrs. Sheldon Whitehouse caused a stir upon her arrival because she was the surprise bearer of the Tiffany Diamond. "She is a noble-looking woman," said Walter Hoving, explaining why he had diplomatically chosen the ball's chairwoman for the honor. Mrs. Whitehouse, who was advanced in years, modestly told reporters, "It might have been more attractive to have a younger woman wearing it." She also remarked that it was "quite comfortable," despite its weight (which the *Times* compared to the heft of an oatmeal cookie). Pistol-packing guards had delivered it to the Whitehouse home earlier that day, and they never left Mrs. Whitehouse's side. Baldrige had to talk them out of following the mortified matron into the ladies' room.

The knowledge that the legendary Tiffany Diamond was going to be in their midst had the effect of a dropped gauntlet on the Newport set, and many women retrieved their most expensive jewelry from their vaults. Consequently, the ladies at Marble House wore an awe-inspiring array of magnificent gems that night, including a cabochon star sapphire pendant "the size of a hand grenade." The ballroom was ablaze with so many diamonds that one of the guards marveled, "I been with Tiffany for forty years and I never saw anything like it." Danny Dugan, Tiffany's top diamond salesman, looked around the room and calculated that he saw a cool $20 million worth of "ice." Even Newport's police chief spoke of the evening in superlatives, calling it "the biggest, most brilliant party seen in Newport since 1929."

John F. Kennedy didn't need diamonds to attract attention; he had Jackie, who looked regal in a beaded strapless gown (cleverly ruched to disguise the fact that she was pregnant). No matter how late the hour, the popular Kennedys were surrounded by a crowd of beaming well-wishers. Despite JFK's apprehensions about the press, not one photographer snapped him with a drink in his hand.

Lester Lanin, another popular bandleader in Newport, played until three in the morning, entertaining enthusiastic dancers with a mix of popular show tunes, such as "Some Enchanted Evening" from *South Pacific*, along with lesser-known songs, including the local favorite, "Rhode Island Is Famous for You." After the event, Lanin jumped on the marketing bandwagon by releasing a record album titled *Lester Lanin at the Tiffany Ball*. The cover showed a beautiful young woman, dressed in a gown and a tiara, dancing with a handsome, tuxedo-clad man. The album said that the ball recalled the days when "the rich

Senator John F. Kennedy and a radiant Jackie (pregnant with Caroline) chat with Noreen Drexel at the 1957 Tiffany Ball.

were very rich and the rest of us could believe in fairytales," and promised an immediate connection to the magical, mythical, and normally unattainable world of Newport. "Shut your eyes and listen," the liner notes suggested seductively. "Your living room is 'The Gold Room' at Marble House during the Tiffany Ball—with music by Lester Lanin." Not surprisingly, the album became a best seller. For a mere $3.89, anyone could experience the Newport dream.

The Jazz Festival and The Preservation Society's glittering soirees lifted Newport from its doldrums and made the city attractive to insiders and outsiders alike. But the event that really put Newport back on the map was the 1958 America's Cup race. Landlubbers find the Cup rules nearly impossible to decipher, but the underlying principle is really very simple. The race is a challenge-based yachting competition. Essentially, one sailor boasts to another, "My boat's faster than yours." The defender says, "Prove it," and then they go out and race, boat against boat, until there is a winner.

The first such race took place in 1851, when the U.S. schooner *America* defeated England's *Aurora* and brought home the trophy that was called the America's Cup in honor of the winning vessel. Sixteen races followed during the next 107 years as English and sometimes Canadian challengers attempted to outsail the winning Americans. The yacht club sponsoring the champion, in this case the New York Yacht Club, always controlled the race. It selected the defending boat, hosted the event, and even set the rules. No challenger was able to overcome this triple advantage, so not surprisingly, the America's Cup remained in America.

In 1930, when *Enterprise* raced against Great Britain's *Shamrock V*, the New York Yacht Club moved the America's Cup race from New York to Newport, the institution's home away from home. In 1937, the sprightly *Ranger* successfully defeated *Endeavour II*, another British challenger.

In 1958, the race was on again, with *Columbia* scheduled to face off against the persistent Brits' *Sceptre*, and Newport was thrilled to host the prestigious sea battle in its waters. The race gave the once great port an opportunity to reconnect with its nautical roots, and everyone, from Bellevue Avenue socialites to Thames Street sailors, wanted to be part of it. *Vogue* covered Newport's exciting America's Cup summer in its September 15 issue. According to the magazine, "Newport this season shimmered in the public gaze." In less flowery prose, the city was jumping. In its fourth smash year, the Lorillards' Jazz Festival was twice as long (four days instead of two) and ten times as big (it attracted sixty thousand people compared to its initial six thousand). Fans who were unable to make the trip to Newport could listen courtesy of Voice of America radio broadcasts, or they could buy newly pressed *Jazz in Newport* record albums.

There was also Tennis Week at the Newport Casino, home of the National Lawn Tennis Hall of Fame. Maurice McLoughlin, a tennis champion known as the California Comet, was an honored guest at this year's event. He was an old-timer who had played in casino tournaments back in 1912 and 1913, and almost half a century later, McLoughlin was surprised to see that the place looked exactly the same, right down to its lush grass and weathered shingles. Even some of the spectators were the same. Mrs. Bruguiere, who watched McLoughlin when she was the young Daisy Post Van Alen, observed this week's tennis matches from the comfort of her Rolls-Royce, which her chauffeur always parked at the edge of the court.

The *Vogue* spread featured an article titled "Newport Decliched," written by Mrs. Bruguiere's daughter-in-law, Candy Van Alen. Assigning a piece to the Newport insider was a clever move on *Vogue*'s part because Candy was an experienced journalist who still wrote an occasional travel article. But more importantly, she was a Van Alen, so, as her husband liked to joke, she was "more kosher" than most of the people summering in Newport. She knew everything about everyone.

Not that she wrote anything objectionable. Candy diplomatically sidestepped gossip and focused on more benign topics. She argued that the city was not the stodgy "stronghold of the Old Guard" that people imagined. In fact, she saw it as "a centre of daring thought, daring action, and daring elegance."

René Bouché's sketch of dark-haired Candy Van Alen and her smiling husband, Jimmy, watching a match during Tennis Week.

Her use of the British spelling of the word "centre" was a little
unusual (and maybe even a little pretentious) for someone who
was born and raised in America, but the Van Alens had always
been notorious Anglophiles. That "Old Guard" frame of mind
was more prevalent than Candy cared to acknowledge.

In the same issue, young George Plimpton, who was making a
name for himself as a journalist, sportsman, and everyone's favorite
bon vivant, penned a spirited piece about Newport's trial races

for the America's Cup. He described the process of selecting the best twelve-meter boat from among the four contenders. Only one would have the honor of defending the Cup against *Sceptre*, and it was exciting to watch the eliminations.

All of Newport took to the sea during the races. Women wrapped gay scarves around their heads, donned sunglasses, and set sail with the spectator fleet that trailed the contenders like an eager school of fish. Not everyone had the stamina to keep up with the program. "The trouble with this whole America's Cup business," one colonist complained, "is that they go out too far. . . . We sailed for an eternity before they even got the races started. . . . I thought, my Lord, we're going to see the cranes of Le Havre pop above the horizon any second now." Still, most Newporters were mesmerized by the boats and their chesslike maneuvers. Smooth sailing was rarely a part of any America's Cup race. The boats spent most of their time locked in a complex dance that involved constant blocking, jockeying, and spinning.

Vogue sent photographer Toni Frissell to take pictures of the yachts and their crews, but the magazine decided against using photographs to depict Newport society at play. Instead, artist René Bouché was commissioned to create impressionistic drawings of iconic Newporters in their signature settings. The popular European-born portraitist and fashion illustrator was a perfect choice. Like John Singer Sargent, the artist to whom he was often compared, Bouché liked rich people. "I consider myself the avant garde, because nobody sings the song of the upper level of society today," he told *Time* magazine "Nobody speaks of the exceptional human being."

Bouché sketched the colony's key "lions and tigresses," the sort of people *Time* described as inhabitants of "a world often so polite that it is rude, and so frantic that it is bored." There was a drawing of Mr. and Mrs. Claiborne Pell, a Newport first

René Bouché's 1958 sketch of Mr. and Mrs. Claiborne Pell lunching at Bailey's Beach. Two years later, Pell was elected to the U.S. Senate

family, enjoying a relaxed al fresco lunch at Bailey's Beach. Then there was Elaine Lorillard, wearing her characteristic oversized sunglasses as she watched musicians jam at the Jazz Festival. In a drawing of a tennis match at the casino, the highly recognizable Van Alens chatted up friends in the stands. The most glamorous illustration showed couples dressed in haute couture evening clothes at a Newport ball. With every stroke of his pen, Bouché captured the elegance, the impenetrability, and the offhand opulence of the enclave. While Newport was busy watching its races (and enjoying all the other activities the 1958 season had to offer), once again, the world was busy watching Newport.

20

The Changing of the Guard

The handsome senator from Massachusetts won the presidential election in 1960, and every time he and his first lady vaca-
tioned at Hammersmith Farm, the spotlight on Newport got a
little brighter. Jack and Jackie Kennedy brought youth, energy,
power, and sex appeal to the city, although some old-fashioned
colonists continued to grumble that he was "pink" (their term for
Democrat) and not nearly as patrician as his wife. Newport was not
impressed by presidents, although they had been visiting the city
as long as anyone could remember. President Chester A. Arthur,
according to local folklore, was snubbed by all, including the servants at the casino, who made him call for his own carriage.

In modern times, presidents played golf at the Newport
Country Club, and if they were very distinguished, or very lucky,
were treated to an outing on the *Blue Dolphin*, the Cushing family's lobster boat. Dwight D. Eisenhower had the privilege of
doing both. Jack Kennedy was accepted, partly because he was

a member of the respected Auchincloss clan, and partly because Newport society was getting younger, and the old-timers, with their old prejudices, were dying out.

An up-and-coming photographer named Nancy Sirkis decided to use her camera to immortalize the Old Guard and their world before they disappeared forever. She was an art student at the Rhode Island School of Design in Providence when she first started visiting Newport in the late 1950s. Many magnificent houses were still standing, but some of the landscape was changing before her eyes. Stone Villa, the estate owned by James Gordon Bennett during the Gilded Age, had been razed and turned into a trendy shopping center on Bellevue Avenue. The Rhode Island Episcopal Diocese now owned Miramar, the beautiful French palace Horace Trumbauer had built for the Widener family, and Mamie Fish's beloved Crossways, the scene of so many legendary parties during her lifetime, had been stripped of its costly chandeliers by vandals, and subdivided into prosaic apartments for navy personnel.

Nancy Sirkis was so fascinated by decaying Newport that in 1960 she decided to make it the subject of a book. She lived and worked in New York, but her plan was to spend ten days a month in Newport, where she would photograph anything and everything that interested her. Sirkis packed up her little Volkswagen Beetle, drove to Aquidneck Island, rented a room from a retired supermarket manager, and immediately got out her camera. Exterior shots were easy because she was young and fearless. She thought nothing of driving to a remote location at four in the morning to capture a particular kind of light. The fog was unusually heavy that year, so many of her shots were moody and imbued with romanticism. One day, she crawled under the massive gates at The Breakers to get the angle she wanted. The local police were suspicious when they saw her in odd places at odd times, but they soon realized that she was a harmless photographer and looked the other way.

Nancy Sirkis's moody photograph of The Breakers, with its unwelcoming "No Trespassing" sign prominently displayed.

Sirkis naively thought that she would have equally easy access to the interiors of Newport's manses. She called some of the city's personages, only to discover that they never answered their own telephones. Butlers dutifully took her messages, but no one ever called back. Frustrated, Sirkis consulted a friendly antiques dealer in town. He advised her to visit Mr. and Mrs. George Huntington Hull, who observed the quaint custom of being "at home" to their friends at teatime every day. They were a prominent old Newport couple. Mrs. Hull, in fact, was one of the original Four Hundred on Ward McAllister's famous list.

Sirkis hopped into her Beetle and drove over to Roselawn, the Hulls' cottage. They were taken aback by the bold young woman at their door—especially since she was wearing shorts—but they graciously invited her to join them for tea. Sirkis was so charming, and her photographs so beautiful, that the Hulls agreed to a sitting, striking a stately pose beside a marble bust of an ancestor.

Then they introduced her to all their friends. With the Hull stamp of approval, the barricades came down, and Sirkis was showered with invitations from eager Newporters who wanted to be included in her book. She photographed Miss Edith Wetmore presiding over her silver tea service at Chateau-sur-Mer, and Sirkis observed that for Wetmore, it was still the Gilded Age. The nonagenarian maintained a large household staff, including a butler, footman, cook, secretary, nurse, houseboy, gardener, and assorted maids.

Wakehurst, the Van Alen estate, was similarly untouched by time. The exacting Mrs. Daisy Bruguiere (whose lavender hair and imperious manner prompted young people to refer to her as "the purple people-eater"), insisted to Sirkis that her house "was the last in Newport to be run properly." "Properly" meant having a French chef, two dozen servants, and strict rules for every occasion. A first invitation to Wakehurst for tea or cocktails was essentially an audition, an opportunity for Mrs. Bruguiere to determine if there would be a second invitation. Anyone who dared to be tardy would not be invited back. Mrs. Bruguiere's icy formality even extended to her feuds. She and Maxim Karolik had such a tempestuous relationship that the only way they could maintain a semblance of civil communication was to "speak" through their butlers.

Sirkis became a popular guest at the best tables in Newport. She'd don her simple little black dress and attend dinners where there was a heady combination of formal service and great gossip. The winter was long and gray, and a fresh young face at these gatherings kept life interesting for the older set. Their houses were still exquisite and beyond opulent, Sirkis noted, but she was content with her role of observant outsider. In the presence of all that money, "I didn't envy anyone anything," she said. Meanwhile, when she wasn't socializing, Sirkis was creating extraordinary photographs for her book.

Her timing was perfect because, toward the end of her stay, she became eyewitness to what writer Cleveland Amory would call the

Daisy Van Alen Bruguiere posing imperiously for Nancy Sirkis.
Newport's most exacting society matron was so concerned about
her image that she demanded retouches.

Crucial Battle of Modern Newport. The fate of the remaining "properly run" houses had grown uncertain because their elderly owners
were on their last legs. Spinster Edith Wetmore contemplated the
future of Chateau-sur-Mer and eightysomething Alice Brayton was
still considering her options. Her heirs were not interested in taking
care of her beloved animal topiaries, and Brayton was reluctant to
send them away to a new home. The New York Botanical Gardens

had already petitioned to adopt them, but Brayton told Sirkis that she couldn't bear the thought of her giraffe leaving through the front gate.

Ninety-six-year-old Julia Berwind, who died in 1961, left The Elms to her nephew, Charles E. Dunlap, who promptly sold it to a New York real estate syndicate the following year. To be fair to the seemingly unsentimental Dunlap, The Elms was not the kind of house an ordinary person could keep as a weekend retreat. The fifty-room palace required a fleet of servants, and that kind of household help was either unavailable or unaffordable.

The syndicate planned to subdivide the property, and whether they put up tract housing or commercial buildings, Bellevue Avenue would never be the same. "Finished, done for, and kaput" was the way Amory described the city's prospects in a lengthy *New York Times* piece. "Whichever way The Elms blew, Newport was going," he wrote. Katherine Warren and other concerned preservationists saw the handwriting on the wall and resolved to save The Elms. The problem was that they had to move very quickly if they were to raise sufficient money to buy the property from its new owners.

While they scrambled, Dunlap arranged for the Parke-Bernet Galleries to come to Newport to auction off the house's fabulous contents. The Elms welcomed the public on June 27 and 28, and most of its treasures, such as Joss Von Cleve's painting *Madonna and Child*, furniture upholstered in rare Aubusson tapestry, and Della Robbia terra cotta reliefs, were for sale. Throughout, Sirkis was there, busily photographing the buyers as they studied the contents of the grand rooms. One man coolly smoked a cigar while examining the underside of a valuable rug. Two ladies debated the merits of an antique marble bust. And an anonymous couple—possibly friends or family members who had fond memories of the house—held each other close as they gazed across a room. The most active shoppers were representatives of film and television companies who wanted the antiques for their prop departments. The sale brought in $115,620, and the Von Cleve, which sold for $10,000 to a New York art dealer, was the big-ticket item.

Luckily for Newport, the stock market took a sudden dip, and the real estate syndicate got cold feet about its much-reviled plans for The Elms. The Preservation Society made a bold cash offer of $75,000 for the main residence, and miraculously, on July 23, 1962, it was accepted. Warren and her group went into high gear, giving themselves only a few weeks to whip the house into shape for an August 30 gala opening. Most of the original furniture and decorative objects from the house were already living happily ever after on Hollywood sets, so the preservation team had to raid their own well-appointed attics and basements, and those of local friends and museums, for spare antiques. The Metropolitan Museum of Art in New York, the Museum of Fine Arts in Boston, and the Fogg Museum in Cambridge, Massachusetts, were happy to help with some loans. Against all odds, The Elms opened on schedule, and the evening was a sellout. Eight hundred well-wishers gathered to celebrate The Preservation Society's amazing victory. Sirkis photographed the party, and the images provided an eloquent ending for her book, *Newport Pleasures and Palaces*. Her artistic creation served as an elegy for a vanishing world.

Meanwhile, the "new" Newport was becoming a "happening place," as they liked to say in the sixties, especially in the summer. In fact, the Kennedys were spending so much time at Hammersmith Farm that there was talk of making Newport the permanent location of a summer White House. In 1962, Rhode Island's senator Claiborne Pell suggested that a citizen's group donate an appropriate house for this purpose, and there was some wisdom to the idea. When Eisenhower visited Newport, he was accompanied by twelve staff members, seventeen Army Signal Corpsmen, and an enormous security force. The White House's traveling circus required a minimum of two hundred telephones just for basic communications. Kennedy traveled a little lighter than his predecessor, but it was still a strain on the community to accommodate the president, his staff, and the hundreds of newspaper and broadcast journalists who followed him everywhere. An official summer residence in Newport, or anywhere else, for that matter, would be easier to maintain and to secure. In the words of one bodyguard, it would be "a Secret Serviceman's dream."

Ultimately Kennedy rejected the gift for a number of reasons. First of all, it was difficult to predict how a subsequent president might want to vacation. What if he preferred the mountains to the shore? Then there was the nasty problem of public perception. Everyone knew Kennedy was rich enough to buy his own house and didn't need a gift that would cost his supporters $250,000. As the *Washington Post & Times Herald* pointed out in an editorial, the president already owned three homes (in Virginia, Palm Beach, and on Cape Cod) and "needs another summer residence about as much as the Department of Agriculture needs more grain in storage," referring to the controversial U.S. grain surplus in 1962. Accepting a free house would have been very bad for his image.

However, Kennedy was at liberty to arrange for his own place in Newport, and that's exactly what he did. In 1963, with Senator Pell's help, he reserved Annandale Farm (formerly known as Armsea Hall), the very property that had been proposed as the country's official summer residence, for the following summer. The twenty-two-acre estate was next door to Hammersmith Farm, so Jackie could be near her family. It had a spectacular view of the bay. And it looked very "presidential" because it resembled the White House. The Kennedys agreed to pay $2,000 per month to rent the property for August and September 1964.

Pell called the arrangement "one of the greatest single accomplishments for Newport in many years." He was particularly excited by the prospect of a Newport dateline on stories coming out of the authentically white summer "White House." Pell, the consummate gentleman, congratulated the Realtor for graciously waiving his commission on the deal, and urged his fellow Newporters to be respectful of the first family's privacy during their visit.

The Kennedys were enjoying the summer of 1963. They appeared regularly at St. Mary's, the church where they were married, for Sunday Mass. The president swam in the brand-new heated pool at Bailey's Beach, and went sailing with his five-year-old daughter, Caroline. His staff members had a good time, too, although they sometimes caused raised eyebrows. One day, members of the Newport Casino watched in horror as White House press secretary Pierre Salinger played tennis on their hallowed grass courts. He stuck out like a sore thumb because he was dressed in a yellow shirt and blue shorts. "At least they could wear white" was the disapproving consensus of spectators.

Suddenly the resort had an appealing new generation of young men and women who, like the Kennedys, were stylish, athletic, and downright sexy. Large-bosomed dowagers in overly upholstered gowns had been replaced by sleek socialites in form-fitting designer sheaths. The July 1963 issue of *Town and Country* featured a glamorous, fur-clad Lee Radziwill on its cover. The accompanying headline was "What's New in Old Newport?"

No less an outlet than the *New York Times* decided it was a question worth answering. They dispatched Charlotte Curtis, the paper's top society reporter, to get the story. Outfitted in chic little suits, Chanel pumps, and her signature pearls, Curtis operated with the stealth of an undercover agent. Born in Columbus, Ohio, and educated at Vassar, where she studied history, she looked and sounded like a lifelong member of high society. But Curtis's refined exterior disguised a razor-sharp wit and a unique reporting style. It was neither her ambition nor her inclination to write for the dreaded "women's pages"— a section of the newspaper that was generally the final resting place for fluff pieces and press releases. But when Curtis became a full-time society reporter for the *Times* in 1963, she made the best of her situation by approaching each story as if it were hard news. Her anecdotes and observations about the rich, the powerful, the famous, and the infamous evolved into a lively form of sociology.

When writing about a party, for example, she noted every detail, including how many bottles of champagne were consumed. According to Curtis's personal manual of style, not all brides were beautiful and not all cows were sacred. She could be depended on to enliven her reportage of a wedding by naming the previous love interests of the bride or the groom. Curtis had other talents, too. *Women's Wear Daily* said she could "spot a phony as quickly as a blue blood," and Punch Sulzberger, her publisher, credited her with "skinning" high society "without Novocain." Yet, as he observed, "they never felt a thing."

The summer of 1963 was a busy one for Curtis because she was writing a multipart piece about society in America. Newport was not the only upper-crust resort in transition. In Southampton, a horrified beach club manager grumbled that society was upside down. "I'm not sure where it's all going to end," he told Curtis. "Why, some of the mothers bring their own children to the beach these days." After Southampton, she moved on to Saratoga to cover the resort's annual multimillion-dollar horse auctions and attendant festivities. Then she headed to Newport. The big story there concerned eighteen-year-old Janet Auchincloss, Jackie Kennedy's half sister, who was having her coming-out party on August 17.

Curtis arrived a few days before the event and began her Newport tour at the casino, where Tennis Week was in full swing. The opening line of her first dispatch was "Money is still in style in America's social capital. Especially if it's inherited." She chatted up Mrs. Bruguiere, whose money was particularly "stylish" because it had been bequeathed by two important families, the Van Alens and the Vanderbilts. Then Curtis listened attentively as Katherine Warren and Candy Van Alen explained the nuances of the social calendar. The daily routine had not changed much since the last century. It still involved an appearance at Bailey's Beach for lunch, followed by a visit to the casino or the golf club, and finally, dinner party commitments five or six nights a week. Blessedly, there weren't many cocktail parties (which were considered very Southampton) because most people felt they ruined the day. Curtis wrote up a witty summary of quotidian Newport and in her headline selected one very telling adjective to describe the city: "gilded."

The raison d'être for Curtis's stay in Newport—and the big night on every colonist's calendar that summer—was young Janet Auchincloss's debut. She was being presented to society, and somehow this private affair at Hammersmith Farm was of great interest to the outside world. The fact that President and Mrs. Kennedy were expected had something to do with it. Both Bouvier sisters, Jackie and Lee, had been major debutantes in their day, so young Janet was entering the social scene at a very high level, and with a mother who was a veteran at launching her lovely daughters.

The party had a Carnival in Venice theme, and New York designers, imported especially for the occasion, spent two full days transforming Hammersmith Farm into a Venetian garden. They installed gondola poles and decorated them with garlands and firefly lights. They hung lanterns everywhere and draped tables with vibrant Venetian-colored cloths. A thirty-foot red and black gondola was set up in front of the bandstand, and small gondola-shaped centerpieces overflowing with fruit, feathers, and grape leaves were positioned on the buffet tables. The caterer (also from a Manhattan-based firm) transported the food to Newport in a speeding refrigerator truck. Breast of chicken supreme with wild rice, and other delicacies, would be prepared in special field kitchens set up on the Auchincloss property.

On Saturday, August 17, so many invitees jetted in to Newport for the festivities that the tiny airport was a hub of private planes carrying "sun-bronzed men and long-necked beauties." They crossed paths with women who were jetting out for quick hair appointments in Manhattan and hurrying back to dress for the night. Considerate hosts had hairdressers on hand for the occasion. Mr. and Mrs. John R. Drexel III, for instance, asked Kenneth of New York's most exclusive beauty salon to send one of his best associates to their Bellevue Avenue home to coif a select group of ladies.

As it turned out, President Kennedy and his wife did not attend because they were mourning the death of their infant son, Patrick, who was born on August 7 and died two days later. But they did send a bouquet of white roses and stephanotis to Janet and promised to host a party for her at the White House later in the year.

Outfitted in a white Christian Dior gown, the hardworking debutante graciously greeted a thousand guests—friends, relatives, socialites, bluebloods, diplomats, captains of industry, politicians, and assorted other notables. Orchestra leader Meyer Davis and his twenty-four musicians, who were up late the night before playing at another deb party in Newport, good-naturedly dressed as gondoliers for this event. Underscoring the humor of his situation, Davis asked a reporter, "Did you ever see a Jewish gondolier?" The band performed until 5 a.m., and thanks to a substantial wee-hours breakfast of sandwiches, pancakes and sausages, scrambled eggs, and bacon, and chocolate and vanilla layer cake, the dancers were able to keep up with the music. A few brave souls ended the evening at Bailey's Beach, where they welcomed the dawn by swimming in the chilly waters. Reporters from *Time* magazine, the *New York Times*, and the *New York Journal-American* were there to record all the important details, including the moment when a young man fell into the orchestra pit and had to be extracted from a large flower pot. Cholly Knickerbocker, America's favorite gossip columnist, proclaimed Newport the "in" resort of 1963.

But the city never realized its dream of becoming the nation's unofficial summer White House. President Kennedy's assassination on November 22 put an end to that idea. After the tragedy, Mrs. Kennedy had difficulty deciding if she would proceed with the lease on Annandale Farm. In July 1964, her press secretary told reporters that the former first lady would stay at her mother's place instead, because "she feels the children have had too many environmental changes lately." Barclay Douglas, the owner of Annandale Farm, was so distressed by the news that he refused to refund Mrs. Kennedy's deposit. Offended by his ungallant behavior, Newporters found an effective way to strike back. The local tax assessor paid a sudden visit to the Douglas estate and promptly raised its property taxes.

Minnie

In 1964, *Town and Country* returned to Newport to extol
the city's many virtues. This time the fresh-faced beauty
on the cover was Mary "Minnie" Cushing, granddaughter of
artist Howard Gardiner Cushing and daughter of Howard
G. Cushing of New York and Newport. With her windswept
dark hair, emphatic eyebrows, glowing complexion, towering
height, and aristocratic bearing, Minnie looked as if she could
go from the beach to a ballroom without missing a beat. In
fact, both settings were her natural habitats.

Minnie summered with her handsome brothers, Fred,
Howard, and Thomas, at The Ledges, the Cushing family

home that was as beautiful in 1964 as it had been a hundred years earlier. "Most American families go to bits by the third generation; the Cushings haven't," said a Newporter, in praise of the family. The Cushings maintained traditions, whether it was checking their lobster pots in the waters surrounding the house, or spending time in the magnificent studio where their artist grandfather created some of his best works. Late at night, the former atelier turned into a hot spot for the party-loving young Cushings and their friends.

Slim Aarons, a professional photographer who was famous for shooting "attractive people, doing attractive things, in attractive places," came to Newport several times in the 1960s. When he was looking for iconic images, he trained his lens on the Cushings. Aarons visited Bailey's Beach, where he photographed a trio of Viking-like Cushing men masterfully riding the waves on their surfboards, gifts their father brought to them from Hawaii. Aarons also photographed The Ledges with the brilliant blue Atlantic Ocean as its background. The simple white edifice looked as regal as any castle, and Minnie was its fun-loving princess.

Minnie always made for good copy because, in addition to being a stunner, she was adventurous and irreverent. *Vogue* described her as "a beauty in a lineage of beauty" and ran an eight-page spread of photographs that emphasized her dramatic looks and boundless energy. "Marvelous in motion," the magazine said, showing Minnie barefoot on a horse and leaping over rocks at the beach. *Town and Country* called her a "travel addict" and noted that, this summer, she would be jetting off to Spain to follow the corridas. Minnie played in exotic locales in Europe and the Far East, and eventually, in 1965, went to work in New York City, where she became muse and amanuensis to up-and-coming fashion designer Oscar de la Renta.

Minnie was a real-life precursor to the spirited ingenue in *That Girl*, Marlo Thomas's popular 1966 television series. Dressed in chic little outfits, she rode her bicycle to her Seventh Avenue office because she wanted to have a daily workout, and she said that the chorus of appreciative honks from taxi drivers always made her smile. Despite the fact that she was a fashion insider with access to the kind of wardrobe other girls could only dream about, she often designed her own clothes, or picked up pieces without even looking at their labels.

As de la Renta had hoped, she inspired him to think younger. At his fashion show, Minnie gleefully modeled his most outrageous numbers herself, including an evening bikini, a bejeweled coat that bared the midriff, and a gauzy chiffon caftan that left little to the imagination. The *New York Times* credited the designer with proving that "couture clothes can be kicky, not stuffy." In fact, "stuffy" was the last word anyone would use to describe de la Renta's spring collection that year, and he had Minnie to thank.

21

Anything Goes

Newport was "no longer the place of the lifted pinky," quipped a journalist in *Venture* magazine. Now, with its "it girls," pop fashions, and posh parties, "Newport swings," he said. With trendsetter Minnie Cushing in the news all the time, Newport turned into a style center, just as it had been in the Gilded Age. Suddenly reporters and their readers wanted to know what was in those fancy Bellevue Avenue closets. "20 Gowns and 2 Perfumes" was the answer Charlotte Curtis came up with when she asked her Newport sources that very question. Daytime attire was informal, from Minnie's aptly named miniskirts to blue jeans designed by Jax and Lily Pulitzer sheaths. Even the most abbreviated bikini failed to shock anyone at Bailey's Beach anymore.

But evening was another story. "Mrs. Drexel's hair goes up promptly at 5 p.m.," Curtis wrote. The setting sun signaled all casually attired socialites that it was time to turn into a brilliant butterfly. That's when the Balenciagas, the Saint Laurents, and other couture creations came out of captivity to perform their nightly magic. A well-dressed woman could get by with twenty gowns in rotation as long as she had an assortment of jewels (old family diamonds and contemporary pieces designed by David Webb and Kenneth Jay Lane) to accessorize. As for the two perfumes, every woman needed a light, fresh scent for day and a sexier one for night. Wardrobe requirements were a little less punishing than they were when a woman was required to change her clothes nine times a day, but it was still important to look good, especially with all those journalists and photographers routinely coming to call.

In 1966, Minnie was back in the headlines when her globe-trotting father became ill while on safari in Kenya and she raced to his side. While she was there, she met Peter Beard, a dazzlingly handsome photographer and wildlife conservationist who had recently written *The End of the Game*, a book that exposed the consequences of big-game hunting in Africa. Not surprisingly, these two beautiful people fell in love and, after a whirlwind courtship, announced their engagement and upcoming Newport wedding. They would be married on August 13, 1967, at historic Trinity Church. But it was not going to be a traditional Newport affair, not if Minnie and Peter had their way.

Their prewedding party at Bailey's Beach was unconventional from start to finish. The bride and groom, resplendent in a caftan and tuxedo, respectively, made a dramatic entrance with sparklers in hand. The beach was illuminated by flaming torches, and the evening's entertainment (no Meyer Davis for these trendsetters) consisted of Liberian dancers who performed the Watusi and the Fanga to the insistent beat of ceremonial drums.

If the Bailey's Beach party evoked mating rituals in exotic Africa, the marriage ceremony the next day was pure jet set. There were 416 guests at the flower-and-candle-filled church, where a special pew (in the back) had been reserved for six women who worked at

The Ledges, the Cushing family's historic estate on a spectacular promontory in Newport.

The Ledges. The bride wore a long white organdy gown designed by her dear friend de la Renta, and her headdress was a cascade of white flowers created by Adolfo, New York's hottest hatter.

After the ceremony, guests gathered in a large green-and-white-striped tent that had been set up on the Cushing lawn. For music, Cushing and Beard called on Peter Duchin (whose mother was an Oelrichs), the popular young bandleader who had played at Truman Capote's Black and White Ball the year before. Toni Frissell, a photographer who worked for all the top fashion and lifestyle magazines, including *Vogue*, *Life*, and *Sports Illustrated* (and who photographed the Kennedy-Bouvier wedding), was there to take pictures. According to Minnie, the guests drank champagne, "the usual Heidsieck, or whatever it is," and ate hot and cold hors d'oeuvres.

Liberian dancers aside, what was really untraditional about Minnie and Peter's nuptials was that their "wedding movie" was made by Jonas Mekas, an avant-garde filmmaker. Mekas was a Lithuanian Holocaust survivor who moved to New York in 1949. He bought himself a camera, immediately started filming his own life, and amassed impressive credits over the years. Mekas edited *Film Culture*, wrote for the *Village Voice*, and cofounded both the Filmmakers' Cooperative and the Filmmakers' Cinémathèque, which made him an important architect of the New American Cinema, as he named it. Peter Beard, who was a close friend, asked Mekas to film the wedding, and the acclaimed international artist happily agreed.

Mekas arrived in Newport a few days before the wedding, so he had time to explore. Like President Eisenhower, he was treated to a spin on the Cushing lobster boat and learned the history of the island from its captain, the proud father of the bride. He spent two days filming the happy couple, and eventually cut the footage into a thirteen-minute film he called *Peter's Wedding*. Set to the rousing and romantic strains of the "Blue Danube," by Johann Strauss, Mekas's impressionistic work turned the conventional society wedding upside down, literally and metaphorically. His camera practically swooned while it followed the bride and groom, their families, and their guests through the classic rituals—the ceremony, the receiving line, the congratulatory handshakes and kisses, the first dance, the cutting of the cake, and the getaway, when the newlyweds flew off in a helicopter. But in typical Mekas style, the filmmaking was completely spontaneous, so there was no real narrative or structure. His avant-garde sensibility underscored the giddy exuberance of the celebration and made it come to life.

Mekas was privy to a funny scene the day after the wedding, when Beard, probably inspired by his athletic bride and brothers-in-law, tried to master the sport of surfing. At some point the horrified groom realized that he had lost his wedding ring in the sand. But even he found it funny when his friends scoured the beach, searching for the proverbial needle in a haystack. Mekas turned on his camera and captured the comic finale to the big wedding weekend.

The fact that Minnie Cushing and Peter Beard fell in love in Africa may have added a note of divine kismet to their relationship. But the truth was that sooner or later they probably would have gotten together at Bailey's Beach. When it came to mating, all roads still led to Bellevue Avenue, and with every passing generation, the connections between cottagers became more and more complicated. "This place is loaded with cousins," pointed out Jimmy Van Alen, who could boast ties to assorted Vanderbilts, Astors, and Goelets, among others. Even Proust would have trouble keeping it all straight, quipped a confused journalist.

A few weeks after the Cushing-Beard wedding, Van Alen hosted a party that was a Venn diagram for a certain husband and his many ex-wives. John Jacob Astor came to the Van Alens' soiree because his teenage daughter, Mary Jacqueline (Jackie) Astor, was the guest of honor. But no one expected the oft-married and oft-divorced man to walk in with his first wife, Ellen Tuck French Astor Guest. With Tucky in tow, Astor greeted his former second wife, Gertrude Gretsch Coletti-Perucca, who was Jackie's mother. Later, at the Tennis Ball, Astor ran into his former fiancée Eileen Gillespie Slocum. Remarkably, Astor reunited with most of his significant others on the same night, and in the same zip code.

Writer Cleveland Amory described a similar situation in a humorous article he wrote for *Harper's* magazine titled "Newport: There She Sits." Without naming names, he enumerated the guests at a not-so-unusual wedding ceremony in Newport. The bride and the groom were joined by the daughter of the bride and the bride's ex-husband. On the groom's side, there were his two children, his ex-wife, and her new husband. The new husband's ex-wife was not in attendance. Not that she disapproved of the marriage—she planned on attending, but couldn't make it at the last minute because she was ill.

Everything was up to date in Newport, and not just the cottagers' short skirts, long hair, and the "Bob & Carol & Ted & Alice" approach to relationships. In general, life was a little less formal and a lot more fun. These days, most houses had streamlined staffs, so hostesses had to bring in outside help for parties. Their savior was an enterprising ex-butler named Eric Henry Evitts. Mr. Evitts was English, and his past was colorful. Back in 1953, during Queen Elizabeth's coronation, he visited a family member who was employed at Buckingham Palace. Mr. Evitts arrived to find total chaos in the royal kitchen, so he took off his jacket, rolled up his sleeves, and pitched in to help, as if it were his civic duty to assist in putting together a meal for the new monarch.

Back in America, Mr. Evitts considered his options. He had worked for Mrs. Bruguiere, so he knew how to please a finicky employer and manage a demanding household. He decided to put his skills to good use by starting a catering business, essentially becoming a butler for many employers instead of one. Smart hostesses called him first to reserve a date. If Mr. Evitts was busy, they had to pick another night.

Once he was on board, Mr. Evitts did all the work. He assembled a staff from among the qualified domestics in the area, and oversaw all the nagging little details regarding the help, the setting, and the food. He was famous for his cheese puffs and his clicker. Mr. Evitts always stationed a uniformed maid at the front door to click off each dinner guest as they entered the house. When the clicker indicated that the expected number of guests had arrived, the maid signaled him to start serving dinner.

Mr. Evitts is "the real power" in Newport, wrote one journalist who was penning a story about "insider" Newport. "He taught us all manners," reminisced Marion "Oatsie" Charles, a former Washingtonian who knew more about etiquette than most people. Mr. Evitts proved that it was still possible to live like a queen or a king in modern-day Newport, even if it meant renting a retinue.

A few old-timers, such as Mrs. Bruguiere, managed to hold on to their butlers and footmen, even though the concept of liveried servants was beyond quaint. One young man who needed a job accepted the position of pantryman at one of the properly run cottages. He was paid $250 a month to work about four and a half hours a day, and most of the time his duties consisted of washing the dishes of the three people who lived there. Other servants cared for his clothes and made his bed, and he had so much free time that he didn't know what to do with himself. When a coworker urged him to ask for a raise, he was aghast. "I didn't have the gall," he said.

There were other perks for modern-day servants besides free time. Jane Pickens Langley, the singer/celebrity/socialite who was the new owner of Maxim Karolik's house, believed that being a domestic was a "lovely way of life" and pointed out that she let her servants "have telephone calls and things of that type." Having permission to use the phone was nice, but there were privileges that were much more meaningful to staffers. Like the character Fairchild in Samuel A. Taylor's play *Sabrina Fair* (which was made into the movie *Sabrina*, starring Audrey Hepburn), Newport's chauffeurs were in the proverbial catbird seat when it came to accessing insider information about the stock market. While they were driving their wealthy employers around town, they were given—or overheard—stock tips that feathered their own nests. Some of the chauffeurs pooled their findings, and, with the right "blue chip" advice, their small investments grew into small fortunes.

When chauffeurs could get rich, change was definitely in the air. Even the musty ritual of afternoon tea had been renovated by the newly "with it" cottagers. In a *New York Times* article titled "Newport: One Never Serves Coffee at Teatime," readers learned that tea was served every day at the homes of the Firestones, the John Jermain Slocums, the John Nicholas Browns, and other families on and around Bellevue Avenue. Hu-Kwa was poured from a silver pot, and little butter-and-peppered-lettuce sandwiches were passed around. It was never polite to request coffee at teatime, but these days, it was just fine to ask for a highball. "I think we need this to keep going," Mrs. Slocum, observed, referring to the breakneck pace she and her friends faced during the season. Today the dress code was come as you are and the music was likely to be the beat of Herb Alpert and his Tijuana Brass.

At the very moment Newport was becoming younger and hipper, the city was incubating a hot new band with a cool new sound. The Cowsill brothers—Bill, Bob, Barry, and John—were former navy brats who lived with their parents, Bud and Barbara, and their younger siblings, Susan, Paul, and Richard. They organized a classic garage band and played Beatles' songs at school dances, colleges, and local clubs.

It was a family affair through and through. Bud Cowsill managed his teenage sons and shuttled the group around in an old station wagon. They played regular gigs at Bannister's Wharf in downtown Newport and in the clubby basement of the Munchinger King Hotel on Bellevue Avenue. One lucky day, a *Today* show staffer was in the audience, and he was so impressed by the group's clean look and appealing, sunshine-pop sound that he invited them to appear on the show. The Cowsills charmed the television audience and won a contract with MGM Records. Eventually they invited their mother to become an official band member and expanded to include sister Susan and brother Paul.

The Cowsills perfected bouncy, four-and five-part harmonies that made their songs upbeat and infectious. It was a "Newport" sound, high-spirited and redolent of blue skies, fresh breezes, and good times. "The Rain, the Park, and Other Things" (frequently referred to as "the most tune-worthy song of all time") soared to number 2 on the *Billboard* chart, and "Indian Lake" and "Hair" were both top sellers as well. The family band even inspired the hit television series *The Partridge Family*, which starred Academy Award winner Shirley Jones and her teen idol stepson, David Cassidy.

In these relaxed times, some of the cottagers were surprisingly unperturbed about issues that would have had them up in arms in the past. In 1968, the Rhode Island Supreme Court ordered Bailey's Beach to remove a three-hundred-foot-long chain-link fence that blocked public access to the ocean. Of course, some outraged club members protested this invasion of the club's privacy. Katherine Warren said, "It's sort of cruel not to let us have just one tiny beach," and T. Wiley Buchanan warned that "It can only cause ill will," implying that Bailey's Beachers might retaliate by not being as generous to the community in the future.

Yet there were more enlightened members who understood the need to tear down the barricades. Senator Claiborne Pell said that people had made "a mountain out of a sandhill" and added that he was "happy to abide by the court's ruling." Eileen Slocum, while protective of the club's "members only" buildings and swimming pool, agreed that the seashore was another story. "I feel the ocean is open to the public anywhere in the world," she said.

Forward-thinking Newporters acknowledged that it was difficult to be a "Shangri-la" and a "happening place" at the same time. To be truly new, old Newport had to make some concessions to progress, and there was real work to be done. The city needed a face-lift, especially in its seedy waterfront area, and a more visible welcome mat. The solution was to open up the island to the outside world, and the best way to accomplish this would be to build a great, big, beautiful bridge.

Doris

Doris Duke inherited $100 million from her tobacco tycoon father when she was twelve years old, earning her the moniker "the richest girl in the world." In Newport she spent time at Rough Point, her family's baronial home on the Cliff Walk, and made her debut there in 1930, with six hundred guests in attendance. Eileen Slocum recalled seeing young Doris and her pal Woolworth heiress Barbara Hutton, "the gold dust twins," drinking ice cream sodas at the local drugstore.

The press always covered Doris's colorful, gold-plated life. She married twice, first to politician James Cromwell and then to international playboy Porfirio Rubirosa, she had affairs, and she lived extravagantly and eccentrically in homes all over the world. But in Newport in the late 1950s, Doris Duke was best known for her ongoing battle with the city over the Cliff Walk.

That dispute began in 1958, when Doris ordered her staff to put up a barbed-wire fence, thorny bushes, and a "No Trespassing" sign on the ocean side of her property. The Cliff Walk in front of Rough Point had been destroyed by hurricanes, so passersby were treading on her grass and walking up to the house to peek in her windows. The city refused to stop them, invoking "the privileges of the shore," Newporters' constitutional right to unimpeded access to the sea.

Doris wasn't the only cottager to be annoyed by the rude behavior of pushy pedestrians. One property owner on the Cliff Walk came up with a novel solution to the problem after one too many picnickers spread blankets on her lawn and sat there enjoying their lunch, oblivious of—or insensitive to—the fact that they were trespassing. One day, the exasperated lady of the house instructed her chauffeur to follow the interlopers home. A few weeks later, she parked herself on their small, suburban front lawn with a picnic of her own. They got the point.

Doris was forced to remove her fence, but like William Beech Lawrence, the cottager who used an angry bull to deter trespassers, she brought in two German shepherds to patrol her property. In May 1964, her guard dogs took their jobs a little too seriously and bit two intruders. The police stepped in and ordered her to get rid of the dogs.

The Cliff Walk continued to be a bone of contention between Doris and the local authorities until one evening in October 1966. That day, she had been with her close friend and constant companion Eduardo Tirella, an interior decorator and Hollywood set designer who was helping her redo Rough Point. Doris liked having a confidant on call, so she was a little disturbed when Tirella started talking about returning to Los Angeles to work on a new Tony Curtis movie.

Following an afternoon of autumn gardening, Doris and Tirella got into a rented Dodge station wagon and he drove the car down the long driveway leading out of Rough Point. For security reasons, the estate's thick iron gates were fastened with a padlock and chain and had to be unlocked by hand, so Tirella set the car in park and got out. Meanwhile, Doris took his place at the wheel. Seconds later, the car shot forward, slamming Tirella up against the gate, moving with such force that it pushed him and the gate all the way across Bellevue Avenue and into a tree. Tirella died instantly.

Doris told the police that she had no idea how the car raced out of control and insisted that her foot was planted firmly on the brake. The only explanation she could offer was that she was unfamiliar with the Dodge because it was a rental. The police listened, and then handed over the wagon to experts, who inspected the throttle and the breaks and tested the gas pedal. They found that everything worked perfectly.

It seemed implausible that Tirella's death was an accident. There were rumors that the couple had been drinking the night before and arguing earlier that day. Yet, only three days after the incident, Newport police chief Joseph Radice closed the case, stating there was "no cause to prefer charges," a shockingly speedy resolution.

Then, on October 15, the *Newport Daily News* ran another front-page story about the heiress. "Doris Duke Gives $25,000 to Restore Cliff Walk," read the startling headline. The same woman who had been at odds with Cliff Walk advocates for almost a decade was now writing a large check to help them meet their goals. The article suggested that the donation had been in the works before the accident, but conspiracy theorists swore that Duke's sudden burst of civic-mindedness resulted from a last-minute, back-room deal she made to avoid prosecution for the fatal crash. Five months later, the story became even more intriguing when Police Chief Radice suddenly retired.

22

Tourist Attractions

There were only three ways to enter Newport in the 1960s, and not one of them was easy. A visitor approaching from the north could go over the Mount Hope Bridge (built to "take the 'island' out of Rhode Island!" the guidebooks said). Or they could cross the Sakonnet River Bridge in Tiverton. Both of these routes were a little challenging because they involved long stretches on single-lane roads that had a high volume of traffic in the summer. And many drivers couldn't forget that the Mount Hope Bridge had to be dismantled and rebuilt just a few months before its opening in 1929 because its supporting cables were cracked—a bit of historical trivia that usually occurred to them when they were midway across it.

The southern route, with its scenic farms and glimpses of beautiful Narragansett Bay, was more picturesque, but equally taxing when it came to crossing the water. It involved a white-knuckle drive from the mainland to the nearby island

of Conanicut via the precarious Jamestown Bridge. Not only
was the bridge high and slippery, but also its two narrow lanes
were made of an open steel grid that rattled and showed nervous drivers glimpses of the ocean below. After suffering this
stressful crossing, travelers faced an inconvenient wait at the
Jamestown docks before taking a twenty-minute ferry ride
into Newport Harbor. Upon landing, they found themselves
on a decrepit old wharf in the most unattractive part of the
city. This was the dangerous, high-crime area known as "Blood
Alley," where sailors caroused when off-duty. The surrounding Colonial streets were narrow and difficult to navigate, and
visitors who attempted to exit Newport late at night were often
stranded when they missed the ferry by a few hair-raising minutes. One regular commuter swore that the deckhand always
smiled sadistically at the desperate latecomers when he signaled
the last boat to pull away from the dock.

Jet-setters could fly in from the mainland, a fine solution when
the wallet and the weather cooperated. But all in all, the message
to visitors was an unwelcoming "Come to Newport . . . if you
dare." The solution was to build a new, state-of-the-art bridge that
would turn the trip into a speedy twelve-to-fifteen-minute ride.
Construction started in January 1966. There had been some debate
as to what the bridge would look like. Fortunately, John Nicholas
Brown, one of the city's most prominent citizens, and a man of
exceedingly good taste, headed the commission. He had a personal
stake in the bridge's design because his house had a spectacular
view of Narragansett Bay, and he wanted to keep it that way. His
attitude was that if he had to see the bridge every day, it had better
be beautiful.

When the Newport Bridge was completed in 1969 it was,
as Brown hoped, a beautiful sight. At 2.1 miles long, and with
two majestic "cathedral" towers rising 400 feet (roughly 37 stories) above the water, the silvery suspension span registered

The Newport Bridge, renamed the Claiborne Pell Bridge in 1992 in honor of Rhode Island's beloved senator.

as a graceful work of sculpture in the harbor. It was the fourteenth-largest bridge in the United States, and it was going to have a tremendous impact on the city. Experts estimated that 1,140,000 vehicles would drive across it in its first year.

Meanwhile, Newport was busy making itself pretty for all those expected callers. An urban renewal plan was in the works to transform the blighted wharf into a scenic, efficient, and tourist-friendly waterfront. Some buildings were razed.

Others, as was the custom in old Newport, were upended and moved to new locations. Trinity Church was enhanced by a brand-new, classically styled village green, which looked authentically Colonial. Ironically, with its new boulevards, promising commercial districts, and unobstructed view of the harbor, the renovated Thames Street area was similar to the model proposed by Nathan Fleischer in his 1947 pamphlet *Newport: Blueprint for a City That Must Do, Develop, or Die.* Fleischer believed that the improvements would attract tourists, and he was right. Now that Newport was more accessible, a record-breaking one hundred thousand visitors came to see The Breakers in 1970. And The Preservation Society added Chateau-sur-Mer, Rosecliff, Kingscote, and Miss Alice Brayton's beloved farm to its already popular roster of attractions such as The Elms and Marble House.

Thanks to Katherine Warren and her fellow preservationists, these Gilded Age properties were in good shape. But Colonial Newport needed a helping hand, and the person to extend a very well manicured one was Doris Duke. According to local legend, Duke sat down to tea one day with Warren and they divided the task of preserving historic Newport. "All right Katherine, you take the nineteenth century and I'll take the eighteenth," she announced to her friend, as if they were sharing toys.

In 1968, Duke launched the Newport Restoration Foundation to "restore as much as it is possible of the beautiful Colonial architecture of Newport." The foundation planned to acquire old properties in areas that had gone to seed, rebuild and restore them, and rent them to members of the community. Her intentions seemed noble, but some Newporters were still scratching their heads over Duke's sudden rapprochement with the city after her battle over public access to the Cliff Walk.

Despite the cloud surrounding Duke's motivation, the foundation was a sunny development for Newport, especially for its historic wharf area known as The Point. The once-beautiful neighborhood had turned into a slum over the years, albeit a colorful one, populated by families who had lived there for generations. Duke bought its ramshackle Colonial houses and handed them over to her staff for a makeover. In most cases, the buildings were stripped down to their frames and rebuilt according to Colonial "code," which meant nails were left exposed, as they were in olden times, and exteriors were painted in a palette of authentic period colors. Each finished product bore a plaque commemorating its restoration.

The good news for Newport was that Duke's buildings remained on the city's tax rolls, as opposed to the tax-exempt ones owned by The Preservation Society. The bad news was that once a historic house was reclaimed, it attracted affluent tenants to the neighborhood, and low-income residents could no longer afford to live there. Since the foundation used private funds, it was not publicly accountable for its policies, and had the right to select its own tenants. "It's easy to get in if you are a retired navy commander," a Newport resident griped to the *New York Times*, "but so far as I know they've never rented to a black."

Apparently the city didn't dwell too long on the fates of its displaced. Beautification and the boosting of tourism became even greater concerns when in 1973 the navy closed its destroyer base and pulled fourteen thousand sailors out of Newport. Most people thought their departure would be devastating because so many consumers would be leaving the area. Instead, Newport became cleaner and quainter without all those sleazy sailor bars and rooming houses. The city was now a real destination for tourists, and visitors were enchanted by the beaches, the climate, and the cottages, just as they had been during the Gilded Age. The big difference now was that any tourist with the price of admission could actually enter the finest of those once-exclusive homes.

Newport's star was rising, and a long-anticipated movie and a new novel by Pulitzer Prize–winning writer Thornton Wilder may have had something to do with its ascent. *The Great Gatsby*, F. Scott Fitzgerald's masterpiece about wealth and disillusionment in the Jazz Age, was finally coming to the big screen. Directed by Englishman Jack Clayton and starring Robert Redford and Mia Farrow, the production was so heavily promoted and marketed that it even had its own studio-authorized line of pristine white "Gatsby" pots and pans, although there was no indication that the character Jay Gatsby ever cooked.

In the novel, Gatsby's fabled mansion was in "West Egg," Fitzgerald's substitute for Long Island's new-moneyed community of Great Neck. For the movie, the filmmakers decided to use Newport's Rosecliff as the location for Gatsby's home. Paramount Pictures spared no expense in recreating the lavish parties Fitzgerald described. Rolls-Royces and other luxury cars filled the driveway, and the cast wore gowns from the 1920s and Cartier jewels. The extras had to be authentically posh, too, so the film's casting director turned to the Newport cottagers for the right look. "Wanted: Aristocrats, $1.65 Per Hour," was the call. Just for the fun of it, Candy Van Alen, Oatsie Charles, and Nuala Pell signed on, and they were shocked to discover that moviemaking was hard work. "We were paid $1.65 an hour, and I'll probably have to pay a surgeon God knows what to repair my legs," said Charles after a "day" that began at six in the evening and ended at dawn.

Newport figured prominently in all the media's stories about Gatsby. The Rhode Island Development Council saw the wave of publicity as an opportunity to reach out to tourists. "Live like 'The Great Gatsby' in Rhode Island," it promised in a series of advertisements in high-end publications such as *Town and Country*.

Thornton Wilder was also a busy ambassador for Newport that same year with the publication of his best-selling novel *Theophilus North*. His classic plays *Our Town* and *The Skin of*

Our Teeth and his novel *The Bridge of San Luis Rey* were so popular that Wilder was always bombarded by interview requests. He found that the only way he could concentrate on writing was to move to a hideaway for a few months, and Newport was one of his favorites. He was stationed there briefly during World War I, and he returned during the summer of 1920. Young Wilder rented a room at the YMCA and supported himself by tutoring the scions of the rich in Latin. But his real objective that summer was to write his first novel, *The Cabala*, a tale about Rome's decaying aristocracy. Wilder probably thought that Newport's rotting rich would be a fine substitute for the ancient Italian ones.

That summer was so productive that Wilder returned to Newport many times after that. He'd check into a hotel—sometimes the Castle Hill on Brenton Point and sometimes the Muenchinger King or the Viking Hotel on Bellevue Avenue—and set up his typewriter. Wilder didn't know many people in town, so he encountered few distractions. He said he came to Newport because he loved spas out of season, and, "no," he told the *Newport Daily News* in 1960, he wasn't going to "'do' Newport in any of the works he has been writing here."

It turned out that Wilder was stealthily writing *Theophilus North*, which, despite his earlier remarks, was him "doing" Newport. He diplomatically set *Theophilus North* in the past (in the book, the eponymous hero has a series of adventures on and about Bellevue Avenue during the summer of 1926), but some of the situations Wilder depicted were utterly contemporary. A rich father tried to prevent his daughter from running away with a socially and economically inappropriate man. Greedy children fought for control of their father's fortune. And then there was the sad tale of the misunderstood husband who was controlled by his wealthy wife—a plotline that actually paralleled a real-life drama unfolding in a beautiful residence on Bellevue Avenue.

So visible were Sunny and Claus von Bulow, the occupants of Clarendon Court, that it is possible Wilder was inspired to include a version of their story in *Theophilus North*. She was Martha "Sunny" Crawford, an American heiress who, like Consuelo Vanderbilt, May Goelet, Louise Van Alen, and other "dollar princesses" before her, married European nobility in her pursuit of happily ever after. Her first husband was a real-life prince, Alfred of Auersperg, and their union produced two

Sunny (Martha) von Bulow, outfitted in feathers and finery, strikes a dramatic pose at a society party in 1968.

children, Annie-Laurie and Alexander Georg, but little happiness. The couple divorced in 1965, and, in 1966, with a fortune estimated at $75 million, Sunny married Danish businessman Claus von Bulow.

There was some controversy as to who put the "von" in von Bulow. Claus was born in 1926 with the surname "Borberg," but he abandoned it after his parents divorced, and his father, Sven Borberg, was sentenced to four years in prison for having been a Nazi collaborator during World War II. Claus's mother was a member of the distinguished Danish-German Bulow family, so that was the name he used. The "von," an indication of noble birth in Germany, did not appear until after he married Sunny Auersperg. When their daughter was born in 1967, they named her Cosima, paying homage to the infamous second wife of composer Richard Wagner, who was the first Cosima von Bulow. Moving forward, the whole family used the surname "von Bulow."

Sunny's mother, Annie Laurie, and her second husband, Russell Aitken, enjoyed summering in Newport. First they rented, and then purchased Champ Soleil, the downsized, twenty-two-room cottage Robert Goelet moved to after he left Ochre Court. Sunny followed her mother in 1971, when she and her family took possession of the stately Horace Trumbaeur–designed Clarendon Court on Bellevue Avenue. Thanks to the groundwork her mother had done, Sunny and her clan entered Newport at the top of the proverbial social ladder—Bailey's Beach, the Reading Room, and all the desirable club memberships were theirs without asking. The von Bulows seemed to live a charmed life in their fairytale castle.

Von Bulow had been working for oil tycoon J. Paul Getty at the time of his marriage, but his job required him to spend a lot of time in London and Los Angeles, and his bride refused to live in either place. Ultimately, von Bulow left Getty's employ to become a full-time husband and companion to Sunny. He threw himself into respectable activities in Newport, serving on the board of various institutions, such as The Preservation Society and the Newport Casino. Von Bulow even penned a history of Clarendon Court for a historical journal.

"The author of this article has lived happily at Clarendon for the past four years," he wrote. "He hopes some future writer will cover the occupancy of his family at Clarendon with as much wistful charity as he has endeavored to extend to its previous owners." A witty conclusion to a lively little article turned out to be words of profound irony. Von Bulow would be written about, but rarely with charity.

In 1979, the von Bulows were not living happily and the problems in their relationship were deep-rooted. The chains that bound him, though made of gold, were chafing. Tired of being a "hired ornament," in the words of William Wright, author of *The Von Bulow Affair*, he wanted to work at making his own money. He also thought he might like to start a new life with his beautiful young mistress, actress Alexandra Isles, who had made a name for herself as the appealing ingenue on television's daytime serial *Dark Shadows* (the exteriors of which were shot at Newport's own Seaview Terrace). There was the possibility of divorce, but would he be able to walk away from all that money? Sunny discussed her failing marriage with her children, who later recalled that she was coolheaded about a divorce. That was before her first unexplained health crisis, on December 26, 1979, when Sunny lost consciousness while her seemingly unconcerned husband lay by her side. His odd behavior, especially the way he hesitated to call for help, caused Sunny's personal maid, Maria, and her children to wonder if von Bulow had a nefarious agenda. Was he trying to kill his wife? One year later, they believed their worst suspicions were confirmed when, on December 21, 1980, Sunny von Bulow slipped into a coma and never woke up.

After a lengthy investigation, a Rhode Island grand jury delivered the words Claus von Bulow never expected to hear. "Financier Indicted on Charge of Trying Twice to Kill Wife" was the headline in the *New York Times*. For months, readers followed the real-life soap opera, eagerly awaiting the latest news about Sunny, the comatose, ultrawealthy wife; Claus, her self-absorbed husband with the beautiful young mistress on the side; Ala, Alex, and Cosima, Sunny's pampered children with multiple trust funds; and Maria, the ghoulish but devoted housekeeper who went to the police with suspicions of foul play.

The press faithfully reported every detail of the trial. Hundreds of journalists installed themselves in Newport. All the big news services were represented, along with major newspapers, magazines, book publishers, members of the foreign press, and broadcasters. Superior Court judge Thomas H. Needham did not prohibit discussion of the case, nor did he sequester the jury, so everyone involved was free to move about and speak, creating an almost partylike atmosphere. "This town is too small for this big a trial," complained one local taxi driver. But the city was reaping the rewards of its media circus. Television viewers and tabloid readers all became familiar with aerial shots of Clarendon Court and the nearby palaces on Newport's Cliff Walk, sights they wanted to see for themselves.

Private Newport—the wealthy cottagers—were reserving judgment until the verdict was in. Meanwhile, a framed caricature of von Bulow, a symbol of acceptance at the Reading Room, was still hanging on the wall. And if it had been July instead of February, von Bulow would have been free to use his membership at Bailey's Beach. One friend observed that von Bulow was too meticulous to fail at anything (let alone murder) twice. "Bumbling something like this would be ridiculous," he pointed out.

But von Bulow was found guilty on March 16, 1982, and was subsequently sentenced to thirty years in prison. He engaged the high-profile attorney Alan Dershowitz to champion his appeal, and the Supreme Court of Rhode Island reversed his conviction and ordered a new trial.

The von Bulow retrial was scheduled to begin on Monday, April 8, 1985, but when the location was announced, it was Providence, the state capital, instead of Newport. Locals were outraged, not because they harbored any sentimental feelings for Claus von Bulow or were concerned about crime and punishment. Having experienced the economic windfall of the first trial, they were unwilling to part with all that tourist revenue. Viking Tours estimated that their buses carried fifty thousand tourists past Clarenden Court each year. Then there were the restaurants; the souvenir vendors; and, of course, the hotels. The Viking Hotel in Newport had been home to the press corps during the first trial. Now all that business would go to the Biltmore in Providence. "Newport will never be happy about it," said Dr. Earle Cohen, the owner of the Viking.

If Newport seemed a little desperate to host the von Bulow sequel it was because the city was still smarting from the recent loss of another crowd-drawing event, the America's Cup. The New York Yacht Club, still the holder of the America's Cup, had been undefeated for 132 years, the longest winning streak in the history of sports. In 1983, the challenger for the Cup was *Australia II*, from the Royal Perth Yacht Club. Newporters went through their traditional rituals to prepare for the races— dignitaries were invited, dinners and parties were planned, and everyone got out their nautically themed clothing to show their support for the home team. They were betting on *Liberty*, the American defender helmed by Dennis Conner, the Captain Ahab–like skipper who had successfully defended the cup against Australia in 1980. With so many victories behind them, local supporters were a little complacent about the races, and the whole experience had gotten a touch stale.

But all bets were off when the Australians arrived with a tip-top, commando-styled crew and a boat with a secret weapon—a hidden, revolutionary keel design. No more nightly pub-crawling for the Australian challengers, as was their habit during previous races. Under the direction of Captain John Bertrand, the *Australia II* crew trained like marines and studied the local waters until they could sniff the wind and sail like natives. As for the boat's secret winged keel, the key to its speed, no one was allowed to see it. The yacht was protected by armed guards twenty-four hours a day. Divers who got too close were arrested and charged with trespassing.

All of this drama made for a thrilling race. *Time* magazine reported that "a superboat and a bunch of hungry sailors from Down Under" transformed a race that "is usually as exciting . . . as a tennis game without a net . . . into a tingling cliffhanger of a sport." After days of dazzling maneuvers and countermaneuvers on both sides, the upstarts won, and there were twenty-two television crews and thirteen hundred reporters on hand to record their victory. Fans in Perth were especially happy to see the competition come to an end because, on race days, radio coverage started at midnight and ran until early the next morning. Victory meant that Australians would finally be able to get a good night's sleep.

Newporters behaved graciously, but they were dazed and depressed by their defeat. No one could remember life without the America's Cup, and its departure represented the loss of a cherished award and an industry. "It was our prize," bemoaned Mary Walsh, an eminent Cup follower who was in her seventies. "For a New Yorker it would be like losing the Brooklyn Bridge." Even one of the main roads in Newport was named America's Cup Boulevard, after its long-held treasure.

While the von Bulow trial was not the America's Cup, it represented an economic shot in the arm worth fighting for. State representative Paul W. Crowley (who was also a Newport restaurateur) quickly filed a bill that would require felony cases to be tried in the county where they happened. But Governor DiPrete shot it down by saying, "I'm all for tourism, but I don't think that should be the deciding factor where a trial's going to be held."

Newport lost the battle for the retrial, but it retained custody of the story. Long after von Bulow was acquitted, and had moved on to a new life in London, his comatose wife was Newport's very own Sleeping Beauty. Sunny von Bulow's quiescent body may have been in a hospital room, or a nursing home, in another state, but she would forever be associated with Clarendon Court, the castle that was her final home.

23

Who Wants to Be a Millionaire?

The Newport of the early 1990s was a little low on spectacle and glamour. "Even the scandals aren't what they used to be," a reporter wrote wistfully. There was no domineering Alva Vanderbilt Belmont or crazy Mamie Fish, no marrying Wilsons or divorcing Frenches, no junk-collecting Sullivans, no ostracized Coogans, no Kennedys, and no notorious Claus von Bulow.

Doris Duke added a little color in 1993 when, at age of eighty, she died and left $5 million to her butler, Bernard Lafferty. She also appointed him coexecutor of her $1.2 billion estate, a position that came with an annual salary of $500,000. Lafferty, an amiable Irishman, had been her faithful companion for several years, but Duke's advisers protested that he was an illiterate alcoholic who did his employer harm. They said he fostered bad behavior while Duke was alive, and they accused him of "the butler did it" foul play after her death. But one of Duke's neighbors said that Lafferty added lightness and laughter to the poor little rich girl's tragic life.

Lafferty wasn't the first servant in Newport to inherit a windfall. Many cottagers set aside generous bequests for their domestics, who, after decades of faithful service, were sometimes treated like members of the family. But one ambitious household worker wasn't satisfied with being treated like a family member; he wanted to be one.

The players in this long-standing soap opera were more Palmolive than Puccini. In 1959, Ruth and Harold Tinney purchased Oliver Belmont's Belcourt for $25,000. The sixty-room house (described by one Realtor as a forty-five-thousand-square-foot one-bedroom) was no longer the showplace it had been in Belmont's day. It needed a great deal of work, but fortunately the Tinneys, along with their son, Donald, were enthusiastic do-it-yourselfers. They restored the interior, filled it with an eclectic mixture of antiques and collectibles, and gave the house the grand name Belcourt Castle. Like the nearby Preservation Society attractions, the property, now referred to as a museum, was open to the public for a fee. Seventeen-year-old Harle Hanson came to Belcourt Castle as one of its first tour guides, but became the young mistress of the house when she married Donald in 1960.

The Tinneys were a closely knit family who enjoyed working on their white elephant. If a stained-glass window needed to be repaired, they learned everything there was to know about stained glass until they became leading professionals in the field. Despite considerable capabilities, the Tinneys' talents didn't extend to plumbing, and every home—especially one the size of a castle—needed a dependable plumber. In 1974, an agreeable but unlicensed one named Kevin Koellisch reported to Belcourt for duty.

Koellisch was versatile and started taking care of odd jobs around the castle. The place was so big, and the work so constant, that it made sense to make him the resident handyman. Then, after Harold Tinney died in 1989, Koellisch assumed a disturbing new role. Though he claimed to have a "wonderful mother-and-son relationship" with the recently widowed Ruth Tinney, family members and friends feared that Koellisch was pretending to woo the bereaved woman, who was in her eighties. She started wearing youthful clothes and acting flirtatious, and she coyly referred to Kevin, a homosexual, as her "lover."

In time, their odd courtship took an even stranger turn. Ruth Tinney announced that she was adopting thirty-seven-year-old Kevin and that his name would be added to the Belcourt Castle deed. Donald and Harle objected, but there was no arguing with the smitten matriarch. When Ruth died in 1995, all hell broke loose.

There was no will. That was the first problem. And the more Kevin Tinney, as he now called himself, insisted that he deserved one third of "Mom's" $3.2 million legacy, the more Harle and Donald opposed his claim. Belcourt Castle became an armed camp, home to Newport's version of the Hatfields and the McCoys. The "siblings" lived on different floors in the same house, but fought constantly. "I'm a Tinney now, and I'm a Tinney for the rest of my life," insisted Kevin. "He's never been family in my heart," snapped Harle, "and his plumbing work wasn't that good either." He accused her of embezzling funds, and she responded with accusations of her own.

Although Kevin Tinney always claimed to love Belcourt Castle like a native son, he callously asked the court to force a sale so he could collect his share of the profits. The judge thought the better of his request, especially after Koellisch-Tinney's own mother was quoted as saying, "He'd sell his own name for a buck." Donald and Harle Tinney won the right to call Belcourt their castle, but Kevin Tinney promised he would take the case all the way to the Supreme Court, and it appeared that there would be many more installments in the sordid serial. There was something a little distasteful and low-rent about the Tinney debacle, despite the fact that it involved a Richard Morris Hunt cottage with a Bellevue Avenue address.

Newport was more appealing when it was synonymous with "rich," which is why the city became a popular venue for weddings. Getting married there was an extension of taking a mansion (no one used the term "cottage" anymore) tour. Parents and their children walked through Rosecliff, Beechwood, and even Belcourt Castle, imagining what life was like for the occupants of these fabulous homes. Weddings enabled them to actually live that life firsthand. On that special day, in one of those special places, albeit for a fee, every bride could be as good as Mrs. Astor's daughters. Courtesy of Camelot Gardens, the company that purchased Hammersmith Farm from the Auchincloss family in 1977, brides were able to rent the historic house and toss their bouquets from the exact spot where the newly married Jacqueline Kennedy stood on her wedding day.

Whether sightseeing or walking down the aisle, many visitors came to Newport to reenact the splendors of America's Gilded Age. Others saw the city and all that it represented as a trophy. Like the America's Cup, it was waiting to be claimed, and as the old millennium came to a close, some serious challengers were on the way.

On April 1, 1997, Newport Realtor Judy Chace sat in her office, trying to summon the energy to go home. She had been in a car accident that left her somewhat immobilized, so she had to wait for someone to give her a ride, and she was getting a little impatient. It was 9 p.m., time to turn off the lights, but when the telephone rang, Chace answered it. "Oh, halloo," said the heavily accented British voice on the other end of the line. "I'm calling from my lanai in the Bahamas." "Sure," she said to herself. "You're calling from an asylum—or a prison—in upstate New York." Ever since her real estate firm started advertising their high-end properties in magazines targeted at the rich, they received crank calls from convicts and lunatics with imaginary fortunes. The convicts generally revealed themselves by asking for floor plans, information they could put to good use upon their release. The crackpots were a little harder to identify, and this one sounded like he was up there with the best.

He told Chace that he was interested in a Bellevue Avenue listing called Vernon Court. Chace was an unusually erudite broker who knew the histories of all the great cottages in Newport, and Vernon Court was a beauty. The fourteen-thousand-square-foot residence was built in 1898 by Carrère and Hastings, the distinguished architects who designed the New York Public Library and the Henry Clay Frick house, and it had been further enhanced with a swimming pool and two tennis courts. The Gambrill family lived there until 1956. Later, when so many of Newport's best cottages turned into institutions, it became Vernon Court Junior College. The school closed in 1972 and subsequently the estate had several different owners. Now it was back on the market.

Chace patiently explained that there was already a $2.1 million offer on the table. Just to make conversation, she asked the caller when he planned on coming up to see the house. He told her that he was familiar with the property, didn't need to look at it, and was ready to act. "I'd like to buy it," he announced.

At that moment, Chace realized it was April 1, and she waited for the man (who was probably a friend playing a trick on her) to drop his phony accent and say "April Fool's!" Instead, he identified himself as Peter de Savary, the owner of Skibo Castle in Scotland. His offer was real—in fact, he raised the previous buyer's bid by $100,000—and he said he was willing to wire a cool $1 million into the seller's account with the understanding that the money was theirs even if the deal fell through. And by the way, he also asked if Chace knew of any other grand properties in the area. Peter de Savary, whoever he was, was on a shopping spree. It dawned on Chace that she was speaking to the buyer of her dreams, maybe the buyer of a lifetime. When she looked him up on the Internet (and subsequently watched him being interviewed on the television news program *Sixty Minutes*), she realized that de Savary was the real thing.

If Judy Chace hadn't answered the telephone that fateful April Fool's Day, she would have missed a call from a modern-day buccaneer who was as high-rolling and freewheeling as any of the Gilded Age tycoons. "PdeS," as he liked to be called, had more in common with the ambitious men who built Newport—the Astors, the Vanderbilts, the Goelets, and the Belmonts—than their complacent descendants who lived there today. He was the son of a British furniture maker, but he rejected the family business and, at age seventeen, set out to seek his fortune. He found it in Nigeria in the import-export business. The first $1 million was easy, but PdeS's career was like a roller-coaster ride, subject to extreme highs and lows. He'd make millions in oil trading and lose millions in oil refining, said the *New York Times* by way of illustrating the colorful Brit's financial vicissitudes.

In 1979 he opened the exclusive St. James Clubs, a chain of high-end private hotels in London, Paris, New York, Los Angeles, and Barbados. No matter where he hung his hat, PdeS was a citizen of the world. He first visited Newport in 1983, when he led the British sailing team in their challenge for the America's Cup. The team lost to *Australia II*, but PdeS spent enough time in Newport to know that he would be back someday.

He sold his clubs in 1990 and used the money to buy Skibo Castle in Sutherland, Scotland, the site of another de Savary "members only" venture. This purchase (a completely spontaneous move, he said) was especially meaningful to him because Skibo had been the home of Andrew Carnegie, the patron saint of the self-made man. Carnegie moved to America from Scotland when he was a child, built a fortune from railroads, steel, and iron, and used his "can do" philosophy to spur other would-be achievers on to success. PdeS demonstrated that same entrepreneurial spirit in his endeavors. Sometimes he made a fortune and sometimes he lost one, but he always moved on to the next opportunity. In 1997 that opportunity was Newport.

PdeS loved clubs. He understood the mentality of wanting to belong to a select group of like-minded people, and his clubs were founded on the principle that wealthy people will pay handsomely for the privilege of exclusive membership. The problem in Newport was that the old clubs were off-limits to most newcomers, regardless of the applicant's financial status. "Nobody buys their way into Newport," cautioned Eileen Slocum. There was the occasional exception, like the von Bulow family. But many rich aspirants packed up and left town after a few seasons simply because they couldn't get "in." The fact was that without a club life, there was not much to do in Newport. In this respect, nothing had changed in the past hundred years.

PdeS's solution was to introduce a new club to the city, and experience had taught him that to be successful, a club had to seem old, not be old. His plan was to transform historic Vernon Court into a private sanctuary for the visiting rich. He closed the deal on that house and two other lots in the area. And while he was at it, he bought Wildacre and Oakwood, two classic estates that he wanted to renovate. Wildacre had been the home of Albert H. Olmsted, brother of the famous landscape artist Frederick Law Olmsted, and Oakwood had belonged to a member of the Astor family. PdeS was not intimidated by the prospect of all that work because he was used to living in places he described as "large, old houses that have character and something to say." In fact, he found it exhilarating to give an old house new life. "Very often these properties have lost their way," he sentimentalized.

He was ready to roll up his sleeves and get to work, but he instantly ran into trouble with Vernon Court. The city's remaining Old Guard, and its New Old Guard, did not want strangers sleeping in their midst, even if they were strangers who could afford a posh bed at a high-class club. Zoning was denied. PdeS acknowledged temporary defeat and hatched a different plan.

He sold Vernon Court to art dealer Judy Goffman Cutler, whose specialty was American Illustration (a rapidly growing market that she helped to create), and her husband, Laurence Cutler, an architect and Harvard professor. They were looking for a place that could serve as both home and museum for their vast collection of illustrations, including important works by N. C. Wyeth, Norman Rockwell, and Maxfield Parrish.

The Cutlers returned Vernon Court to its former Beaux Arts splendor, displayed their magnificent art on its freshly painted walls, and proudly announced the opening of the National Museum of American Illustration. It was but a short distance from established Bellevue Avenue attractions such as Rosecliff and Beechwood (a venue for weddings, murder mystery tours, and performances featuring a cast of Astor re-enactors who pretended not to know about their *Titanic* future). Inexplicably, a group of influential Newporters expressed "concern" about the new, nonprofit museum's potential effect on the neighborhood. They spearheaded a movement to block the necessary zoning, and the Cutlers had to fight vigorously to win the right to open their meticulously restored French doors and gleaming marble halls to the public.

Meanwhile, in nearby Portsmouth, PdeS purchased undeveloped land from an abbey of Benedictine monks (right up the road from Alice Brayton's farm, now called Green Animals) and built Carnegie Abbey, a luxury retreat modeled after Skibo Castle. Its official address was Portsmouth, not Newport, but in this case, "Newport" was a state of mind. Prospective members were invited to join and, upon acceptance and an initiation fee ranging from $75,000 to $150,000, could purchase houses or condominiums on the grounds, play golf and tennis, ride horses, and sail, as if they were in residence at their very own castle. The buildings were shingled in the best Stanford White style, the clubhouse residences were outfitted like the interiors of luxury yachts, and the surrounding acreage appeared cultivated without seeming new. "It smacks of Old World," PdeS said proudly. The occasional dent or chip never bothered him because he knew that the club had to embrace elements of "shabby chic" for it to be truly aristocratic, just like those fading homes on Bellevue Avenue. Outside the main building, silhouetted by the bright blue waters of Narragansett Bay, was a statue of Andrew Carnegie, the club's namesake and guiding spirit.

It was a brilliant concept. The place was exclusive yet democratic, and authentically "aged" without being old. Bailey's Beachers might not have welcomed Carnegie Abbey members into their clubbiest of clubs because their money was too new. But given the lavish facilities at the Abbey and its seasoned charm, these "exiles" never had to feel as if they were missing out on anything. Their philosophy was that new money is better than no money at all, which actually could have served as an ideal motto for Alva Vanderbilt and her friends a hundred years earlier.

In 2004, Philadelphia real estate developer Brian O'Neill took over PdeS's "Newport" empire. Another larger-than-life, self-made man, O'Neill entered the world as one of six children in a closely knit Irish family. Like de Savary, O'Neill left home as a teenager and experienced various rags-to-riches adventures before finding his niche in real estate. "My parents didn't have enough money," he once told a reporter from *Philadelphia* magazine, "so I made money a priority early on in life." With success came more success, multiple homes, and an art collection. O'Neill was drawn to Newport because of its great history. He had big plans to play Vanderbilt to de Savary's Astor, or vice versa. When O'Neill announced his plan to erect the Newport Club, a multimillion-dollar marina with shops and restaurants in the vicinity of Carnegie Abbey, it certainly appeared as if the two tycoons were engaged in a round of contemporary "Vanderbuilding."

24

Everything Old Is New Again

In twenty-first-century Newport, everything old was new again. With the arrival of buccaneers such as de Savary and O'Neill came the start of a new Gilded Age and a renewed sense of *plus ça change, plus c'est la même chose* (the more things change, the more they remain the same). Ralph Carpenter, who was still one of Newport's most charismatic and knowledgeable elders, liked to boast that a time traveler from the seventeenth century would feel completely at home in today's Newport. Many of the Colonial streets and their restored houses would be familiar to him. He could peruse books at the original Redwood Library; ponder the still-debated origins of the Old Stone Mill; dine at the impeccably maintained White Horse Tavern; and, if he were contemplating eternity, get his gravestone carved by the very same Benson family at the John Stevens Shop.

So, too, could a time traveler from the nineteenth century pick up where he, or she, left off. There was still tennis at the casino;

swimming at Bailey's Beach (provided one was a member); golf at the Newport Country Club; and, courtesy of The Preservation Society and its regular galas, there was still dancing in the ballroom at The Breakers.

Many of the great houses built during the "cottage wars" had become official tourist attractions, or part of the ever-expanding campus at Salve Regina University. Daisy Van Alen Bruguiere's "properly run" English-style manse, Wakehurst, once the most formal household in all of Newport, was now the Wakehurst Student Center. Its exacting former owner, who died in 1969, might have objected to the fact that the black-tied guests who lined up promptly whenever she summoned them to a party had been replaced by casually dressed collegians clutching cups of coffee. A few blocks away, on Ruggles Avenue, the residents of an enormous dormitory called Carey Mansion knew that its ghostly exterior was featured in the 1960s soap opera *Dark Shadows*, but it may have escaped them that the building was originally Seaview Terrace, Edson Bradley's famous $2 million summer house.

The size of these cottages dictated that they were best utilized by institutions. The problem from the city's point of view was that the properties absorbed by Salve Regina University, like The Preservation Society's numerous holdings, were tax-exempt. Fortunately for Newport's coffers, some cottages were still privately held, and, in the 1990s, they were actually finding buyers.

As a rule, properties in Newport were less expensive than ones in Nantucket, Martha's Vineyard, and the Hamptons, so "for the rich, the giant 'cottages' of Newport" were "a relative bargain," suggested the *Wall Street Journal* in 1997. The word "bargain" was an exaggeration, but it was true that a multimillion-dollar price tag in Newport was likely to dangle from a house that had a ballroom, bedrooms galore, a lot of history, and a name all its own. Whenever a cottage went on the market, its story was an important part of the sales pitch, and with good reason. Many of the buyers were entrepreneurs born of the New Gilded Age, and, like their nineteenth-century predecessors, when they bought, they bought big and they bought old. They wanted an immediate connection to the past, and in a funny way, if a house belonged to an Astor or a Vanderbilt, some of its former grandeur would trickle down to the owner who lived there today.

That was certainly the case with Hammersmith Farm, which sold twice in two years. In 1997, the first buyer paid $6,675,000 for the real-life "Camelot" where the Kennedys vacationed and enjoyed some of their happiest times. But the new owner had difficulty working visits to the house into his busy agenda, so he sold it in 1999 for $8.25 million. Both owners insisted that they bought the national treasure to preserve its integrity and save it from developers.

The property adjacent to Hammersmith Farm—the one that had been a candidate for the Kennedy summer White House— also retained a lingering touch of the Camelot mystique, even though the Kennedys never actually lived there. The white stucco mansion at Annandale Farm (or Armsea, as it used to be called) was demolished in 1969, but its memory was kept alive by author Peter George Markwith, who wrote *Whatever Happened at Annandale Farm?*, a fanciful mystery that added a Newport-based conspiracy theory to the long list of Kennedy assassination "what ifs?"

Aquidneck's luxury real estate market received a big boost in 2000, when Mark Levin, the CEO of Millennium Pharmaceuticals in Massachusetts, and his wife, Becky Ruhmann Levin, paid a handsome $10.85 million for Gray Craig, the estate where Oliver Belmont housed his menagerie in the 1890s and the setting for the Social Strategy Board's first party. As was the case in Belmont's day, the Levins maintained peacocks who roamed freely around their twenty-six-acre property.

In 2004, Boston businessman Daniel Meyers spent $10.3 million for Jimmy and Candy Van Alen's forty-five-acre oceanside estate, Avalon. But there was nothing historical about this property. It was one of those contempo, hacienda designs that somehow managed to look outdated even when it was brand-new. After the Van Alens died, their house suffered further indignity when it developed a bad case of black mold. Meyers fell in love with the property's unmatched view of the ocean, but he had no use for its ugly wreck of a house. Avalon was just an expensive tear-down, and he planned to replace it with a stone-and-slate design that would be authentically Newport.

Miramar, the legendary thirty-thousand-square-foot French neoclassical castle George Widener commissioned before his ill-fated crossing on the *Titanic*, made headlines all over the world when, in 2006, it sold for a record-breaking $17 million. Newspapers ran an aerial photograph of the gated estate and enumerated its many charms, including 7.8 landscaped acres bordered by Bellevue Avenue and the Atlantic Ocean; a spectacular four-thousand-square-foot terrace overlooking the water; vast salons with sixteen-foot ceilings and marble fireplaces; twenty-seven bedrooms, some with curved doors and exquisitely built rooms-within-rooms; and a ten-thousand-bottle wine cellar outfitted with a special cement trough that could ice two hundred bottles of bubbly at the same time.

There was great drama surrounding the sale because the buyer was unidentified. "Do you know who bought Miramar?" was the most frequently asked question in Newport right after the story broke. "Everyone would like to know," said a curious City Council member who, despite connections and serious snooping, couldn't uncover any information. A real estate agent who had attempted to sell the house two years earlier noted that good buyers could be very hard to find at the high end of the market because a property such as Miramar required a much larger investment than its purchase price. There was staffing, maintenance, giant property taxes, and an infinite number of unforeseen details to address. That's why these limestone giants were called white elephants.

But Miramar had found a very good buyer indeed. And his greatest virtue wasn't his obviously sizable bank account; it was his vision. Financier and philanthropist David B. Ford, the mystery man who proffered the winning $17 million bid, cherished Miramar's past and believed in its future. He and his fiancée, Pamela Fielder, moved in, little dogs and all, and mounted a siege against the ravages of time. In came the experts, some straight from Versailles; up went three stories of scaffolding; and down came Miramar's signature iron gates, which were sent to a specialist in New Jersey for a two-year refurbishment. Thus the painfully slow process of a "scientific" restoration began. Ford was not interested in giving the house a superficial face-lift. What he had in mind was a total resurrection. The couple was so enthusiastic about the undertaking that when they hosted a cocktail party in August 2008, they distributed commemorative hard hats to their three hundred guests. The scaffolding stood proudly in the background—not an eyesore, but a symbol of Ford's commitment to the cause.

In 2007, Gray Craig became the subject of great speculation when, after seven years of renovating and redecorating, the Levins put their estate on the market, and it was rumored that a movie star was the prospective buyer. The moment the name Nicolas Cage was bandied about, the Academy Award–winning actor became Newport's version of Waldo, as in "Where's Waldo?" a popular children's game that required sharp-eyed players to locate the character's image in a challenging visual landscape. Cage was spotted everywhere, and with such frequency, that it had to be wishful thinking on the observer's part. According to the daily rumors, Cage was at the pizza parlor, by the wharf, in the supermarket, and on the campuses of schools he was supposedly considering for his son.

Bogus sightings aside, Cage was Gray Craig's buyer. He paid $15.7 million for the secluded country estate. Like Gertrude Niesen, the singer who told reporters that "our family kind of collects houses" when her mother purchased Rosecliff in 1941, Cage owned residences all over the world, including an island in the Bahamas, a castle in England, and a fairy-tale Bavarian *schloss*. The first indication that his latest acquisition had gone Hollywood was that it was approved for a private helicopter landing pad. Now no one would be able to track the star's comings and goings.

That same summer, The Ledges, the majestic Cushing house that photographer Slim Aarons found so captivating in the 1960s, was prominently featured in the movie *Evening*, which boasted an all-star cast led by Clare Danes, Vanessa Redgrave, and Meryl Streep. The centerpiece of the story was a 1950s wedding that changed the life of a young, impressionable bridesmaid, played by Danes. When the characters gathered on the Cushing lawn, with the house and the sea in the background, they immediately brought to mind Jonas Mekas's pioneering footage of the Minnie Cushing–Peter Beard wedding in 1969. In both films, the house stole the show.

Evening's set designers had very little to do to get The Ledges ready for its close-up. That's because the house had excellent "bones," and its interiors had been refreshed by Newport's busiest tastemaker (and most in-demand "extra" man), John Peixinho. A "Don't Miss Movie Décor," raved *US Weekly*'s Thelma Adams in a blog describing the house's rich wall colors, muted fabrics, and "grand, old wasp money, luxe cottage look." That was the essence of Newport style, and Peixinho was a decorator who could deliver it classically, but always with an imaginative twist. Subtle was his specialty. "You don't want to change it so you don't recognize it," he said of the rooms that were his projects. He enhanced interiors, but without gilding any lilies. "Nobody does it better," was the consensus among Peixinho's existing—and aspiring—clients, guaranteeing that his dance card was always full.

The cottages that were not privately owned generated a literal cottage industry for Newport. The Newport Bridge, now called the Claiborne Pell Bridge, after the famous Rhode Island senator, allowed tourists to enter the city with ease—too easily, if you asked the club crowd. "Everything changed when they built the bridge," complained one trust fund baby who was way too young to remember life before the bridge. But it was an enduring topic of conversation in old, insider circles. The Chamber of Commerce estimated that three million visitors came to Newport every year. In July 2008, The Preservation Society proudly announced that it had hosted its thirty-millionth "guest," meaning that thirty million people had bought tickets to its houses. This "little engine that could" organization surpassed the wildest dreams of its small band of organizers, those eleven dedicated Newporters who gathered in Katherine Warren's living room in 1945.

The "guest," or tourist, was so important to the city's economic well-being that in the spring of 2007, Newport dusted off a program from 1963. Operation Appreciation had been a semiannual, one-day training session for workers who were on the hospitality front lines. "You and the gas station attendants have more to do with the success of the tourist industry than anyone else," the executive director of The Preservation Society told a group of waitresses at the time. Many of them were demure and respectful navy wives. Along with businessmen, bus drivers, bellboys, and policemen, they were taught the basics of hospitality because, in the 1960s, tourism was rapidly becoming Newport's most important industry, and they all had a vested interest in protecting it.

Forty-four years later, the Chamber of Commerce launched a new hospitality initiative with the same objective—to give tourists a positive experience. Workers were instructed to be courteous, even if they were directing tourists to the city's hard-to-find public bathrooms, a question that came up with annoying frequency. "You don't have to be toothy nice," emphasized an exasperated city councilman who was having trouble getting his point across to indifferent college students who were working summer jobs. "You just have to be polite, for heaven's sake."

The Newport visitor who decided to spend the night had choices that would have surprised Ralph Carpenter's time traveler. There were big hotels, including the Viking, the Hyatt Regency, and the Marriott, as well as small boutique operations with interesting ties to the past. Once again, scrappy con man Nathan Fleischer proved he was ahead of his time. In the 1940s, he believed that the Chanler house on the Cliff Walk was the perfect setting for a hotel, but he was unable to make a go of it because he was not permitted to serve alcohol. Today, there was a new Chanler Hotel, and it had luxurious bedrooms, a gourmet restaurant, and the elegant bar Fleischer was desperate to open, features that made it a popular destination for tourists and locals.

Fleischer was also ahead of the curve on the "Beatrice" business. With his dramatic son et lumière presentation and his talk of egosexia, Fleischer tried to turn poor, lonely Beatrice Turner and her eccentric paintings into a post-Freudian peep show. But she was much more marketable in her new incarnation as the resident muse of a high-end bed-and-breakfast called the Cliffside Inn. Winthrop Baker, a retired television executive, was shopping for an inn to buy as a gentleman's hobby when he came across Beatrice's former residence, which had become a modest B and B. The house itself was unremarkable, but one of Beatrice's paintings was hanging on the wall. The moment Baker set eyes on it, he fell under the artist's spell. He bought the inn in 1989 and set out on the great Beatrice quest, determined to locate her canvases.

By 1992 he had found thirty-three works by Beatrice—or, more to the point, they found him. People called Cliffside with reports of sightings, and a large stash turned up in Newport. Two locals had found them on a city street, tossed in the garbage by someone who was storing them for Nathan Fleischer. Baker was inspired to turn his inn into a monument to the elegant lifestyle Beatrice enjoyed as a young woman. Guests could relax on the porch, indulge in a sumptuous high tea, and walk up the stairs that Beatrice climbed to the very room where she slept. And her paintings—or copies of her paintings—were everywhere. With the publicity sparked by Cliffside's opening, and a biography written by Sheldon Bart, Beatrice and her art finally achieved the acceptance and fame she was denied in her lifetime.

There was still an intellectual Newport, once the province of Henry James, Julia Ward Howe, and other famous thinkers, and signs of it were evident in the dining room of Ronald Lee Fleming, an urban planner, preservationist, and all-around man-of-the-arts. He enjoyed hosting classic, Gosford Park–like evenings at his home, Bellevue House, a Colonial Revival mansion, which, not surprisingly, was on Bellevue Avenue. It was built in 1910 by Ogden Codman Jr., the architect who coauthored with Edith Wharton the groundbreaking interior design bible *The Decoration of Houses*. Ogden's cousin Martha Codman lived there for years with her husband, Maxim Karolik, the colorful art enthusiast, and the next owner was Jane Pickens Langley, the singer who congratulated herself for allowing her servants to use the telephone.

Fleming bought the house in 1999, and it became a setting for good times and lively meetings of the mind. One of these dinners took place on St. Patrick's Day in 2007. Fleming invited a group of friends and acquaintances to dress in black tie and gather for cocktails in his living room. For his carefully curated guests, the price of admission was their ability to engage in spirited conversation, and once seated at his massive dining table, they were expected to "sing" for their supper. Fleming took the time to introduce each guest to the rest of the group with a few well-chosen words. Then he posed several provocative questions to spark conversation during dinner.

After the meal, Fleming observed the quaint old custom of separating the ladies from the gentlemen, at which time the men were presented with another topic for discussion. "What is the meaning of place?" Fleming asked, although he was cheating a bit with that particular question, having just authored *The Art of Placemaking: Interpreting Community through Public Art and Design*. An animated debate ensued until the wee hours, and everyone went home well fed, sleepy, and a little smarter.

The conversation at parties was not always so elevated. Newport was, after all, the first place in America to have a newspaper that ran a regular gossip column. And during the Gilded Age, the city was a bottomless pit of information for the unscrupulous Colonel Eugene Mann, who printed blind items in his tabloid, *Town Topics*. These same blind items were just as popular today, although usually in the form of conversation. Newporters were often reluctant to disclose the identities of the people they discussed. And there was a virtual gag order imposed on anything that had to do with the goings-on at Bailey's Beach.

What faded beauty was trying to keep a stiff upper lip even though she was indigent and two steps away from being homeless? Which gentleman always crashed the best parties and hurriedly gave his car to the valet, knowing his hostess would never make a fuss after the vehicle had been parked? Which Bellevue Avenue matron prompted the powers-that-be at Bailey's Beach to start locking the cabanas because she was pocketing other members' possessions? The names really didn't matter. Sometimes the items were true, other times they were apocryphal. But there were so many lunches, dinners, and parties to get through during the season that a little gossip helped to pass the time.

There were modern-day Newporters who were engaged in more noble pursuits, and one of them was Dorrance "Dodo"

Hill Hamilton, the owner of the mysterious-sounding SVF Foundation. Hamilton's name was familiar to those who read the annual *Forbes* list of America's billionaires. Her sizable fortune came from Campbell's Soup, the family business. Hamilton was known for her philanthropic activities—she donated tens of millions of dollars to hospitals, schools, and charities. But her SVF Foundation, on the site of the former Arthur Curtiss James estate, may have been Newport's most unusual preservation project.

Bryan C. Jones, a reporter for the *Providence Phoenix*, called SVF "Jurassic Park on Ocean Drive," while George Saperstein, the chair of the Department of Environmental and Population Health at Tufts University (and the scientific director of SVF), said the foundation was a "gift to mankind." What was going on at the old Swiss Village to inspire these odd comments?

In 1913, Mrs. Arthur Curtiss James, the former chatelaine of the Swiss Village, used her bottomless bank account to mount The Masque of the Blue Garden, the party that enchanted Newport and knocked Mamie Fish's nose out of joint. But its current owner, Dodo Hamilton, had different plans for her money. She was using it to save the world. The new Swiss Village was home to a scientific facility funded by Hamilton "to preserve germplasm (embryos, semen, and genetic material) of rare and endangered breeds of livestock." These carefully stored samples would come in very handy in the future if, through disease or disaster, the world lost a popular breed of animal. SVF could rush to the rescue with the genetic material of a hardy Dutch belted cow, or a Tennessee fainting goat, to shore up the food chain.

Not that twenty-first-century Newport was all work and no play. The aforementioned Hamilton accomplished a feat that may have been more difficult than saving the world. In 2007 she managed to open a new club in Newport. She and three partners built Forty 1° North, a state-of-the-art marina and waterfront restaurant named after Newport's latitude. Though it was in the heart of the city's busy Thames Street area, a location best known for its jumble of T-shirt and fudge vendors, the complex was elegant and serene because its owners had come up with a way to keep all those noisy and unsightly tourists at bay. They charged a "Guest Program" fee, $550 for the entire season, or $350 for a week. Part of that fee rolled over into a credit at the restaurant, but the members-only policy prevented the hoi polloi from walking in off the street. Forty 1° North may not have been as exclusive as Bailey's Beach, but it was a club nonetheless, and it drew a young and attractive crowd.

Old or young, Newporters were every bit as athletically minded as they had been in the past. Even beauty-parlor-coiffed matrons managed to shoot skeet at The Clambake Club, whack croquet balls, and play a round of golf or tennis (and sometimes both) without breaking a sweat. Polo, a beloved pastime in Newport in the nineteenth century, was back, and bigger than ever. Dan Keating, a former U.S. luge team member and an aficionado of extreme sports, tried his hand at polo in the 1980s. He loved it so much that it became a full-time pursuit for him. In 1991, Keating and his wife, Agnes (a couple so good-looking that they could have walked straight out of a Ralph Lauren advertisement), asked the town of Portsmouth for a ten-year lease on Glen Farm, a fifty-acre spread. For their part, the Keatings would restore the farm's dilapidated buildings and transform its grounds into an equestrian center for the island and a home for international polo matches.

It took twenty-one truckloads of sod and relentless determination on the Keatings' part to accomplish their goal. The Newport Polo Club was not the biggest draw in the beginning—maybe two hundred spectators showed up on a good day. But the matches developed a real following, and, in time, the "usual" crowd watching the team play against opponents from England, Ireland, France, Spain, and Argentina was two thousand strong. Pass-the-bottle-and-the-chips tailgates turned into proper parties catered by enthusiastic foodies who set tables with linens and floral centerpieces.

The sporting event that was unlikely to return to Newport was the America's Cup race. The New York Yacht Club was alive and well and headquartered at Harbor Court, the former home of John Nicolas Brown, and Newport was still considered one of the best places in the world to sail. But in terms of bringing back the cup, the water wasn't the problem. In 2007, Valencia, Spain, the host city of the thirty-second America's Cup (sponsored by Louis Vuitton), accommodated 5.7 million visitors. The supersized event had become big business, too big for quaint little Newport. There was no room for the multiple challengers, spectator boats, and super yachts. Nor was there an infrastructure to support the crowds who needed hotel rooms and restaurants. For Newport, the golden age of the America's Cup was truly over.

Happily, a tradition that would never die was the fine art of entertaining. Whether it was the summer of 1913 or the summer of 2008, Newporters lived for their parties. There was one bachelor who reverently tallied his invitations the way Silas Marner counted his coins—they were that important. Some parties were so big ("cattle calls," as they were dismissed by insiders) that they didn't require a thank-you note, and others so small that only the lucky attendees knew they were taking place. There were dinners and dances, and galas and barbecues, and bridge parties and, of course, weddings. Once again this summer, people were finding that Newport's season promised to break all records for gaiety.

25

The Season

2008

While the Newport season no longer required a woman to change her clothes a dozen times a day, or to go into purdah to dye her hair red, it was challenging for today's cottagers to keep up with the breakneck pace of a weekend in high summer. Saturday, July 12, 2008, was a perfect example. There were three high-wattage parties scheduled for that night—two gala fund-raisers and one private birthday bash. The Newport Art Museum was hosting "A Summer Soiree" honoring local artist Richard Grosvenor. There was "A New Launch," the International Yacht Restoration School's annual gala. And behind the gates at Seafair on Ocean Drive, Rick Bready was getting ready to blow out his birthday candles with two hundred friends. There were other events, too (ever-popular John Peixinho had three entries in his datebook for that night, and not one of these aforementioned parties figured into his plans). So many invitations, so little time.

It made perfect sense for the Newport Art Museum to honor Richard Grosvenor and to celebrate his body of work with the exhibition "Richard Grosvenor: Newport's Muse and Mentor." His paintings, watercolors, and drawings captured the city's beauty, grace, and spirit. Grosvenor believed that art was pure pleasure. "It's what you see, what you feel, what you smell," he told the *Newport Daily News*.

He shared that philosophy with his classes when he was an art teacher at St. George's School. Grosvenor was a big fan of plein air painting, and he liked to take his students out into the world. One day they found themselves standing precariously on the unfinished Newport Bridge. Even Grosvenor was a little nervous when the wind started gusting so hard that one of the wispy, long-haired coeds looked as if she might blow away. But he believed it was the kind of experience that inspired good art.

Grosvenor's museum tribute aspired to be as unique as its honoree. Guests were invited to dress in "creative black tie" instead of the usual monkey suit. Consequently, it was a night of colors and patterns, and one very eccentric caftan, worn by a man. Grosvenor made a short and witty speech to his 350 admirers, ending with a poem modeled after Dr. Seuss. The evening raised $250,000 for the museum.

Newport's International Yacht Restoration School (IYRS) held its gala in its very own Restoration Hall, a historic waterfront building filled with classic wooden yachts in various stages of restoration. This was where IYRS students (an assortment of college kids, midlifers looking to change careers, and retirees with too much time on their hands) were taught the age-old craft of restoring and maintaining boats and their systems. IYRS's skilled enthusiasts had restored nearly a hundred boats since the school's opening, and at the time of the gala they were hard at work rebuilding the *Coronet*, a historic schooner once owned by Arthur Curtiss James. According to IYRS cofounder John Mecray, the plan was to restore the *Coronet* to "its full Gilded Age splendor," which meant using original materials and techniques.

In 2008, IYRS joined forces with Newport's Museum of Yachting, and turned to trustees Joe Dockery and Carol O'Malley to orchestrate a fund-raiser for the newly aligned institutions. Under the best of circumstances, in robust financial markets, hosting a profitable event was a Sisyphean task. But in 2008's "bust" economy, charity seemed to begin—and end—at home. "Slump Means Less Glitz Per Gala in the Hamptons" wrote the *New York Times* regarding the uncertain fate of fund-raisers in New York's wealthy resort. Organizers who depended on lavish support from rich East Enders saw a marked fall in ticket sales, the article said. Worse still, wealthy sponsors such as Lexus declined the very branding opportunities they once courted, leaving charities holding the bag for their own expenses. If tickets to music impresario Russell Simmons's Art for Life gala, a Hamptons evening honoring big celebrities such as P. Diddy, Ed Burns and Christy Turlington, and Aretha Franklin, were selling at a snail's pace, what hope was there for A New Launch, an event to raise money for yacht restoration in Newport?

Even in a sea of economic downturns, it turned out that IYRS was sitting pretty. In 2007 their annual gala raised an impressive $650,000, and this year, the ambitious cochairs hoped to break that record. Lexus, Sentient Jet Membership, Condé Nast, and Castello delle Regine, a vineyard in Italy, eagerly signed on as sponsors, and the busy hosts assembled a collection of auction items guaranteed to raise paddles high in the air. One of the most coveted prizes was an outing on the *Puma*, a lightning-fast seventy-foot boat skippered by sailing superstar Ken Read. The charismatic veteran of two America's Cup campaigns (in 2000 and in 2003) and Rolex's twice-named Yachtsman of the Year, Read was a living legend in the sailing set. He and his all-star crew were even more newsworthy at the time of the gala, because they were prepping for the grueling, year-long Volvo Ocean Race, a sailing trek that would take them thirty-seven thousand miles from Alicante, Spain, to St. Petersburg, Florida.

Ken Read was at the party, along with Newport's own sailing superstar Jerry Kirby, and America's Cup Hall of Famer Gary Jobson. Kirby was a world-class sailor with a reputation for skill, audacity, dedication, and vision—qualities that carried him through seven America's Cup challenges. When he wasn't at sea, Kirby was a partner in Kirby-Perkins Construction, a company that built some of the most expensive—and expansive—projects in Newport. On any given day, the ruggedly handsome individual-ist, a figure right out of Hemingway, wore at least two hats, and wore them better than anyone else.

Kirby grew up in Newport, but ironically, his family didn't own a boat. When he was fourteen, he developed a passion for sailing and hung around the *Intrepid* during the America's Cup races in 1970. Finally someone took pity on him and gave him a job as a boat boy. Somehow Kirby managed to sustain a surf-and-turf existence for the next thirty-eight years, participating in important boat races all over the globe at the same time that he stayed in the construction business and maintained a home life with his family.

The most revelatory (and oft-repeated) story about Jerry Kirby concerned a race he almost missed. According to local lore, Kirby was speeding across the Newport Bridge, late for a race he was supposed to be in with his old friend and fellow sail-ing dynamo Mike Toppa. As he was driving, it occurred to him that there was a daring shortcut he could take. Kirby pulled over, parked his car, studied the sailboats on the horizon, and, recog-nizing the one he was meant to be on, jumped ten stories into the water to meet it. Toppa saw the crazy man leaping from the bridge and, based on past experience, figured it was Kirby. He swung his boat around and picked up his buddy from the water. In Hollywood's version of the story, he would have asked Kirby,

"What took you so long?" Kirby was Puma's bowman, and a celebrity in Newport and every other port of the sailing world.

The presence of larger-than-life figures such as Kirby, Read, and Jobson (a veritable Holy Trinity for sailing aficionados) magnetized the IYRS gala crowd and worked them into a spending frenzy. During the auction, the *Puma* outing went for $6,500, and there was fierce bidding on other items, such as a vacation at the Castello delle Regine vineyard and a Sentient Jet card. By the end of the evening, IYRS had raised $660,000, which was $10,000 more than the previous year's total. The Hamptons may have been in a slump, but Newport was still fertile fund-raising ground. When asked how the organization was able to reach such a miraculous number, cochair Carol O'Malley pointed out that the gala attracted enthusiastic sponsors because they knew that moneyed IYRS supporters could easily afford to buy a Lexus or a Sentient Jet card. And if the fate of a classic yacht struck someone as an unlikely cause for a fund-raiser, O'Malley suggested that a sail on one might correct that impression.

The words "location, location, location" come to mind at the sight of Seafair, the magnificent, crescent-shaped Louis XIV château that was the setting for Rick Bready's birthday bash that July 12. The house's fieldstone walls and mansard roof suggested nothing less than a formal dwelling in France's château country. But the panoramic vista behind the cottage—Newport's Atlantic Ocean in all of its wild glory—gave Seafair a breathtaking drama all its own.

In 1936, architect William McKenzie designed the house to sit regally on its very own peninsula, and the unusual setting offered spectacular, wraparound views of the sea . . . but at a price. Seafair was so vulnerable to extreme weather that it quickly became known as the Hurricane Hut. The 1938 hurricane battered the house with punishing winds, forcing terrified dinner guests to crawl across the roof to the less imperiled side of the building. The owners were so unnerved by the experience that they abandoned their home for safer quarters.

Seafair's next owners, the William Van Alens, looked death in the face during Hurricane Carol in 1954. Van Alen hastily filled two cars with family and servants, hoping to escape to the higher, more protected grounds of nearby Avalon, his brother's home. But the storm surged suddenly, separating the two cars. The one carrying the servants vanished. Van Alen and his butler survived but ended up in the water, fighting for their lives. The butler proved his mettle by coolly asking his employer if he happened to have a dry cigarette and a light. If they were facing death, they might as well enjoy one last smoke, he said. Fortunately, they were rescued. Another casualty of a Seafair storm was a statue of a peacock that graced a walled garden. Despite the fact that it was made of lead, the four-foot beauty was swept away by angry waves and was seemingly lost forever.

The house changed hands a few times, only to meet a crueler fate in 1986 than anything a hurricane might have wrought. Developers began carving Seafair into six condominiums and removed all its interesting architectural details. Fortunately, the project ran out of money and came to a screeching halt. Even better news for the house was the involvement of Newport Collaborative Architects, a local firm that was experienced in bringing beautiful old homes back to life. In came partner John Grosvenor, the son of artist Richard Grosvenor (and a talented artist in his own right), who set about restoring the once-graceful flow of the house and its wonderful details.

Apparently the long-lost peacock approved of Grosvenor's work. According to Bettie Bearden Pardee in her book *Private Newport*, Seafair's former owner, the one who lovingly positioned the statue in her garden, returned to the house for a visit in the 1990s, after its restoration. She was shocked to see a four-foot lead peacock—*her* four-foot lead peacock—standing in the garden, as if it had never left. When she asked the new owners where they had found it, they told her "it was thrown up on the lawn during a storm."

The new millennium brought new millionaires to Seafair. They were Rick and Cheryl Bready, a high-profile couple from Providence. He was the phenomenally successful head of Nortek, a manufacturer and distributor of building products, and she was a restaurateur who owned several popular eating establishments in Rhode Island. Their first encounter was the stuff of classic movie romances. At the time, Cheryl Roberts was a newly divorced mother of two young children who faced an uncertain future. Resolving not to despair, she accepted a friend's invitation to a party at a local country club. Rick, who was exiting a troubled marriage, saw Cheryl across the proverbial crowded room and immediately walked over to her. "Who are you?" he asked. "Who are you?" she replied. Ten whirlwind days later, on an oddly tropical night in October, Rick proposed. Cheryl accepted so matter-of-factly that he wondered if she had heard him correctly. She had. And she told herself that marrying Rick Bready would be her greatest adventure, or her biggest nightmare. As is the case with most successful relationships, it was a little bit of both.

From that moment on, their future was charmed. When Nortek was bought by a private equity firm in 2004, the company rewarded Rick Bready, its cost-trimming, revenue-boosting CEO, with a multimillion-dollar golden parachute and the right to stay on as chief, leading one business journalist to quip that Bready was able to have his cake and eat it, too. But the Breadys put their good fortune to good use. Both Rick and Cheryl were tireless philanthropists.

Rick had always been sentimental about Newport, and he was quick to fall in love with Seafair. He and Cheryl planned on using it as a retreat, but they were also enthusiastic hosts who envisioned sharing their spectacular seaside surroundings with their family and friends. Rick grew up in an Irish Catholic household in Boston as one of five children. When he wanted something, he had to reach for it and reach fast, or he would come away empty-handed. Birthdays were often overlooked in a family where there were so many vying for attention, so Cheryl promised herself that Rick's special day would never again be forgotten.

One year, she staged a masked ball at Mrs. Astor's Beechwood. Most guests arrived wearing fanciful masks, but Cheryl had commissioned extras, all bearing Rick's face. When the birthday boy walked into the room, he was greeted by multiple versions of himself. In 2004, Cheryl invited over a hundred Bready friends to Seafair to celebrate Rick's sixtieth. Typically, this kind of party might include a dj or a doo-wop band, a corny video with biographical highlights, and perhaps some really good cake. But there was nothing typical about the Bready celebration.

At Seafair, a small army of workers erected a state-of-the-art tent and built a stage on top of the tennis court. One day, surprised neighbors watched as an unusual delivery was airlifted onto the lawn. It was a very precious piano, accompanied by a very alert guard. They both belonged to the singer Elton John, who incredibly was slated to be the entertainment at Rick's party. Cheryl was so excited that she couldn't stop herself from reaching out and touching the piano keys just for a second, while the accommodating guard looked the other way.

The night of the party, Cheryl and Rick's guests gathered in the tent and rocked to such favorites as "Bennie and the Jets" and "Philadelphia Freedom." Transported by the music, they sang, they clapped, they swayed, they danced. All the while, oblivious motorists rode past on Ocean Drive. Most of them admired the view, but they never suspected that Sir Elton John was performing a few hundred feet away.

People talked about the-night-that-Elton-John-played-at-Rick-Bready's-birthday-party until the event reached folkloric proportions. Then, in the summer of 2008, a new rumor circulated that superseded all talk about Elton John. Cheryl was staging another big birthday party for Rick, and this time the musical mystery guest would be . . . Like the cat who swallowed the canary, Cheryl refused to divulge the entertainer's identity. Keeping it secret was part of the fun. There was one question on everyone's mind. Who could top Elton John?

Few of Cheryl's invitees turned down the invitation, which specified that Seafair's gates would close promptly at six thirty. A steady stream of cars—many of them snappy convertibles—paused patiently while a policeman directed traffic and a black-suited security guard carefully checked names against a master list. A fleet of valets welcomed the guests as they pulled up to the house. Inside, a relaxed Rick Bready stood at the top of the stairs, warmly greeting each new arrival. He was comfortably attired in shorts, a loose shirt, and sandals, a respite from his daily bespoke suit.

During a festive round of cocktails and hors d'oeuvres, 220 men and women of all ages, many of them the Breadys' oldest and closest friends, such as Rose Mastrati and Tommy and Barbara Paolino, a university head, some business buddies, and only two or three people from Newport (including one very tall and striking Cushing), gathered on the patio behind the house. It was the best vantage point for Seafair's panoramic view of the Atlantic. When Cheryl asked everyone to go to the tent, there were no stragglers. The big moment—or "the reveal," in the parlance of television reality shows—had arrived.

The big black piano was a dead giveaway. Cheryl, stunning in white, stepped out on the stage, thanked all the people who had worked so hard to make the evening possible, and welcomed the one-and-only "piano man." Billy Joel entered, embraced his hostess, and sat down at his piano, flyswatter in hand, to join his band in a lively rendition of "My Life."

A little context: that very morning, Billy Joel was the cover story of the *New York Times* Arts & Leisure section. Journalist Dan Barry reported that when fifty thousand tickets went on sale for the singer's July 16 concert at New York City's soon-to-be-demolished Shea Stadium, they sold out in exactly forty-eight minutes. An additional show was set for Friday, July 18. Those tickets sold out in forty-six minutes. Joel ranked an impressive sixth on the list of top-selling artists of all time, "behind the Beatles and Elvis Presley but ahead of Elton John and Barbra Streisand," according to Barry. Billy Joel was one of the biggest stars in the history of modern music, and here he was performing at a private birthday party in Newport. It was a true, new Gilded Age moment. Just as Mamie Fish, Tessie Oelrichs, and Alva Vanderbilt Belmont spared no expense in importing world-class talent to their Newport parties, the Breadys continued the tradition by bringing in Billy Joel at the very pinnacle of his popularity.

He was worth every penny. Joel was in top form—relaxed, amusing (even a little risqué), and dedicated to pleasing his very appreciative audience, who couldn't quite believe that the real Billy Joel was *thisclose*. Playing on lyrics of one of his more famous songs, he joked about being in "a Newport state of mind," and encouraged the guests to get up and dance, which they did, especially when he played "Tell Her about It" and "Only the Good Die Young." They were joined by flashy "facilitators" who danced up and down the aisles, performing carefully choreographed moves and encouraging others to follow suit.

Joel played for almost two hours and ended the set with an impassioned rendition of "Piano Man." He received a standing ovation. The concert was finished, but the evening was far from over. The party continued in grand style in yet another tent, where there was a lively band and two singers. The pool, beautiful by day, was covered with ice sculptures that replicated the New York City skyline. In addition to looking dramatic, the decorations were extremely practical because they prevented people from falling into the water.

Guests drank cocktails from a martini bar and feasted on a buffet of lobster tails and prime ribs. Cheryl was so distracted that she missed the food and ducked into the kitchen to down a quick English muffin with cream cheese. No one had a better time than Rick, who reminisced about past birthdays. Buster, the Bready cockapoo, also seemed to enjoy himself. He confidently circled the tables, pausing to greet guests, as he had done so many times before.

The next day, even the most seasoned partygoers searched for opportunities to bring up Billy Joel's name, so they could talk about their fabulous night at the Breadys'.

As for the guests who attended the other parties that Saturday night, after the donations were tallied and the dress clothes put away, Newporters were contemplating their next round of activities. There was sure to be a party or two, followed by dinner at the Clambake Club or that nice Sunday night buffet at Bailey's Beach, the same choices that had been available to their parents and perhaps their parents' parents as well.

Afterword

On July 27, 2008, Eileen Slocum, Newport's most visible bridge to its Gilded past, died peacefully at age ninety-two. Her passing was significant for all the obvious reasons. She was a beloved mother, grandmother, and great-grandmother. She was a lifelong Newporter who wholeheartedly embraced the grandest of that city's traditions. And she was a passionate and tireless supporter of the Republican Party. But what did Eileen Slocum mean to me? She was one of my first interviews, and the outspoken matron who so quickly and enthusiastically rejected my Truman Capote book when I attempted to present it to her. At the time I pondered the question "Was she rude?"

That was two years ago, and the fact that I even raised the point was as clear an indication that I was a Newport outsider as was my inappropriate use of the word "mansion" when I was a child. Real Newporters knew that Mrs. Slocum spoke her mind. At her dignified and intensely personal funeral service at

Trinity Church on a picture-perfect Saturday in early August, one of Mrs. Slocum's grandsons spoke of her most famous character trait. Sherman Scott Powell, the son of Beryl Slocum and Adam Clayton Powell III, said admiringly, "You always knew where you stood with my grandma."

Another grandson (Mrs. Slocum had a seemingly endless supply of smart, eloquent progeny) recalled that family members, regardless of their age, were expected to be knowledgeable about current affairs whenever they sat at her table. Furthermore, they had to be prepared to express—and defend—their opinions. Mrs. Slocum was training future generations to speak their minds.

Sometimes, Powell noted, actions spoke louder than words. When Newport was plagued by a series of break-ins, Mrs. Slocum armed herself with a Colt .38 and learned how to use it. Then she announced to the *Providence Journal* that she was "packing" a pistol, just in case any would-be robbers were reading the news. "I so strongly believe in good families remaining armed," she later told the *Journal*'s M. Charles Baskt.

One of Mrs. Slocum's last wishes was revelatory, too. She wanted mourners to come to her Bellevue Avenue home to view her body. Everyone was welcome—family, friends, neighbors, acquaintances, politicians, fellow Republicans, and others who wanted to pay their respects, no invitation required. Dressed in a peignoir and modestly covered with a fine white sheet, the woman who was always described as the "doyenne" and "gatekeeper" of Newport society received absolutely anyone. She once said of Newport, "By being rather fastidious about the people in clubs, we've managed to control the particular atmosphere of the community." In death, however, exclusivity was no longer an issue.

Eileen Slocum was a bundle of big contradictions, simultaneously impolite and proper, conservative and maverick, entitled and civic-minded, old-fashioned and enlightened, opinionated and tolerant, off-putting and endearing. She was, in fact, a metaphor for Newport itself, for the city could be described by the same seemingly contradictory adjectives.

Rockwell Stensrud, author of *Newport: A Lively Experiment 1639–1969*, has spent a great deal of time contemplating the history, character, and significance of the city. "During the Gilded Age," he says, "'Newport' became a catch-word for elegance, entertainment, extravagance, and escape. But," he adds, "Newport's DNA is stocked with surprises." The same place that gave us white elephants and monkey dinners was a cradle for tolerance and democracy.

As for me, the self-described bird-watcher who coolly set out to observe and classify the rara avis that is the classically rich Newporter, I now realize that I have been more like Dorothy in *The Wizard of Oz*. I traveled all the way to the "Emerald City" and back, only to learn that the Newport I was looking for was always there, as it was at its start. The "lively experiment" was still a city of uncommon beauty and a place where everything old really is new again.

And the rich? They're still there.

BIBLIOGRAPHY

ORIGINAL DOCUMENTS

Carpenter, Ralph, Papers.
Masque of the Blue Garden Scrapbook, at the Redwood Library, Newport, R.I.
Smith, Joseph Lindon, Papers, Project Files re Masque of the Blue Garden, Archives of American Art.
Van Alen Scrapbooks at the Redwood Library, Newport, R.I.

ARTICLES AND PERIODICALS

Numerous issues of the *New York Times*, *Time*, *Town & Country*, *Vogue*, the *Newport Mercury and Weekly News*, and the *Newport Daily News* featured stories about Newport. Specific editions of these and other periodicals consulted include:

Abbott, Elizabeth. "In Newport, the Many-Faceted Legacy of Doris Duke." *New York Times*, September 7, 1997, R5.
Amory, Cleveland. "The Crucial Battle of Modern Newport." *New York Times*, September 2, 1962.
———. "Newport: There She Sits." *Harper's Magazine*, 1948.
———. "Old and Newport." *Town & Country*, September 1958.
"Angels Over Newport." *Time*, July 24, 1939.

"As to Bucking the Social Tiger." *New York Times*, June 30, 1912, X1.

"Auction at Mansion Further Dims the Grandeur That Was." *New York Times*, June 28, 1962.

"The Automobile in Newport." *Town & Country*, September 27, 1902, 14.

Bagdikian, Ben. "A Second White House—For the Summer?" *New York Times*, May 20, 1962, SM52.

Baker, Joe. "Tribute to the Artist and the Man." *Newport Daily News*, July 12, 2008.

"The Battle of Belcourt." *48 Hours Mystery*. CBS, July 20, 2000.

"Beautiful Fantasy at Mrs. Fish's Ball." *New York Times*, August 20, 1912, 9.

"The Big Weekend." *Time*, August 30, 1963.

Boston, Barbara Hudnut. "They Wanted to Be Alone" *Town & Country*, April 1943.

"Boston's Golden Maxim." *Time*, December 22, 1941.

Bulkerly, William. "Newport Real Estate Market Seeks Return to Posh Past." *Chicago Daily Herald*, June 27, 1997.

Bulow, Claus von. "Clarenden Court, Newport, R.I." *Newport History* (1974): 218–226.

"By the Bay." *Time*, October 6 1961.

"Castle Property Is Withdrawn from Sale," *Newport Mercury and Weekly News*, July 19, 1940.

"Cats by the Sea." *Time*, August 2, 1954.

"CEO of Providence, R.I.-Based Building-Products Maker Gets Unique Parachute," *Providence Journal*, November 18, 2002.

Chorley, Kenneth. "Only Tomorrow." Assembly of Newport Citizens. Rogers High School, Newport, March 25, 1947.

Clendinen, Dudley. "Newport Rues Von Bulow Trial Shift." *New York Times*, April 4, 1985.

"Cliff Walk Fence Faces City Probe." *Newport Daily News*, February 17, 1958.

"Crushing Truth." *New York Times*, August 9, 1876: 4.

Curtis, Charlotte. "The Astors Come Out for a Newport Party." *New York Times*, August 21, 1967, 36.

———. "Fashions for Newport: 20 Gowns and 2 Perfumes." *New York Times*, August 9, 1965, 20.

———. "Janet Jennings Auchincloss Presented in Newport." *New York Times*, August 18, 1963, 90.

———. "Newport, One Never Serves Coffee at Teatime." *New York Times*, September 16, 1967.

"The Cushings of Newport." *Vogue*, May 1971.

Demarest, Michael. "The Best Cup Challenge Ever." *Time*, October 3, 1983.

"Diamond Worth $583,000 Is 'Comfortable' to Wear." *New York Times*, July 17, 1957, 43.

"The Dismantling of Newport." *Time*, July 28, 1941.

"Divine Gets President's Sanction to Buy Next-Door Estate but Owner Won't Sell." *New York Times*, August 17, 1939, 1.

"Divine Is Invited To Visit Newport." *New York Times*, July 12, 1939, 8.

"Doris Duke Gives $25,000 to Restore Cliff Walk." *Newport Daily News*, October 15, 1966.

"Doris Duke Kills Friend in Crash." *Newport Daily News*, October 8, 1966.

"Doris Duke Tells Aim Here." *Newport Mercury and Weekly News*, September 26, 1969.

"EO of Providence, R.I. Building Industry Supplier Is Highest-Paid in State." *Providence Journal*, January 1, 2000.

"The Family Where Marriage Is Always a Failure." *Syracuse Herald*, August 19, 1923.

"Father Divine May Get Castle Here." *Newport Mercury and Weekly News*, July 14, 1939, 5.

"Financiers Leave Newport." *New York Times*, August 1, 1914, 9.

"Foundation Created to Restore Houses." *Newport Daily News*, November 20, 1968.

French, Francis O. "The Newport Idea." *Town & Country*, December 1936–January 1937.

"Glitter and Gold of Yesteryear Newport Recalled at 'Marble House' Tiffany Ball." *Newport Daily News*, July 15, 1957, 1.

"Goelet Newport Estate Offered for UNO Capital." *New York Times*, November 17, 1945, 6.

Green, Penelope. "Updating Newport, Ever So Gently." *New York Times*, August 5, 2007.

"The Grist Mill." *Newport Mercury and Weekly News*, June 26, 1953, 4.

Hanlon, John. "Meet Jimmy Van Alen, Newport's Last Grand Homme." *Providence Journal*, August 22, 1971.

"Harry Lehr Protests He Did Not Drug a Monkey." *New York Times*, July 6, 1902, 7.

"Heartbreak of Society." *American Weekly*, September 9, 1949.

Heffner, Stephan. "Doris Duke: Caged by Fortune." *Providence Journal*, September 13, 1987.

"Housing Problem." *Time*, July 6, 1962.

"How Newport Spends Its Day." *New York Times*, August 6, 1905, SM1.

"The Human Poodle." *Cedar Rapids Evening Gazette*, June 2, 1900, 12.

Hurt III, Harry. "Private Sector: King of Clubs, and Maby Castles." *New York Times*, March 28, 2004.

"Hyde Park Denied to Divine." *New York Times*, February 6, 1940, 19.

"Improvements at Newport." *New York Times*, October 24, 1897, 11.

"Is the Proposed Reformation of Newport Possible?" *New York Times*, March 22, 1908, SM8.

"The Isle of Peace." *Scribner's Monthly*, August 1881.

Kahn, Joseph P. "Gilded Age Opportunity." *Boston Globe*, October 1, 2006.

"Kennedys to Occupy Estate Here in 1964." *Newport Mercury and Weekly News*, November 1, 1963, 1.

Kenworthy, E. W. "Society's Shaky Citadel." *New York Times*, September 23, 1962, 21.

Kilkenny, Frances. "At Fashionable Newport." *New York Daily News*, July 12, 1939.

Kirk, Laura Meade. "A Club like No Other." *Providence Journal*, September 3, 2006.

Konigsberg, Eric. "In Hamptons, Slump Means Less Glitz Per Gala." *New York Times*, July 19, 2008.

"Legendary British Entrepreneur Peter De Savary Shares His Excitement Over His New Projects on the Spice Isle of Grenada." *Hello!*, August 19, 2008.

"*Life* Visits a Fading Newport." *Life*, October 16, 1944, 120.

"*Life* Visits Gertrude Niessen's Palace at Newport." *Life*, August 18, 1941, 82.

"Lineage of Beauty: Minnie Cushing." *Vogue*, February 15, 1965.

Marquard, Bryan. "Donald Tinney, Artist and Heir to Famed Newport Mansion." *Boston Globe*, January 28, 2006.

"Maxim Karolik Sings." *New York Times*, October 17, 1925, 18.

McCabe, Carol. "You Can Make It in Newport." *Providence Journal*, August 18, 1974.

McCabe, Lida Rose. "Surprise Valley Farm." *Country Life*, April 1924, 51–53.

McCrillis, John O. C. "The Sullivans of Bellevue Avenue." *Newport History*, Fall 2006.

Mehren, Elizabeth. "Seamy Saga of Belcourt Castle Joins List of Newport, R.I., Scandals." *Los Angeles Times*, June 20, 1999.

"Miss Gertrude Niesen Arrives at 'Rosecliff,'" *Newport Mercury and Weekly News*, October 10, 1941, 8.

"More Trouble among the Four Hundred." *Chicago Daily Tribune*, September 1, 1894, 12.

Morris, Bernadine. "Bicyclist Lends Cachet to Seventh Ave." *New York Times*, April 24, 1965, 21.

"Mrs. Astor Censures Some Society Women." *New York Times*, September 15, 1908, 5.

"Mrs. Fish Opens Her New Ballroom." *New York Times*, July 6, 1913, 11.

"Mrs. Fish's Harvest Ball." *New York Times*, August 23, 1900, 7.

"Mrs. Fish's Triumph in Social Rivalry." *New York Times*, August 23, 1907, 1.

"Mrs. JFK Gives Up Lease Here." *Newport Daily News*, August 1, 1964, 2.

"Mrs. Kennedy Arrives Here on Monday." *Newport Daily News*, July 23, 1961, 1.

"Mrs. Stuyvesant Fish Talks in Pungent Style." *New York Times*, September 27, 1903, 1.

"Mrs. Van Rensselaer's Neighbors." *American Weekly*, July 13, 1947.

"Narrative Note on a Not So Naughty Niesen." *New York Times*, April 23, 1944, X1.

Nemy, Enid. "Court Ruling against Fence Is Making Waves at Bailey's Beach." *New York Times*, August 10, 1968, 19.

"New Divine 'Heaven' Opposed by Negro." *New York Times*, July 13, 1939, 20.

"The New Guest of Honor." *New York Times*, July 6, 1902, 6.

"Newport and Its Summer Life." *Ladies' Home Journal*, June 1889, 5.

"Newport at War." *Life*, April 26, 1943, 31–34.

"Newport Expects Divine." *New York Times*, July 23, 1939, 3.

"Newport Past Is Renewed." *Life*, August 12, 1957, 123.

"Newport Reforms, No More Freak Fetes." *New York Times*, March 15, 1908, 1.

"Newport: Report on the 1958 Season." *Vogue*, September 15, 1958.

"Newport Residence Is Sold for $31,700." *New York Times*, November 30, 1941, 64.

"Newport Socialite's Life Was Made Richer by Love." *Newport Daily News*, November 8, 2001.

"Newport Still Puts on a Good Show." *Town & Country*, June 1974.

"Newport Surprised by Mrs. Astor's Interview." *New York Times*, September 20, 1908, X6.

"Newport Tango-meters the Trot!" *Washington Post*, August 24, 1913, 1.

"Newport: The City of Luxury." *Atlantic*, August 1908, 162–168.

"Newport: The Place to Be, the Clothes to Wear, the People to See." *Town & Country*, August 1964.

"Newport's Dinner Dance—Elaborate Function by Mr. and Mrs. Pembroke Jones at Friedheim." *New York Times*, August 16, 1902, 9.

"Newport's Old Time Season." *New York Times*, July 12, 1908, X2.

"Newport's Season Promises to Break All Records for Gayety." *New York Times*, July 20, 1913.

"Newport . . . Those Days, This War." *Vogue*, September 1, 1942.

"1926 Newport." *New Yorker*, August 21, 1926, 9.

"Oelrichs Auction Begins." *New York Times*, July 15, 1941, 16.

Powel Jr., Harford. "Newport the Supurb." *Harper's Bazaar*, August 1931, 86ff.

"Prince Wilhelm's Odd Dilema at Newport." *New York Times*, August 25, 1907, SM9.

"A Quaint Scotch Game." *New York Times*, September 5, 1893, 10.

"Rain Stops Dance at Prince's Dinner." *New York Times*, August 25, 1907, 7.

Randolph, Nancy. "1,100 at Big Newport Ball and They All Wanted to See Kelly." *New York Daily News*, July 10, 1955.

"Rich Masque Opens the James Garden." *New York Times*, August 16, 1913, 9.

Rimer, Sara. "For Sale: Memories of a Camelot Wedding." *New York Times*, July 17, 1995, A8.

"Robert Goelets Give Villa to Catholics." *New York Times*, March 21, 1947, 18.

Rosenberg, Alan. "Von Bulow Redux." *Providence Journal*, October 14, 2007, D1.

Ross, Lillian. "You Dig It, Sir?" *New Yorker*, August 14, 1954.

"Rules for Blackout Here Established." *Newport Mercury and Weekly News*, December 12, 1941, 2.

Salit, Richard. "Mansion's $17-Million Sale Sets Record." *Providence Journal*, December 2, 2006.

Schuyler, Montgomery. "A Newport Palace." *Cosmopolitan*, August 1900, 361.

Schwardron, Terry. "'Things Are Not Being Done Properly Anymore.'" *Providence Journal*, September 29, 1974.

"Scores Triumph of a Generation." *New York Times*, August 2, 1913.

Sheppard, Eugenia. "Newport May Have Dowagers but You Can't Call It Dull." *Corpus Christi Times*, July 16, 1965, 4C.

"Simple Life at Newport." *New York Times*, September 27, 1908, X10.

Slocum, Eileen G. "Memories of Bellevue Avenue." *Newport History* 67 (1995): 36–50.

"Social War over Prince Still On." *New York Times*, August 24, 1907, 7.

"Social War Stirs Newport." *New York Times*, August 7, 1907, 7.

"Society in Costume at Mrs. Fish's Ball." *New York Times*, August 2, 1913, 7.

"Society Gardeners Win in Newport." *New York Times*, September 18, 1907.

"The Sparrow." *Time*, November 9, 1959.

"Spectacular Entertainments Give Way to Rigid Exclusiveness and Restful Elegance of Earlier Days." *New York Times*, August 7, 1910, C11.

Stephens, Suzanne. "Renewal in Newport." *Architectural Digest*, February 1996: 152.

"Supreme Court Ruling Ends Inheritance Fight over Newport Mansion." *Boston Globe*, November 16, 2006.

"That Was Newport." *New Yorker*, July 20, 1935, 21–23.

"There Are No Idle Rich, Declares Mrs. O. H. P. Belmont." *New York Times*, July 9, 1911, SM3.

"There Are Really Three Newports." *Holiday*, July 7, 1949, 99.

Thomas, Helen. "Mrs. Kennedy Alters Plans on Vacation." *Cedar Rapids Gazette*, July 23, 1964, 12.

Toufexis, Anastasia. "The Case of the Sleeping Beauty." *Time*, January 25, 1982.

Van Alen, Candace Alig. "Newport De-cliched." *Vogue*, September 15, 1958.

"Van Alen Was Game for More Than Tennis." *Providence Journal*, July 6, 1991.

"Vinson Walsh Killed, 5 Hurt, at Newport." *New York Times*, August 20, 1905, 1.

"Von Bulow Story Describes Newport High Society." *New York Times*, February 13, 1982, 9.

"Ward McAllister's Last Service to Society." *New York Times*, May 29, 1904, SM2.

"Warning to Divine Found at Newport." *New York Times*, July 25, 1939, 14.

"Water Works Files Lien Against Rosecliff." *Newport Mercury and Weekly News*, July 3, 1942, 1.

"What's New in Old Newport." *Town & Country*, July 1963.

"The Whirlaway Wedding of Mary Cushing and Peter Beard in Newport." *Vogue*, October 1, 1967.

Whitman, Alden. "Newport, Where Inflation Stings a Little, but It Doesn't Really Hurt." *New York Times*, July 19, 1974, 30.

"Wreckers Taking Newport's Villas." *New York Times*, April 5, 1949, 35.

Zuckerman, Faye. "Gala-Vanting." *Providence Journal*, July 20, 2008.

BOOKS

Aldrich, Elizabeth, and Mina Mulvey. *From the Ballroom to Hell: Grace and Folly in Nineteenth-Century Dance*. New York: TriQuarterly Books, 1991.

Amory, Cleveland. *The Last Resorts*. New York: Harper & Brothers, 1952.

_____. *The Trouble with Nowadays: A Curmudgeon Strikes Back*. New York: Ballantine Books, 1981.

_____. *Who Killed Society?* New York: Harper & Brothers, 1960.

Baldrige, Letitia. *Juggling*. New York: Viking, 1976.

_____. *Of Diamonds and Diplomats*. Boston: Houghton Mifflin, 1968.

Bari, Sheldon. *Beatrice: The Untold Story of a Legendary Woman of Mystery*. Newport: Newport Legends, 1998.

Barrett, Richmond. *Good Old Summer Days*. New York: D. Appleton-Century, 1941.

Belmont, Eleanor Robson. *The Fabric of Memory*. New York: Farrar, Straus, and Cudahy, 1957.

Bentley, Jerry H. *Concise History of the World: An Illustrated Time Line*. Washington, D.C.: National Geographic, 2001.

Birmingham, Stephen. *The Right People*. Boston: Little, Brown, 1958.

Boss, Judith A. *Newport: A Pictorial History*. Norfolk: Donning, 1981.

Bourget, Paul. *Outre-Mer*. New York: Charles Scribner's Sons, 1895.

Boyle, Robert H. *At the Top of Their Game: Profiles from* Sports Illustrated. New York: Lyons, 1983.

Brittan, Belle. *Belle Brittan on a Tour*. New York: Derby & Jackson, 1858.

Brown, Eve. *Champagne Cholly*. New York: E. P. Dutton, 1947.

Bullard, F. Lauriston. *Historic Summer Haunts from Newport to Portland*. Boston: Little, Brown, 1912.

Cable, Mary. *Top Drawer: American High Society from the Gilded Age to the Roaring Twenties*. New York: Scribner, 1984.

Churchill, Allen. *The Splendor Seekers*. New York: Grosset & Dunlap, 1974.

_____. *The Upper Crust*. Englewood Cliffs, N.J.: Prentice-Hall, 1970.

Clegg, Charles, and Duncan Emrich, eds. *The Lucius Beebe Reader*. Garden City, N.Y.: Doubleday, 1967.

Cowles, Virginia. *1913: An End and a Beginning*. New York: Harper & Row, 1968.

Crockett, Albert Stevens. *Peacocks on Parade*. New York: Sears, 1931.

Crowninshield, Francis W., and Louis Francher. *Manners for the Metropolis: An Entrance Key to the Fantastic Life of the 400*. Boston: Ayer, 1975.

Curtis, Charlotte. *The Rich and Other Atrocities*. New York: Harper & Row, 1976.

Dow, Richard Alan, and E. Andrew Mowbray. *Newport*. Providence: Mowbray, 1976.

Downing, Antoinette F. *Architectural Heritage of Newport*. New York: Random House Value, 1987.

Drexel, Elizabeth Wharton. *Turn of the World*. Philadelphia: J. B. Lippincott, 1937.

DuBois, Diana. *In Her Sister's Shadow*. Boston: Little, Brown, 1995.

Elliott, Maud H. *This Was My Newport*. Boston: Ayer, 1975.

Gavan, Terrence. *The Barons of Newport*. Newport: Pinapple, 1988.

_____. *Exploring Newport: The Complete Tour Guide*. Minneapolis: Pineapple, 1992.

Gilbert, Edwin. *Newport*. New York: Bantam, 1972.

Gordon, Lyndall. *A Private Life of Henry James*. New York: W. W. Norton, 1998.

Gregory, Alexis, and John Kenneth Galbraith. *Families of Fortune: Life in the Gilded Age*. New York: Vendome, 2001.

Griswold, Mac, and Eleanor Weller. *Golden Age of American Gardens: Proud Owners, Private Estates, 1890–1940*. New York: Harry N. Abrams, 2000.

Grosvenor, Richard. *Newport: An Artist's Impressions of Its Architecture and History*. Minneapolis: Commonwealth Editions, 2002.

Hammond, Geoffrey. *Showdown at Newport*. New York: Walden, 1974.

Homberger, Eric. *Mrs. Astor's New York: Money and Social Power in a Gilded Age*. New Haven, Conn.: Yale University Press, 2002.

Hopf, John T. *Newport Then and Now*. Trieste: Societa Arti Grafiche Industriali, 1989.

James, Henry. *The American Scene*. New York: Horizon, 1967.

Jefferys, C. P. *Newport: A Short History*. Washington, D.C.: Newport Historical Society, 1992.

Kavaler, Lucy. *The Astors*. New York: Dodd, Mead, 1966.

_____. *The Private World of High Society*. New York: David McKay, 1960.

Knickerbocker, Jacob. *Then and Now*. Boston: Bruce Humphries, 1939.

Lee, Hermione. *Edith Wharton*. New York: Vintage, 2008.

Lehr, Elizabeth Drexel. *"King Lehr" and the Gilded Age*. Philadelphia: J. B. Lippincott, 1935.

Lewis, Rob. *Newport*. Dover: Arcadia, 1996.

Logan, Andy. *The Man Who Robbed the Robber Barons*. New York: W. W. Norton, 1965.

Lowe, Corinne. *Confessions of a Social Secretary*. New York: Harper & Brothers, 1917.

Lundberg, Ferdinand. *America's 60 Families*. New York: Halcyon House, 1939.

_____. *The Rich and the Super-Rich*. New York: Lyle Stuart, 1968.

Mackenzie Stuart, Amanda. *Consuelo and Alva Vanderbilt: The Story of a Daughter and a Mother in the Gilded Age*. New York: HarperCollins, 2007.

McAllister, Ward. *Society as I Have Found It*. New York: Cassell, 1890.

McLean, Evalyn Walsh. *Father Struck It Rich*. Ouray: Bear Creek, 1981.

The Newport Cookbook. New York: Foremost, 1972.

Nichols, Charlie W. *The Ultra-Fashionable Peerage of America*. Boston: Ayer, 1975.

O'Connor, Richard. *The Golden Summers*. New York: G. P. Putnam's Sons, 1974.

Onorato, Ronald J., and Rhode Island American Institute of Architects. *AIA Guide to Newport*. New York: BPR, 2007.

Panaggio, Leonard J. *Portrait of Newport*. Providence: Mobray, 1969.

Pardee, Bettie Bearden, and Mick Hales. *Private Newport: At Home and in the Garden*. New York: Bulfinch, 2004.

Patterson, Jerry. *The Best Families: The Town and Country Social Directory, 1846–1996*. Ed. Anthony T. Mazzola and Frank Zachary. New York: Harry N. Abrams, 1996.

Pearson, Hesketh. *The Marrying Americans*. New York: Coward McCann, 1961.

Pioppi, Anthony, and Brad Faxon. *To the Nines*. New York: Sports Media Group, 2006.

Pottker, Jan. *Janet and Jackie: The Story of a Mother and Her Daughter, Jacqueline Kennedy Onassis*. New York: St. Martin's, Griffin, 2002.

Pryce-Jones, Alan. *The Bonus of Laughter*. London: Hamish Hamilton, 1988.

Rector, Margaret Hayden. *Alva: That Vanderbilt Woman*. Wickford: Dutch Island Press, 1992.

Rhode Island: A Guide to the Smallest State. Boston: Houghton Mifflin, 1937.

Russell, Dr. Preston. *Washington and Lafayette: American Triumph, French Tragedy*.

Santi, Federico, and John Gacher. *Newport Mansions: Postcards of the Gilded Age*. Grand Rapids, Mich.: Schiffer, 2006.

Schwarz, Ted, and Tom Rybak. *Trust No One: The Glamorous Life and Bizarre Death of Doris Duke*. Accord, NY: Vivisphere, 1997.

Simister, Florence Parker. *Streets of the City: An Anecdotal History of Newport*. Providence: Mowbray, 1969.

Sirkis, Nancy. *Newport Pleasures and Palaces*. New York: Viking, 1963.

Sterngass, Jon. *First Resorts: Pursuing Pleasure at Saratoga Springs, Newport, and Coney Island*. Baltimore: Johns Hopkins University Press, 2002.

Strange, Michael. *Who Tells Me True*. New York: Charles Scribner's Sons, 1940.

Tully, Andrew. *Era of Elegance*. New York: Funk & Wagnalls, 1947.

Turberville, Deborah. *Newport Remembered*. New York: Harry N. Abrams, 1994.

Van Rensselaer, May K. *Newport: Our Social Capital*. Boston: Ayer, 1975.

Van Rensselaer, Mrs. John King, and Frederic Van de Water. *The Social Ladder*. New York: Henry Holt, 1924.

Vanderbilt, Cornelius. *Queen of the Golden Age: The Fabulous Story of Grace Wilson Vanderbilt*. New York: George Mann, 1999.

Villars, Elizabeth. *One Night in Newport*. Boston: G. K. Hall, 1981.

Walker, Stanley. *Mrs. Astor's Horse*. New York: Blue Ribbon, 1937.

Warburton, Eileen, Cora Lee Gibbs, and Judith Sobol. *In Living Memory*. Newport: Newport Savings and Loan Association/Island Trust Company, 1988.

_____. *Newportraits*. Hanover, N.H.: University Press of New England, 2000.

Weeter, Dixon. *The Saga of American Society*. New York: Charles Scribner's Sons, 1937.

Wharton, Edith. *A Backward Glance: An Autobiography*. New York: Scribner, 1998.

Wilder, Thornton. *Theophilus North: A Novel*. New York: HarperCollins, 2003.

Worden, Helen. *Society Circus*. New York: Covici Friede, 1936.

Worden, Helen Erskine. *Out of This World*. New York: G. P. Putnam's Sons, 1953.

Wright, William. *The Von Bulow Affair*. New York: Dell, 1984.

Yarnall, James L. *Newport through Its Architecture: A History of Styles from Postmedieval to Postmodern*. Hanover, N.H.: University Press of New England, 2005.

PHOTO CREDITS

INDEX

Page references in *italics* refer to photos and illustrations.

CPSIA information can be obtained
at www.ICGtesting.com
Printed in the USA
LVOW11s2101050317
526225LV00001B/106/P